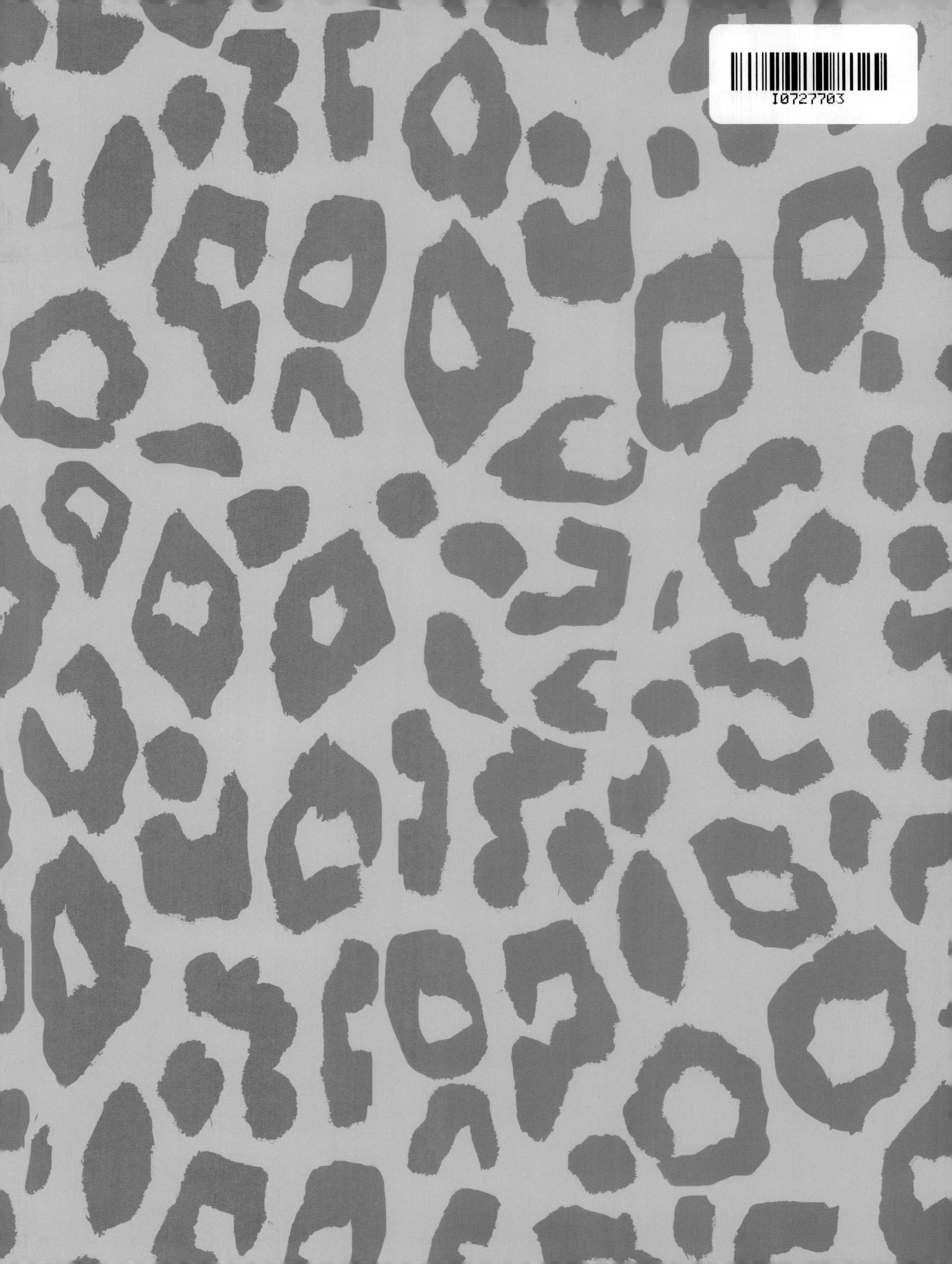
I0727703

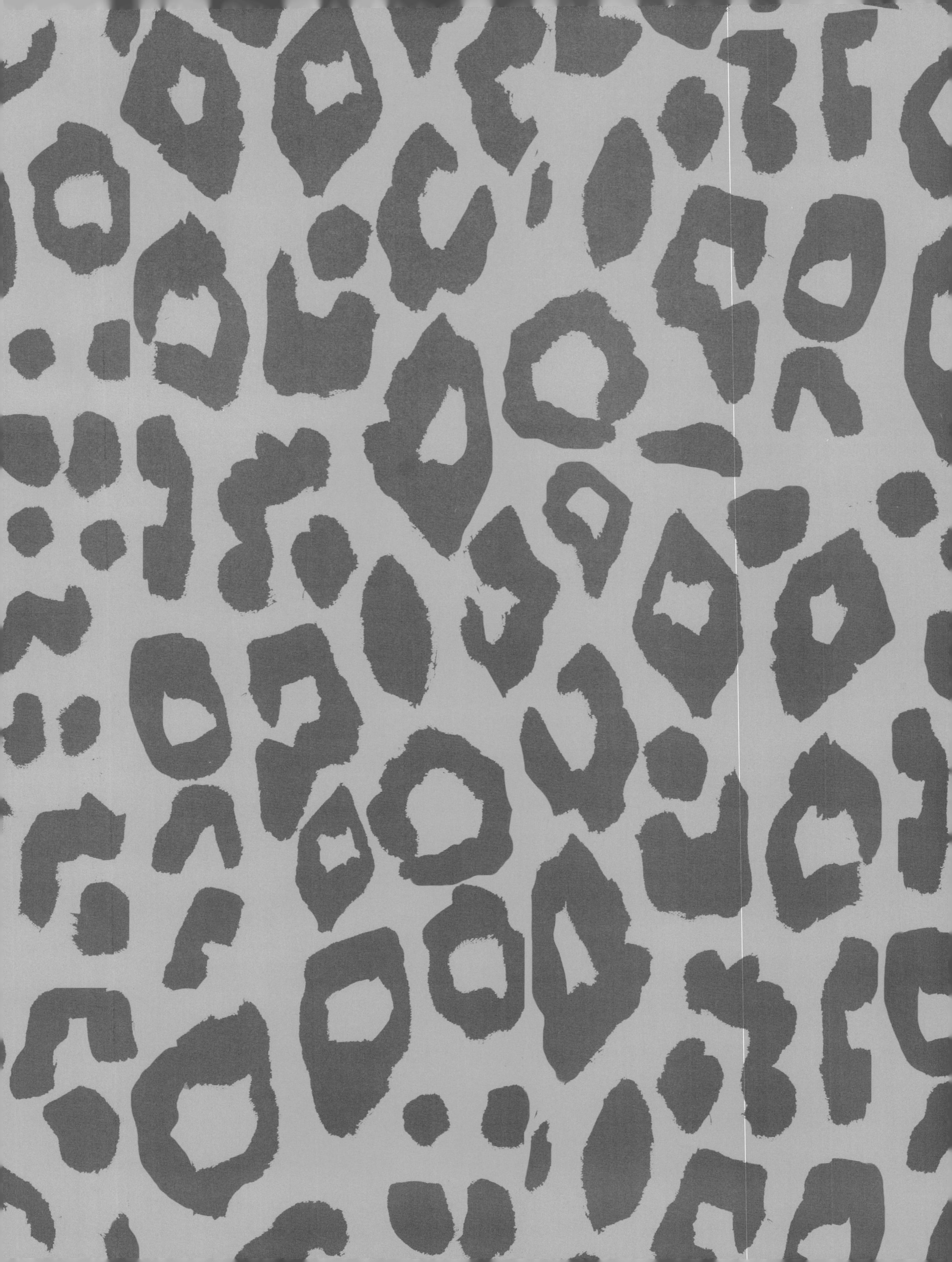

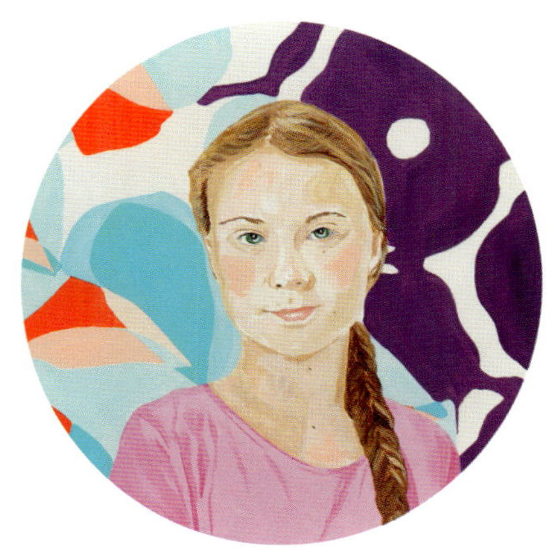

Roar!

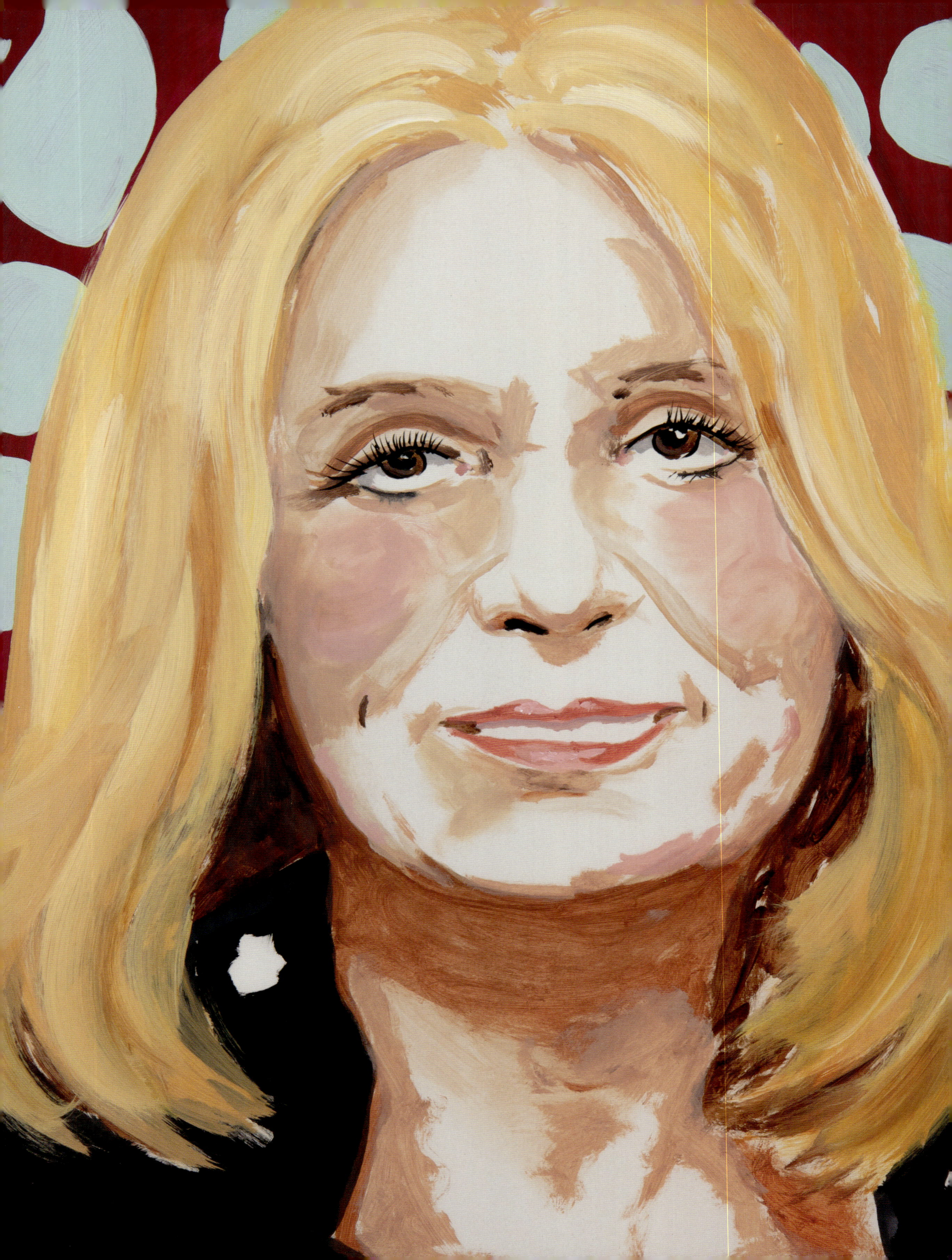

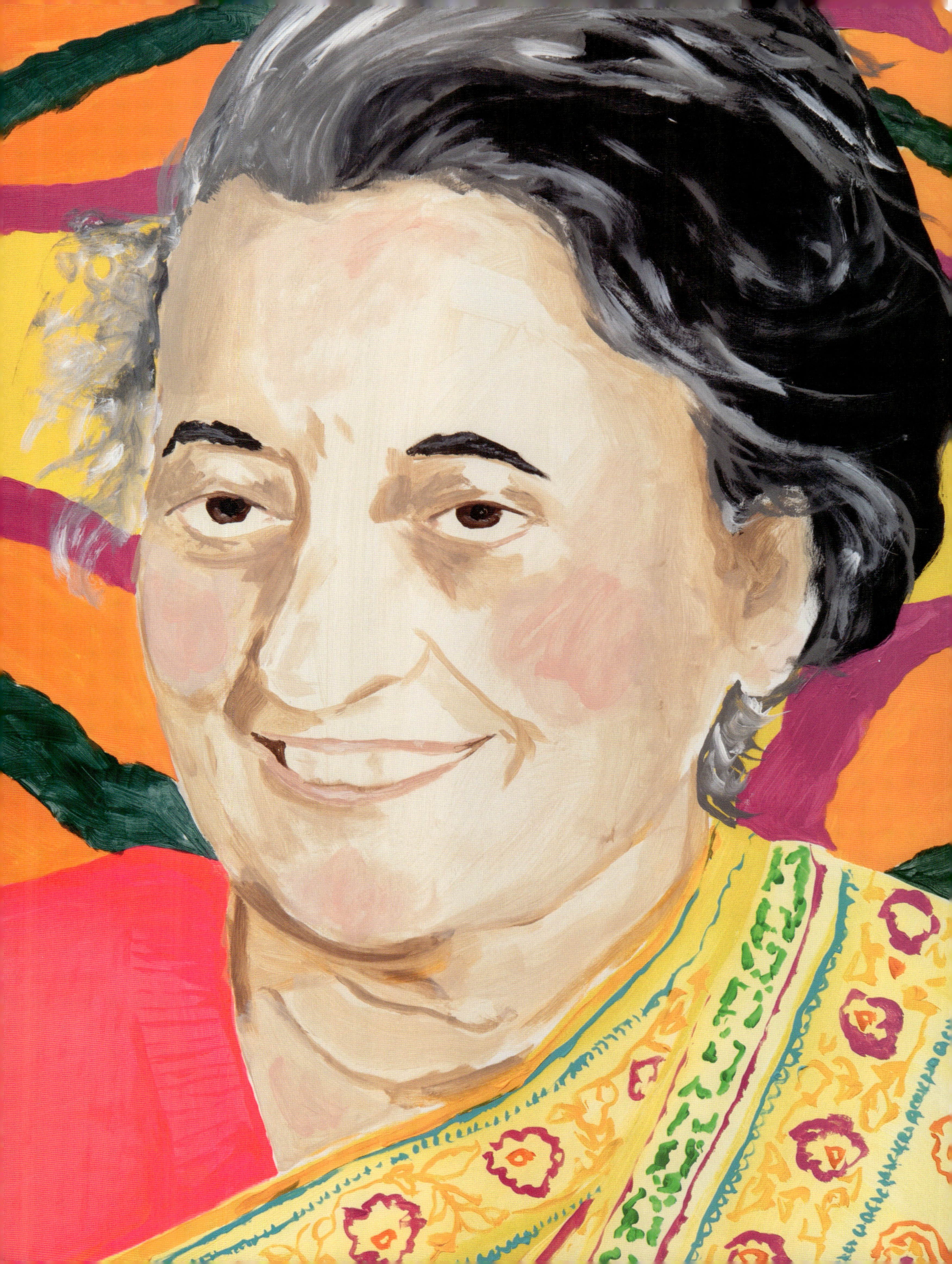

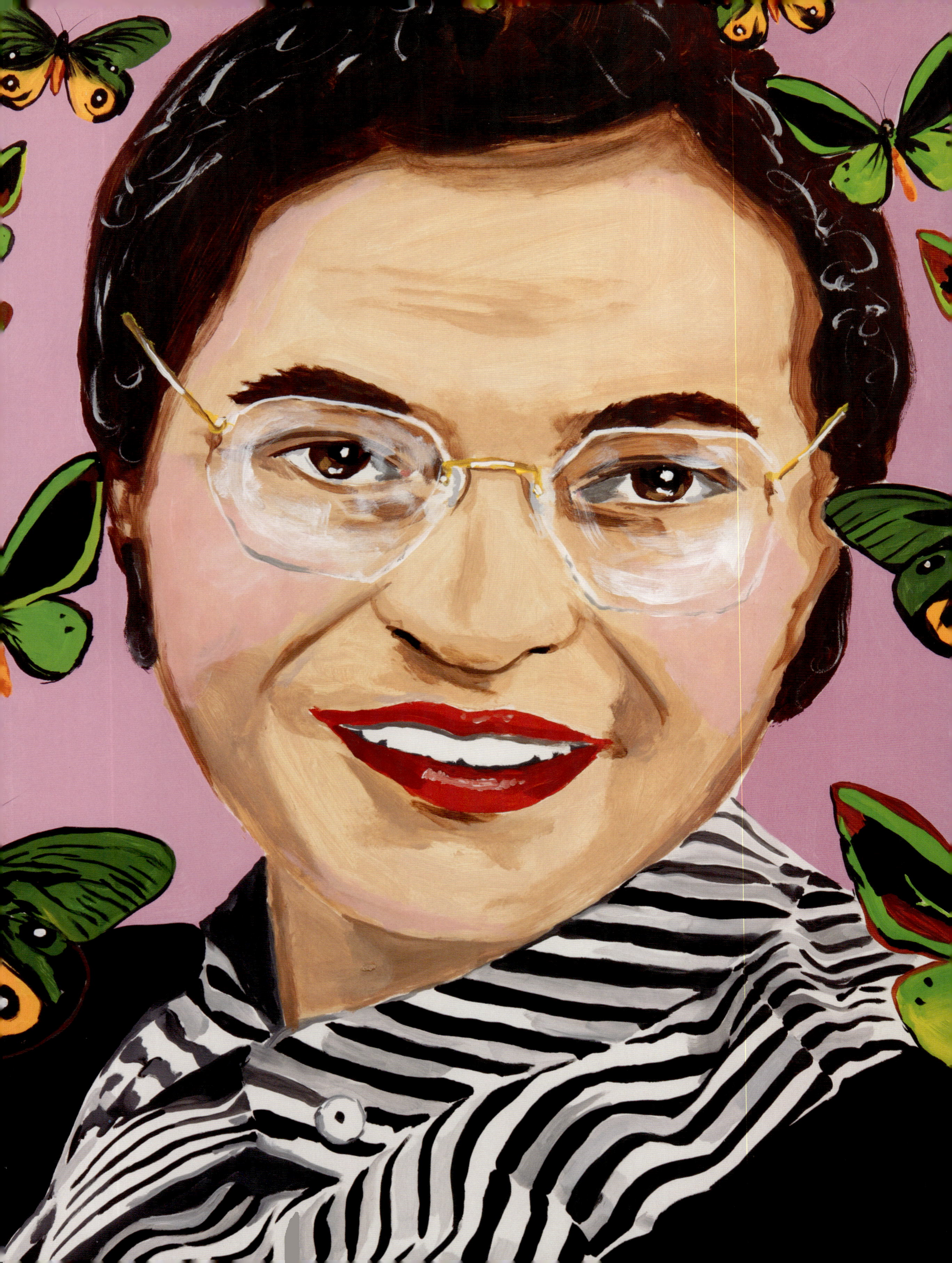

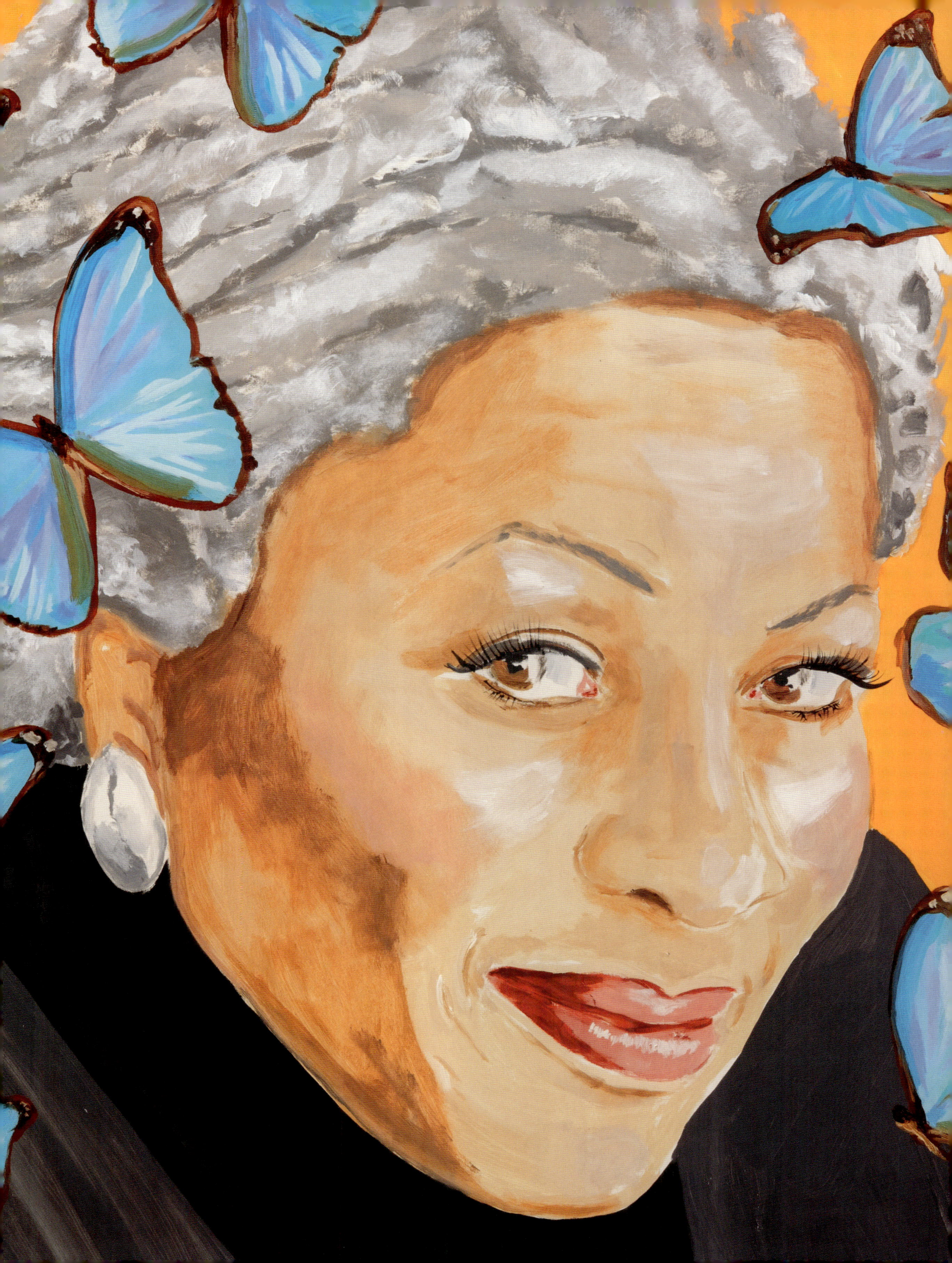

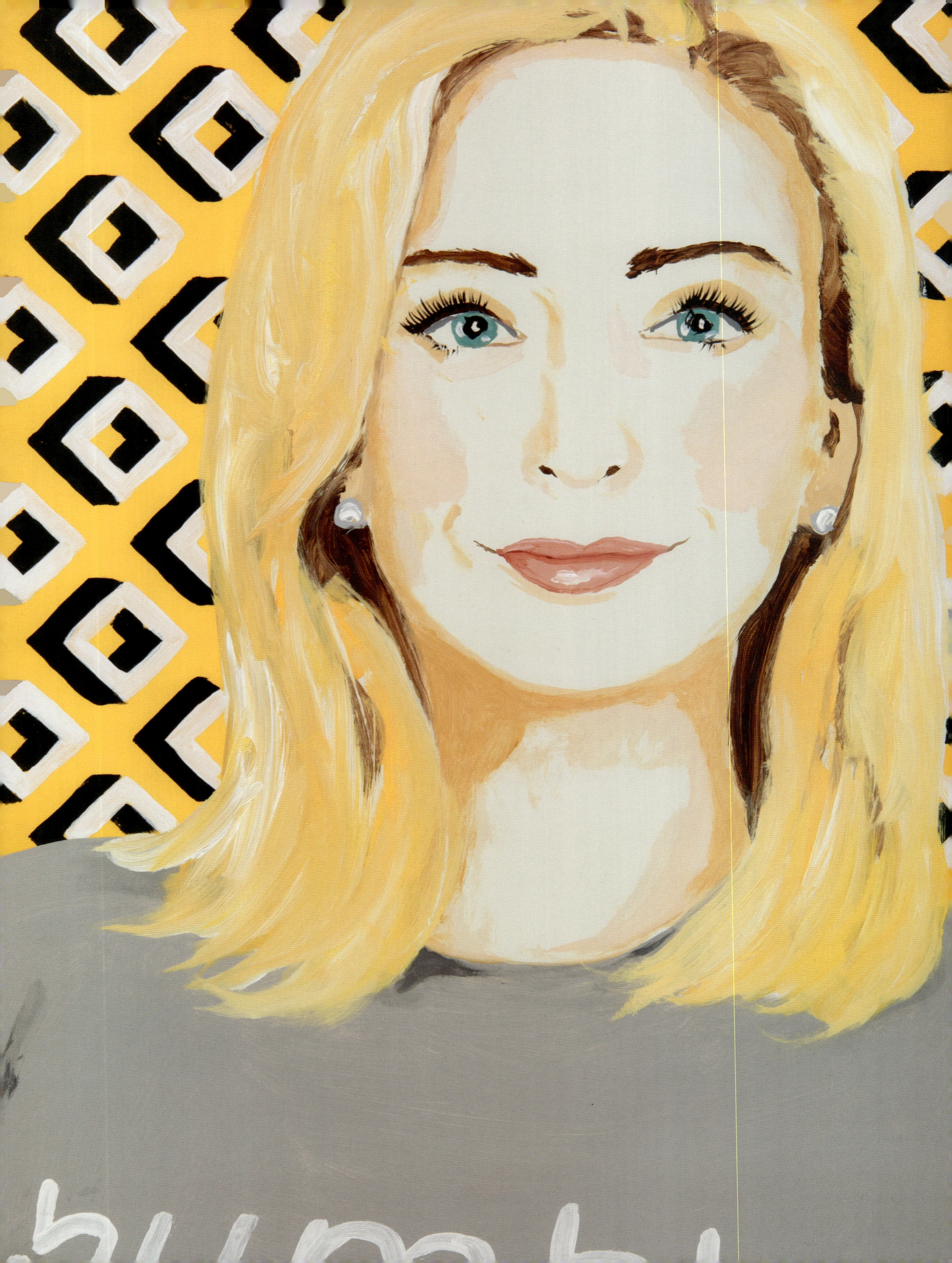

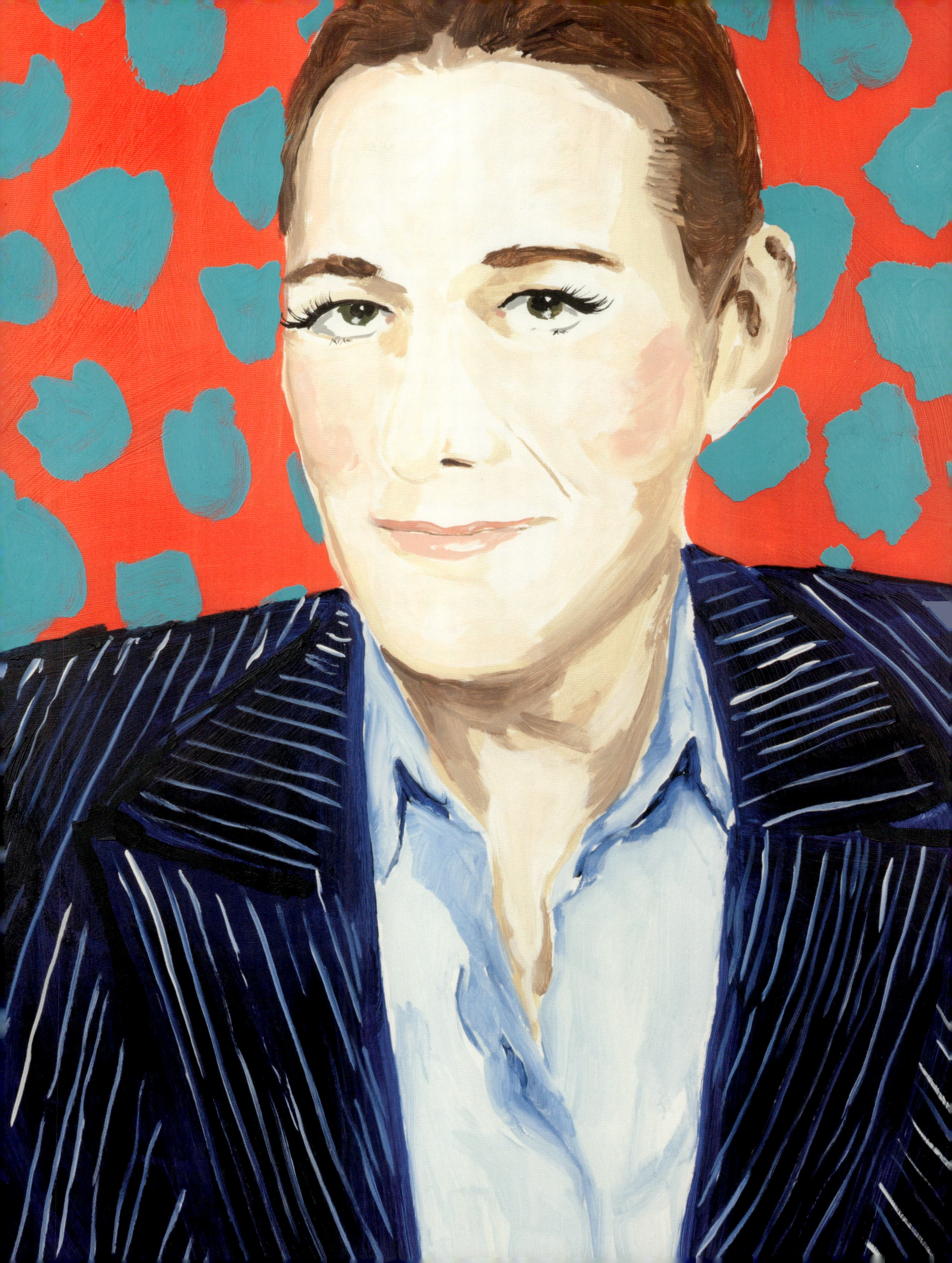

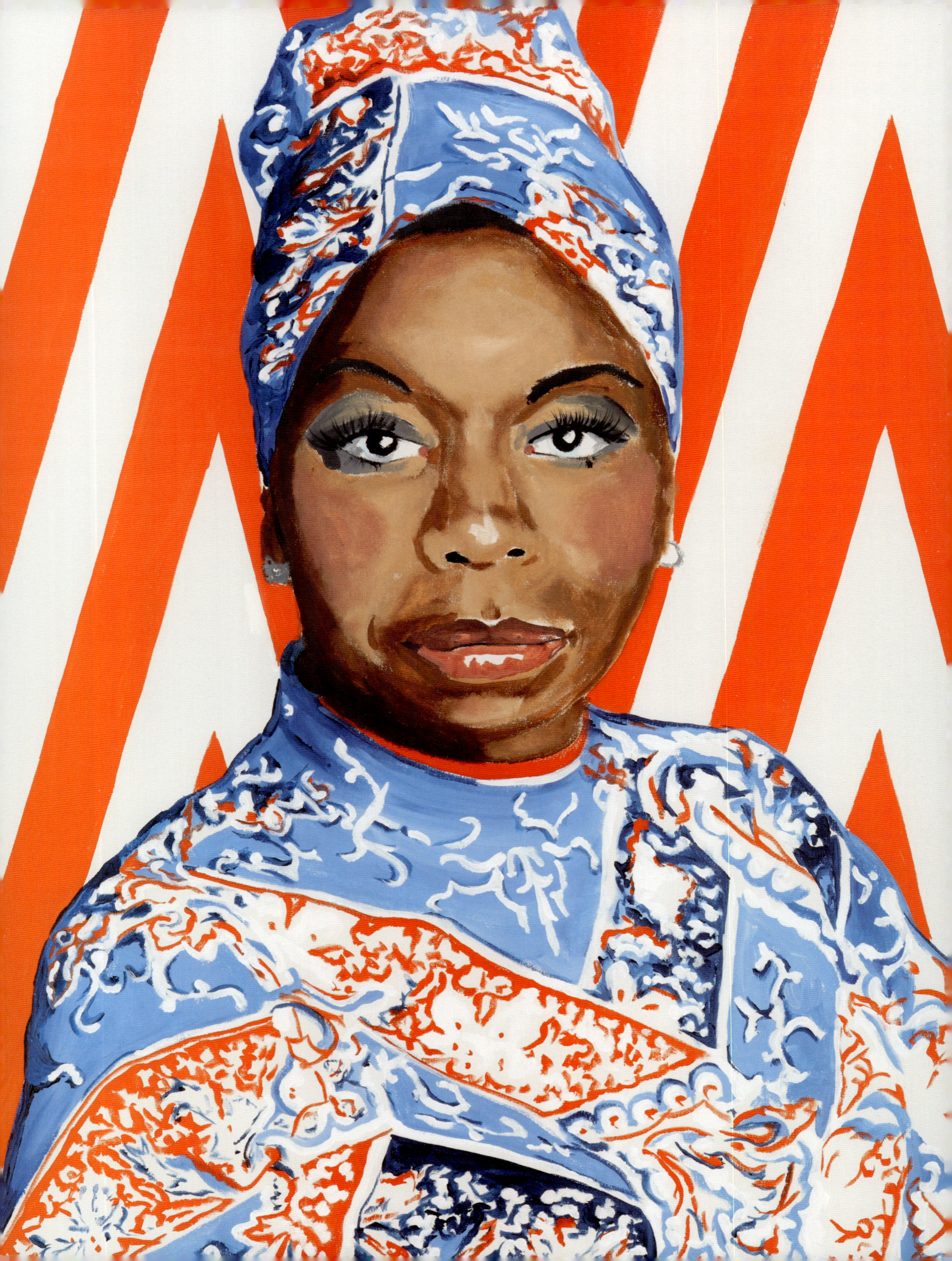

Ashley Longshore

Roar!

A COLLECTION OF MIGHTY WOMEN

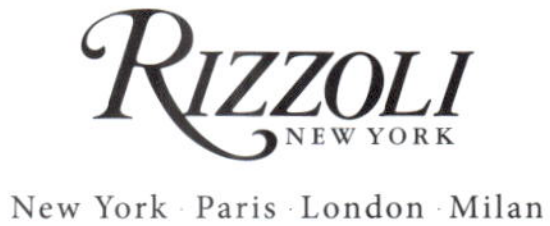

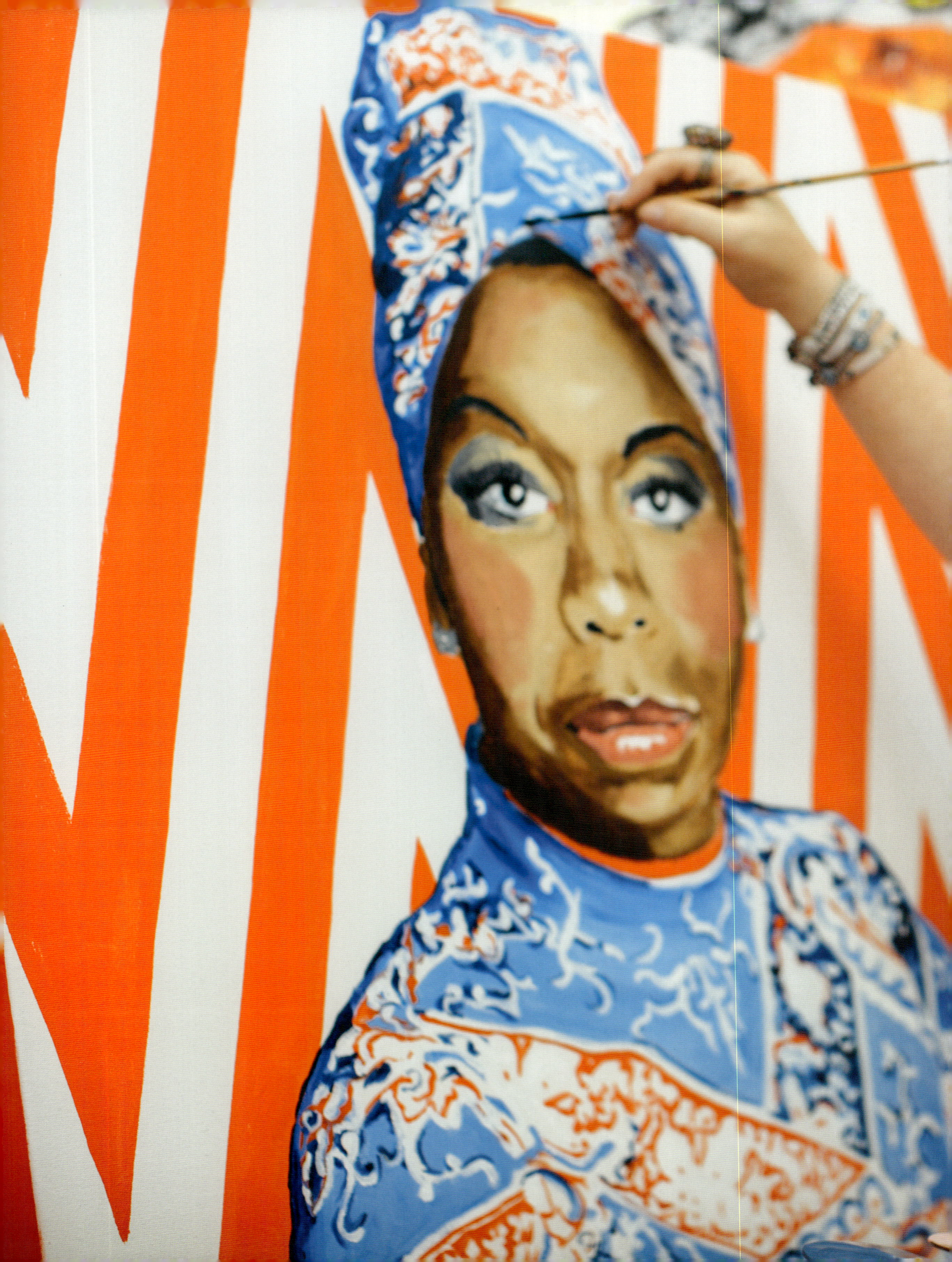

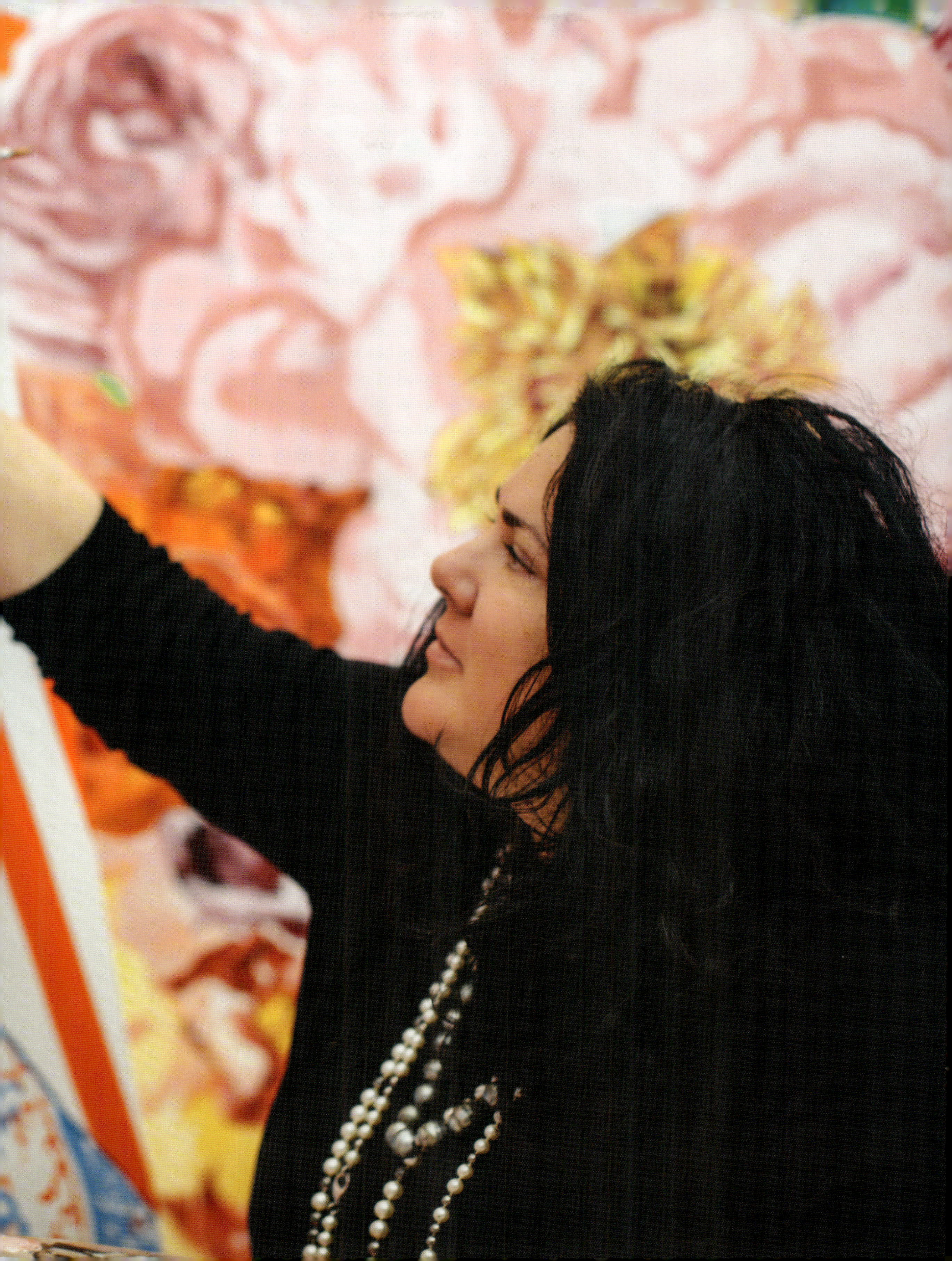

Introduction

I'm excited that Ashley is publishing this body of work, because her paintings make women feel in charge. It underscores that there have been many others who were able to overcome adversity and affect change—that in every woman, there is strength.

When I met Ashley for the first time, in the tea room at Claridge's in London, I was immediately overwhelmed by her enthusiasm and ebullient personality. Over lunch, Ashley provided insights on being a female artist from the South, and we talked about the wonderful women that have inspired us. From this, we had the idea to create an exhibition to venerate women in the gallery at the DVF headquarters.

After our meeting, I made a list of the twenty-five women whom I admired most and who I felt put us on a path to a new and better world—from Toni Morrison, to Wonder Woman, to Oprah—and I gave Ashley some homework. There were some women whom she had never heard of before, like Simone de Beauvoir or Hedy Lamarr, who was widely known as an actress and lesser known for having patented technology that paved the way for the creation of advances like Bluetooth, Wi-fi, and GPS. Much like the other women in the space, we wanted to memorialize her contributions and honor her tenacity.

What I realized about Ashley is that she is someone who is hungry to learn and is open to feedback. She accepted her task and got to creating celebratory portraits of these women—quite quickly too. Within a few days, we'd have completed works, as though she wanted to crystalize her passion for them as soon as her affinity for them developed. As Ashley said herself: with every brushstroke she got to know them better. Her attentive, admiring energy is present in every woman.

The result was a colorful room full of powerful women who had the strength to fight and the leadership to inspire. Gloria Steinem, Harriet Tubman, Marlene Dietrich, Jane Goodall, Greta Thunberg, Lady Gaga, and so many more. Through Ashley's talents we can both respect and celebrate them in the happiest light.

Diane von Furstenberg

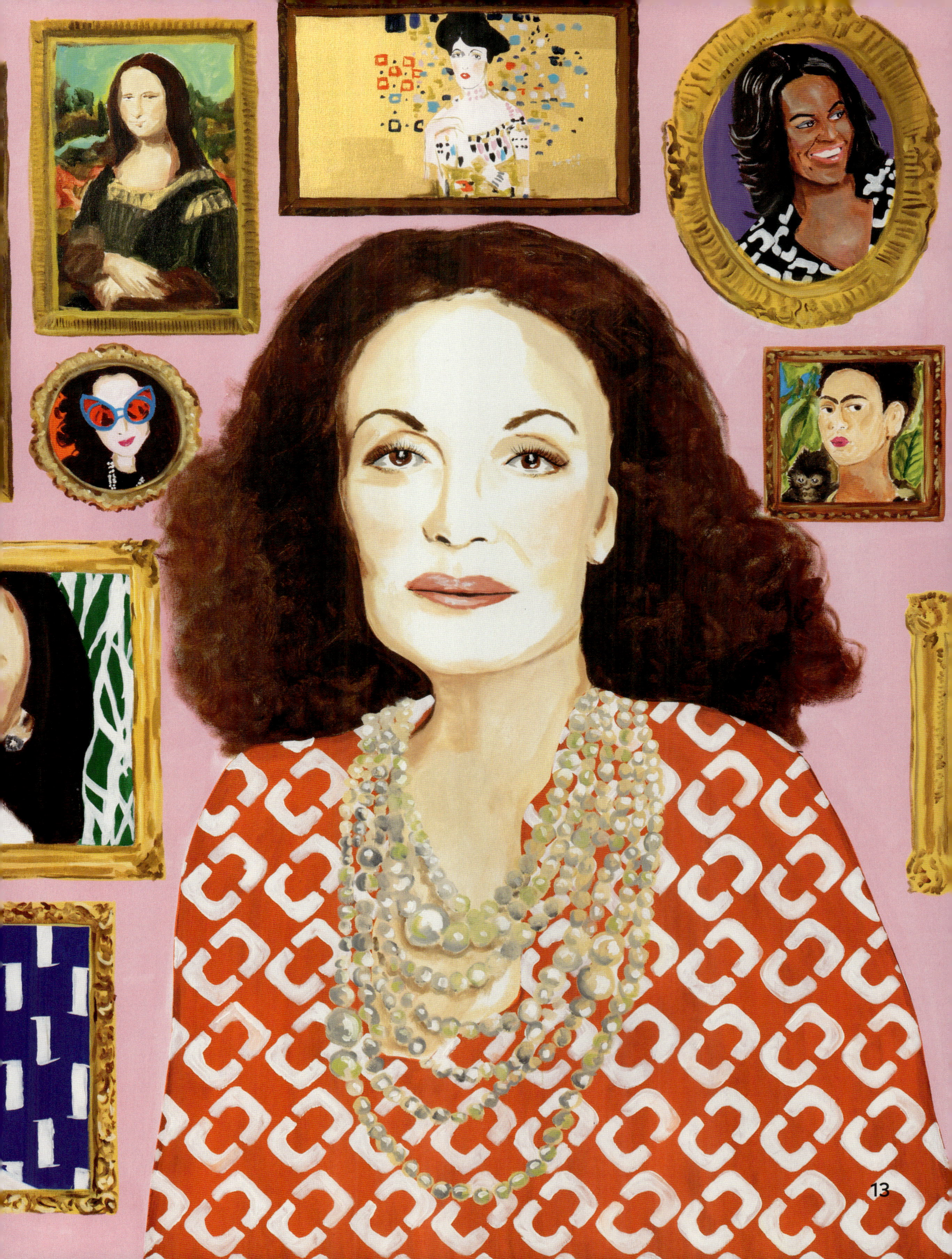

Diane von Furstenberg

Because she has lived her life courageously
and has supported women so enthusiastically.
Because she has style, grace, and beauty.

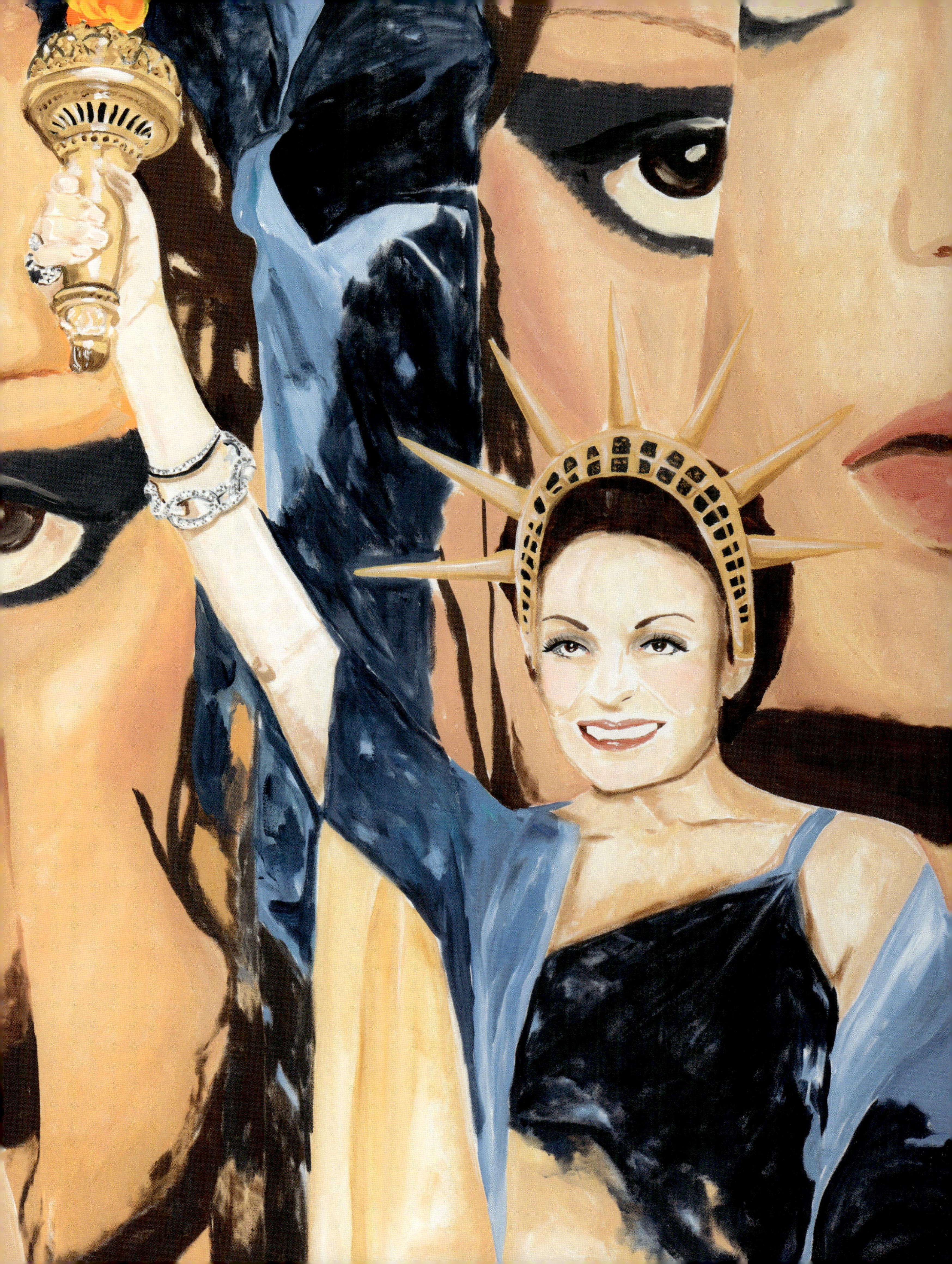

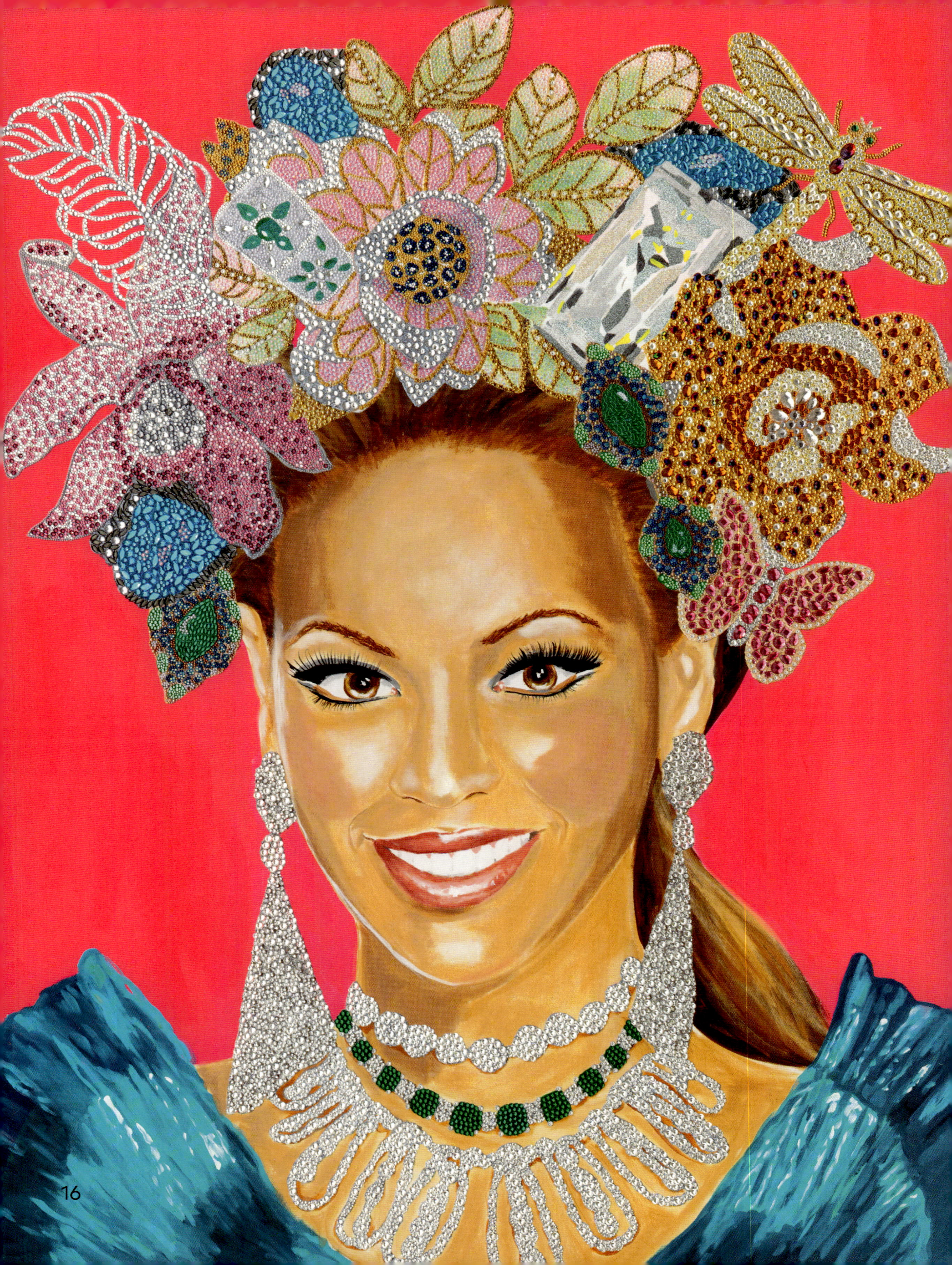

Table of Contents

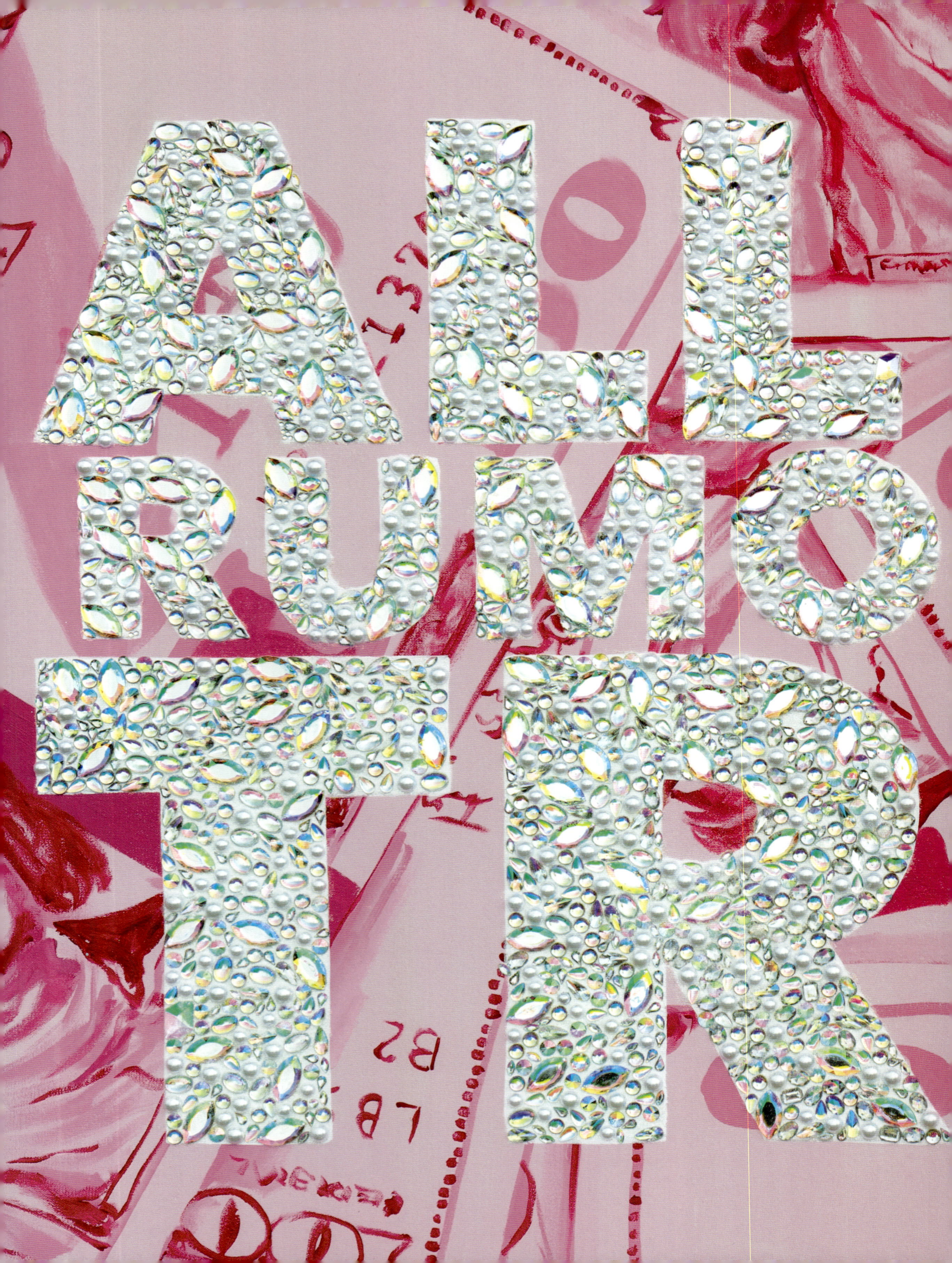

ALL
RUMO
TR

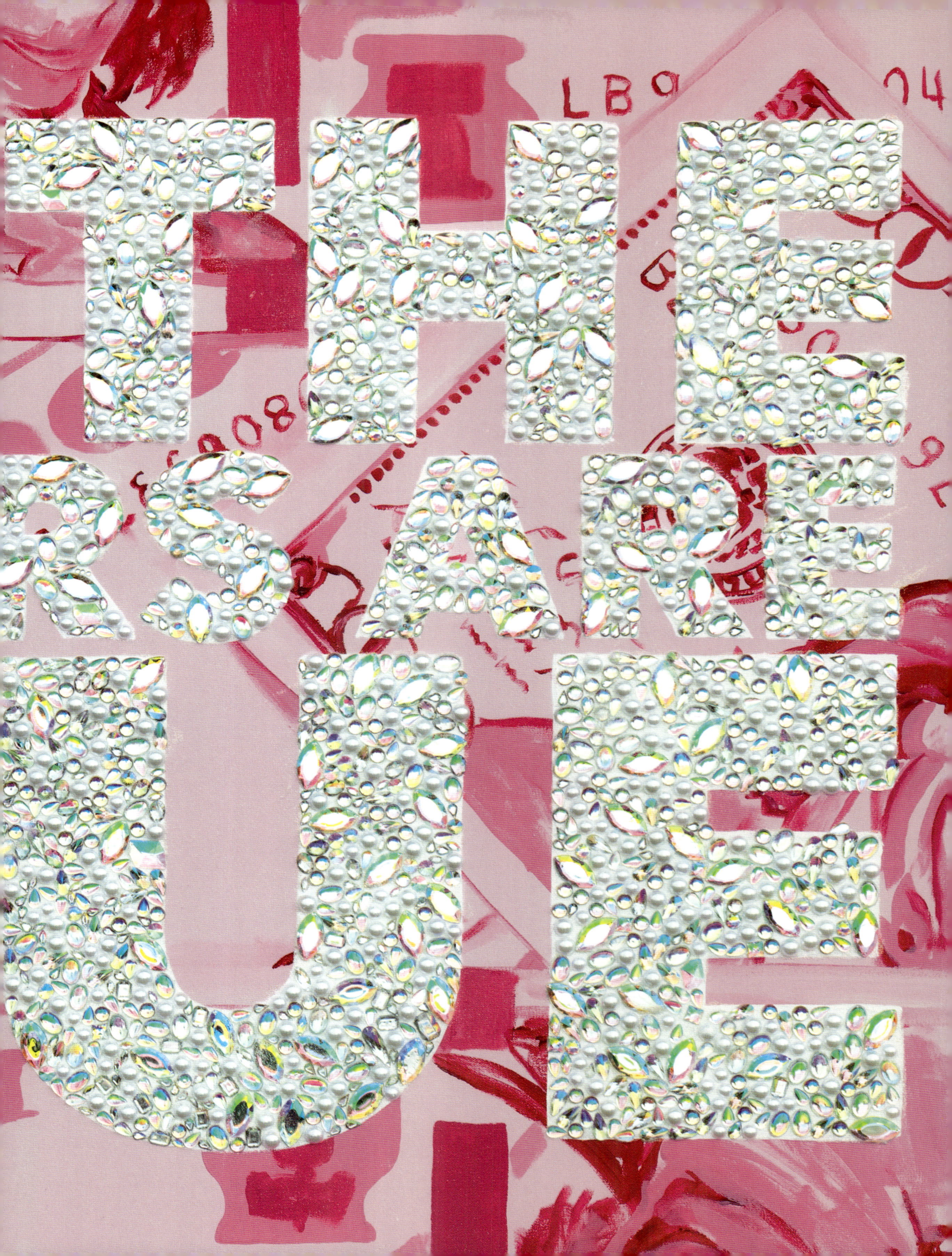

THE
RS ARE
UE

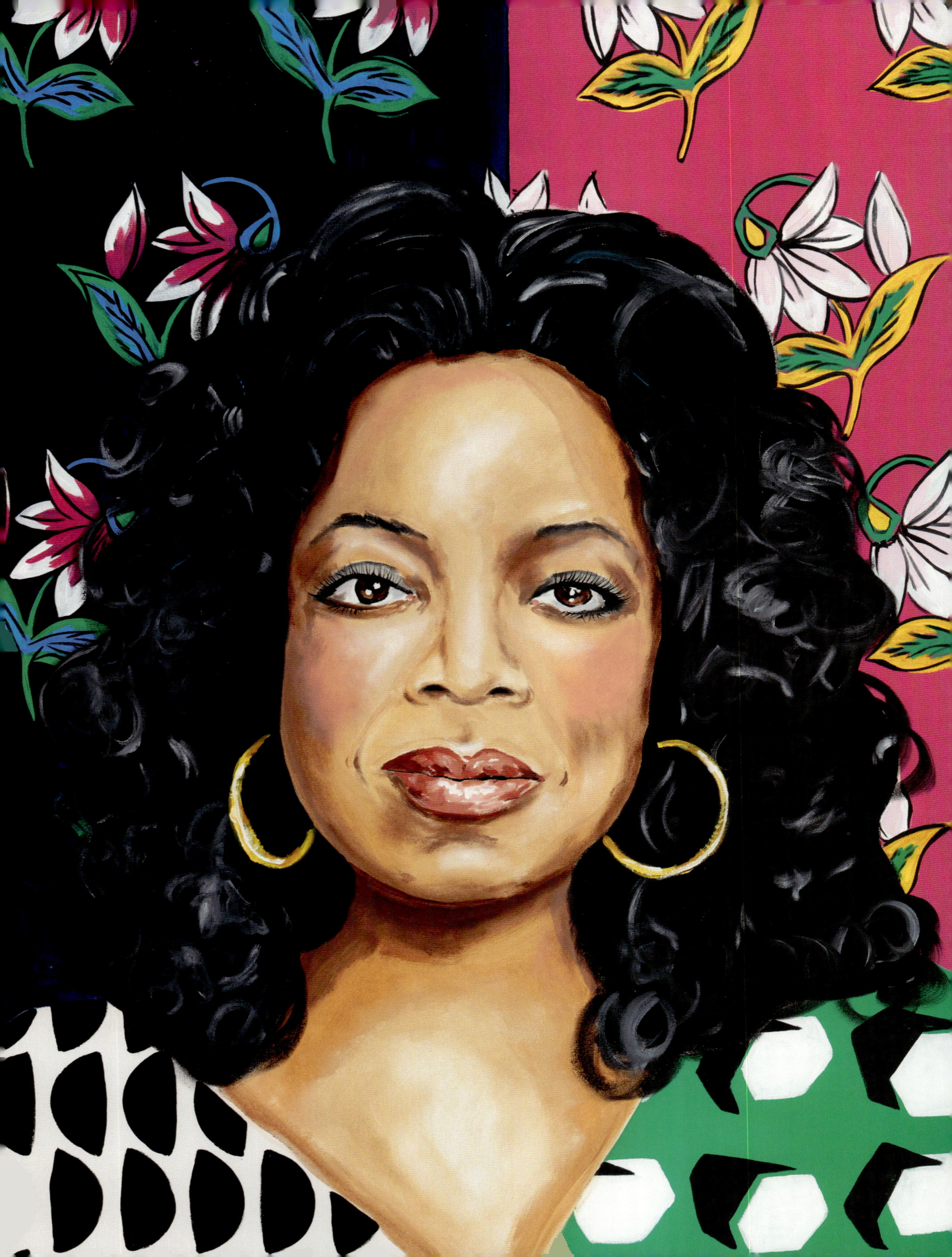

Oprah Winfrey

Because she teaches us how to overcome difficulties and be our very best. She is a force of nature.

Amanda Gorman

Because she has a giant gift and voice, and she is generous enough to share them with us—if we will only listen.

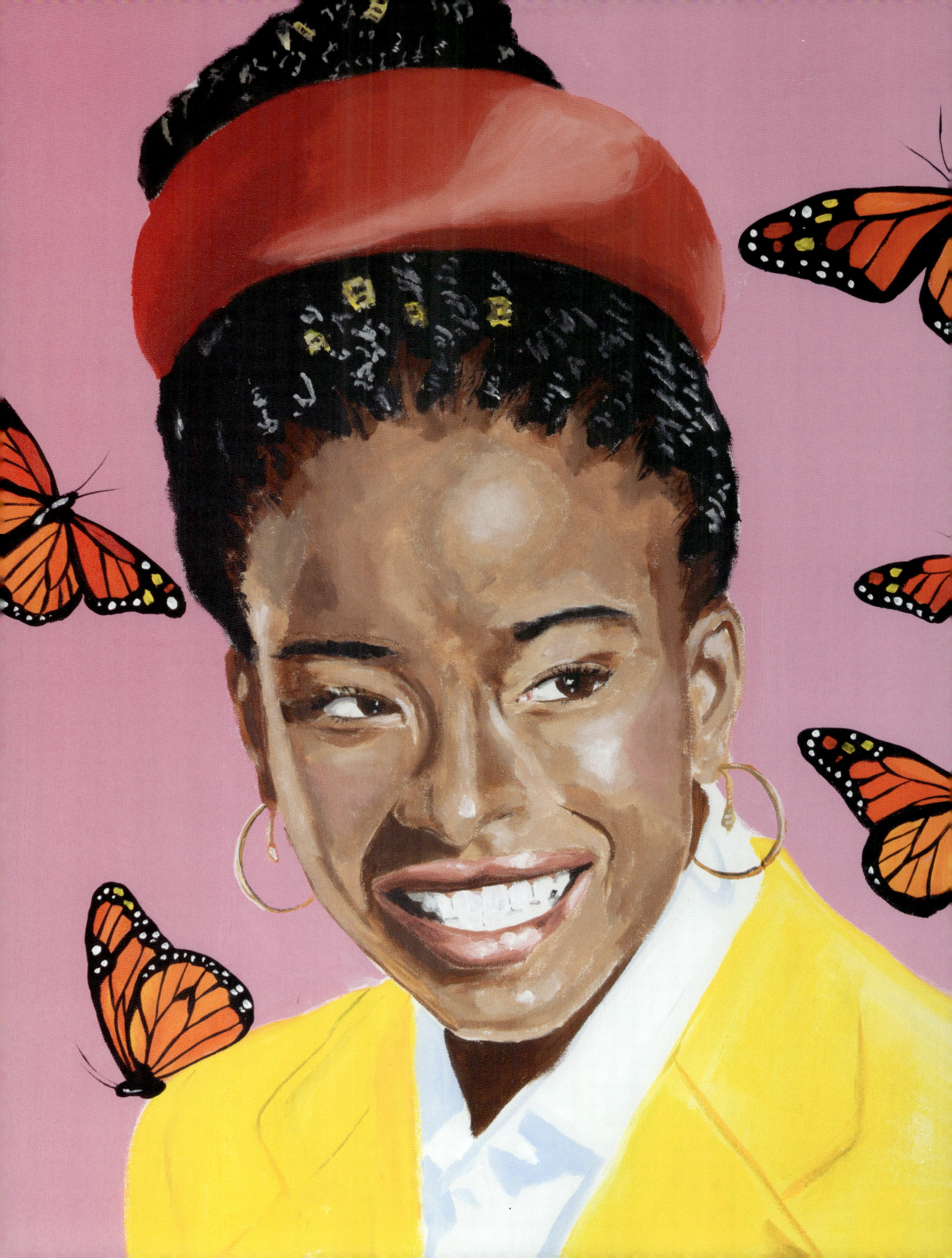

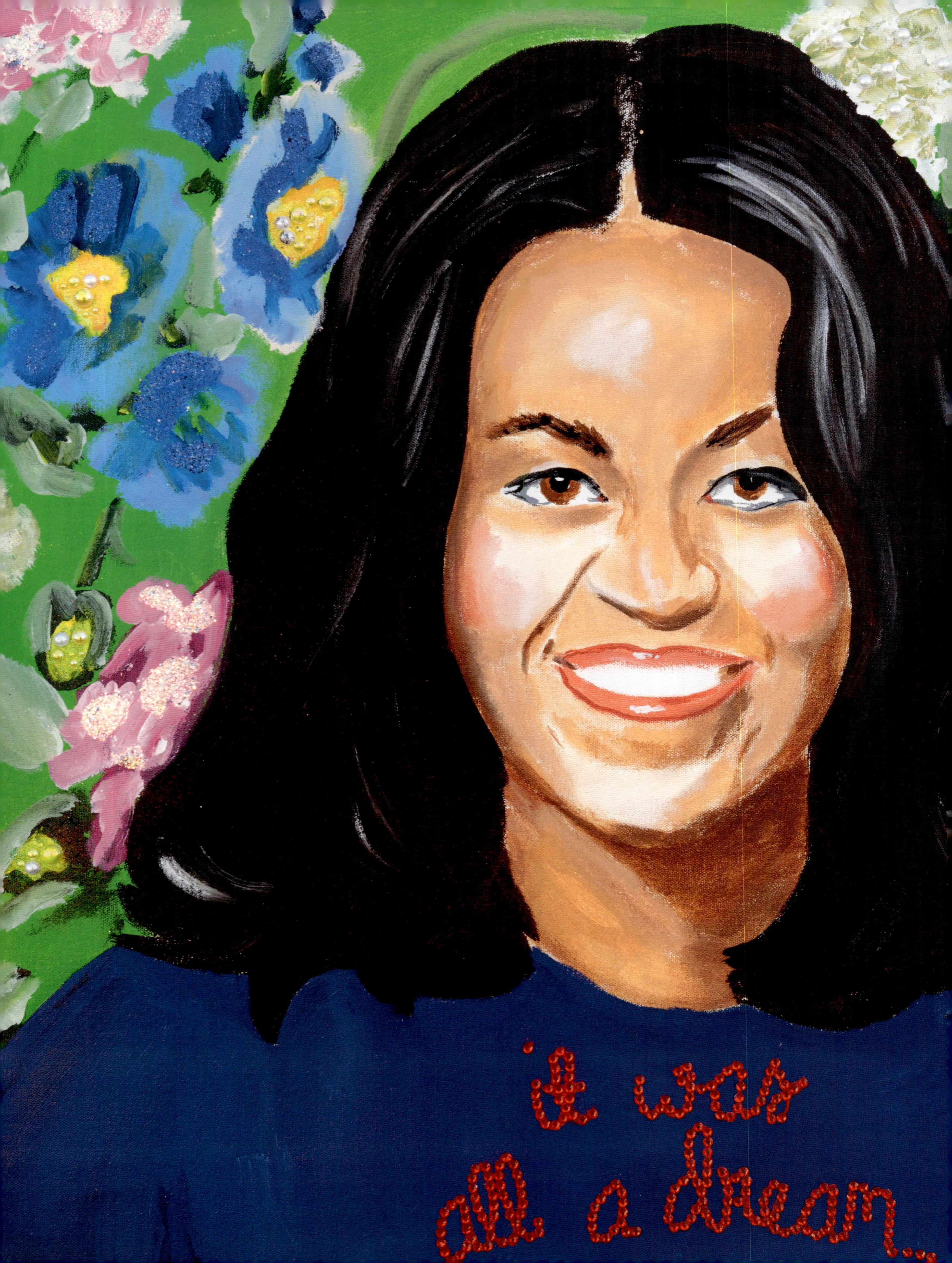

it was
all a dream.

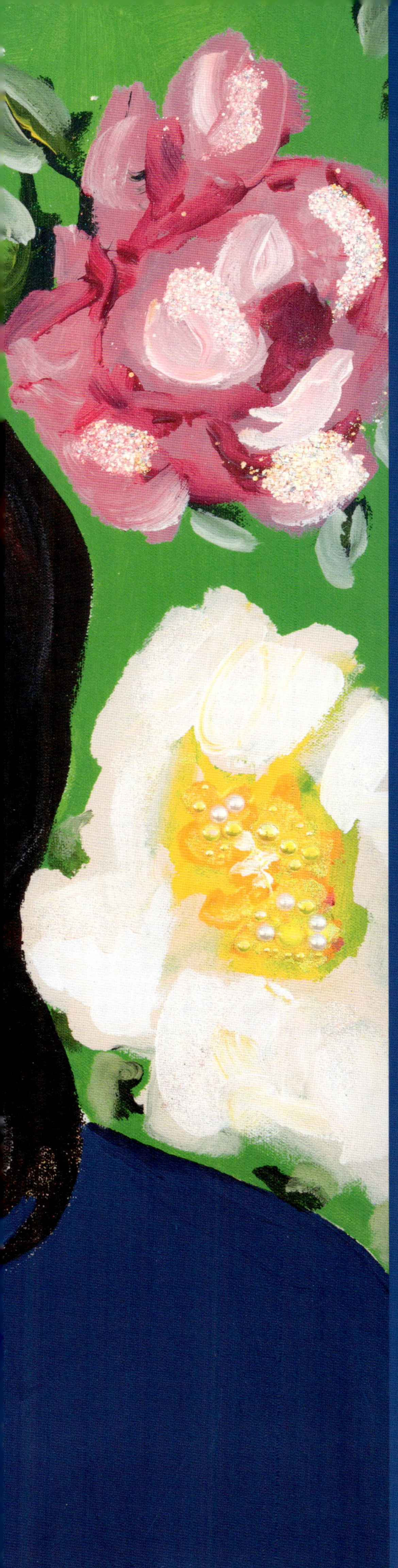

Michelle Obama

Because she leads by example through self-love, hard work, and positivity.

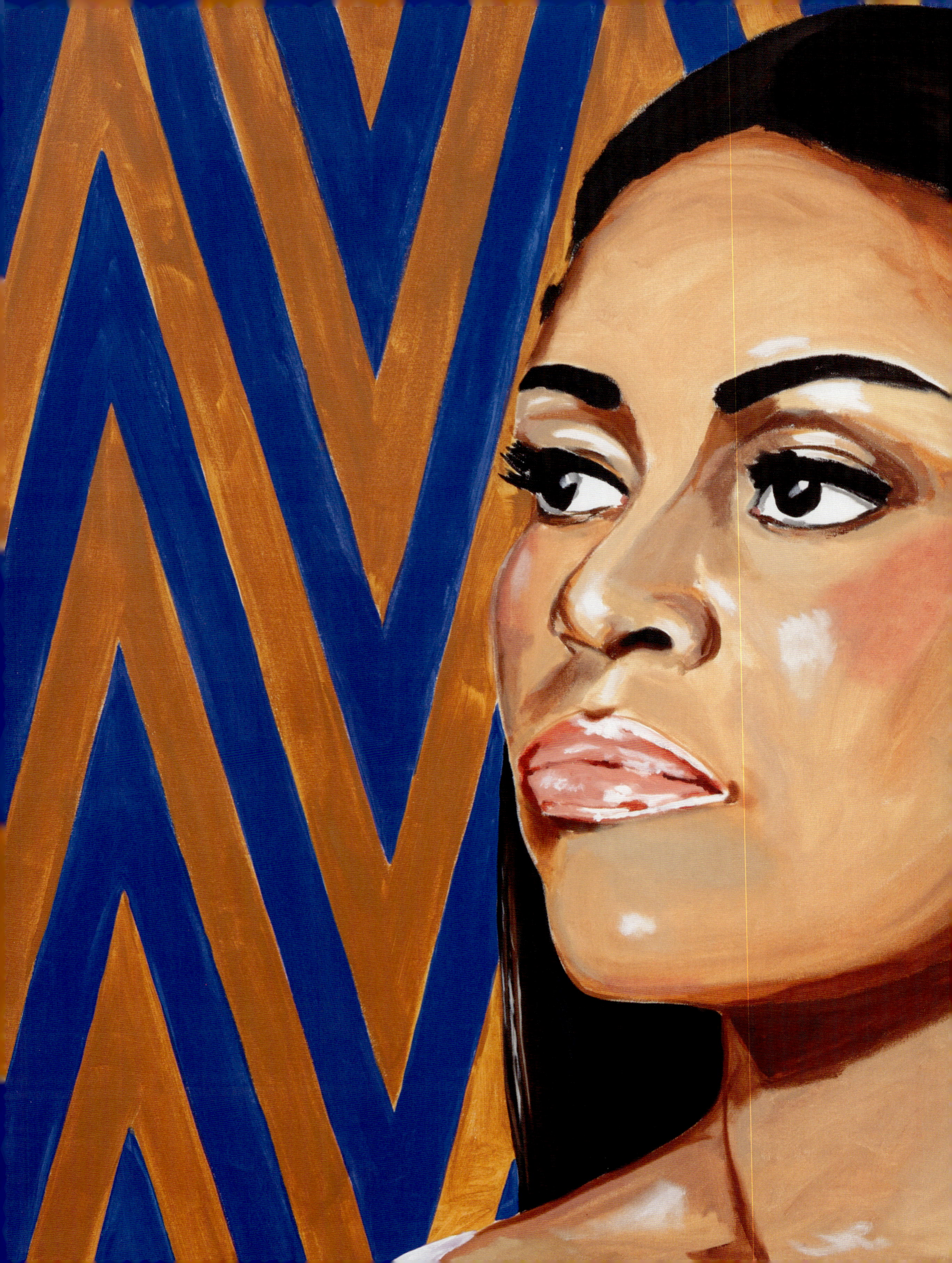

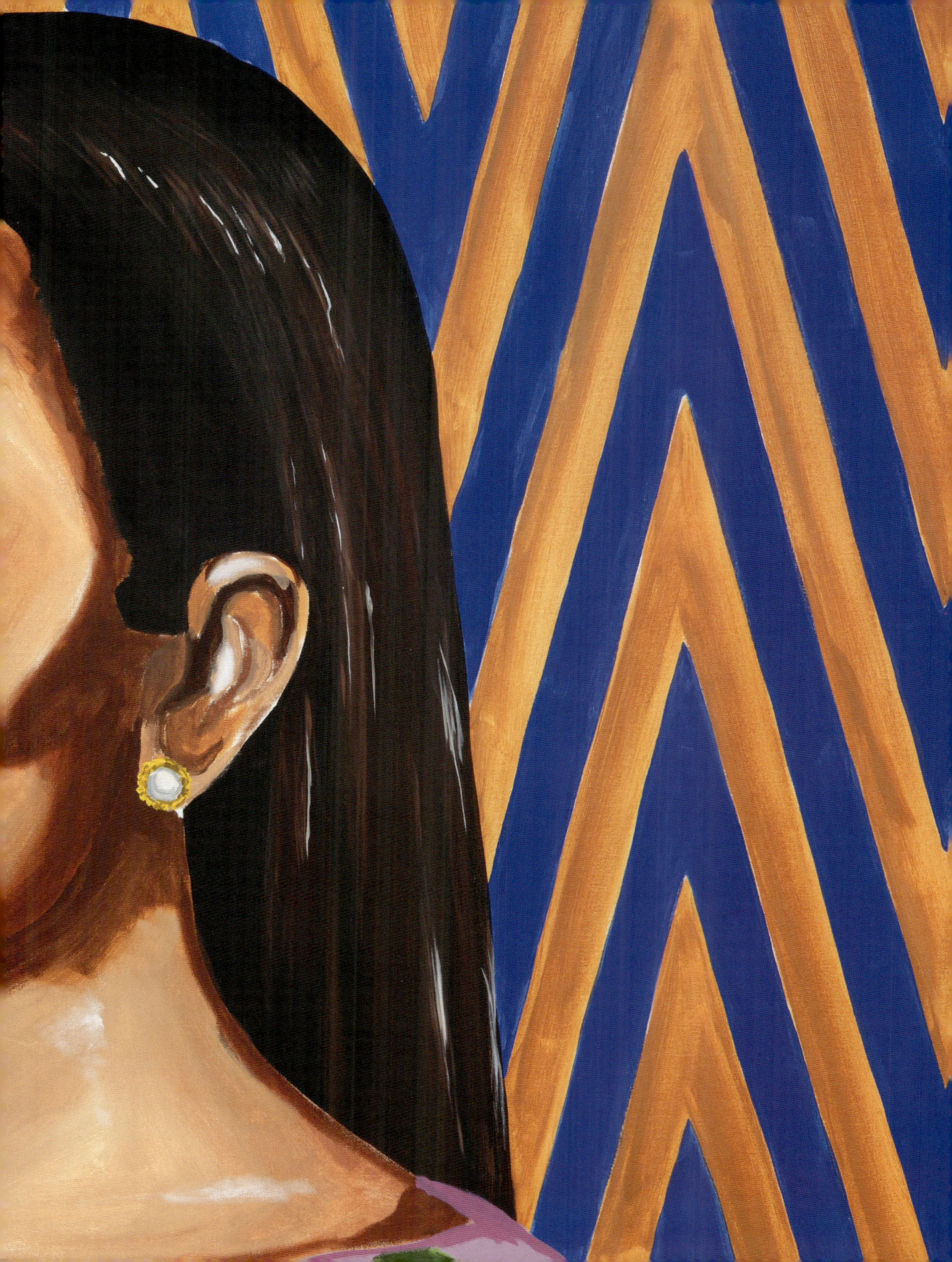

Serena Williams

Because she is strong, beautiful, and fights for her wins both on and off the court.

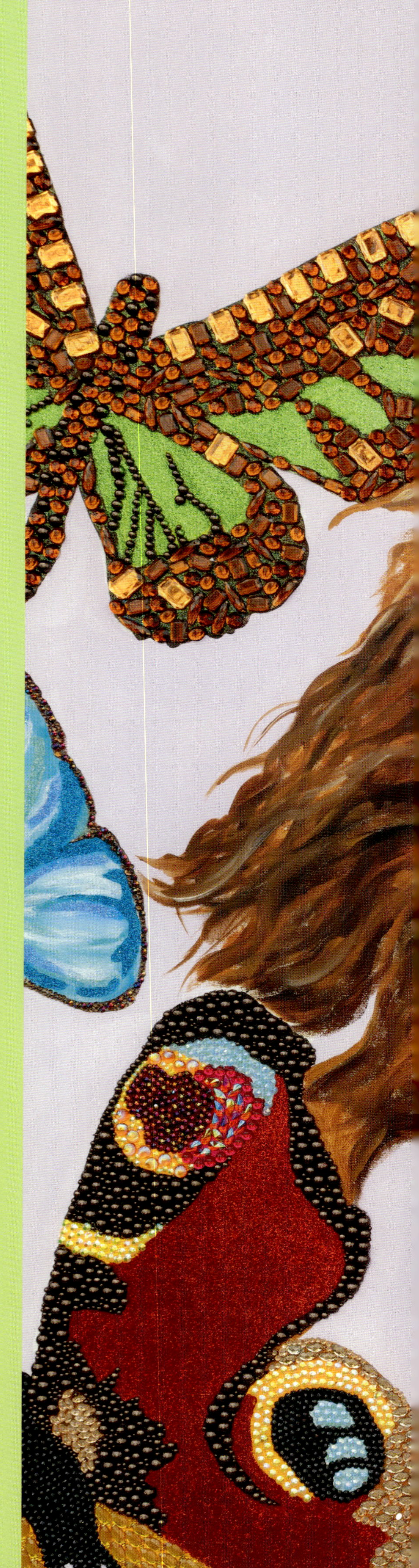

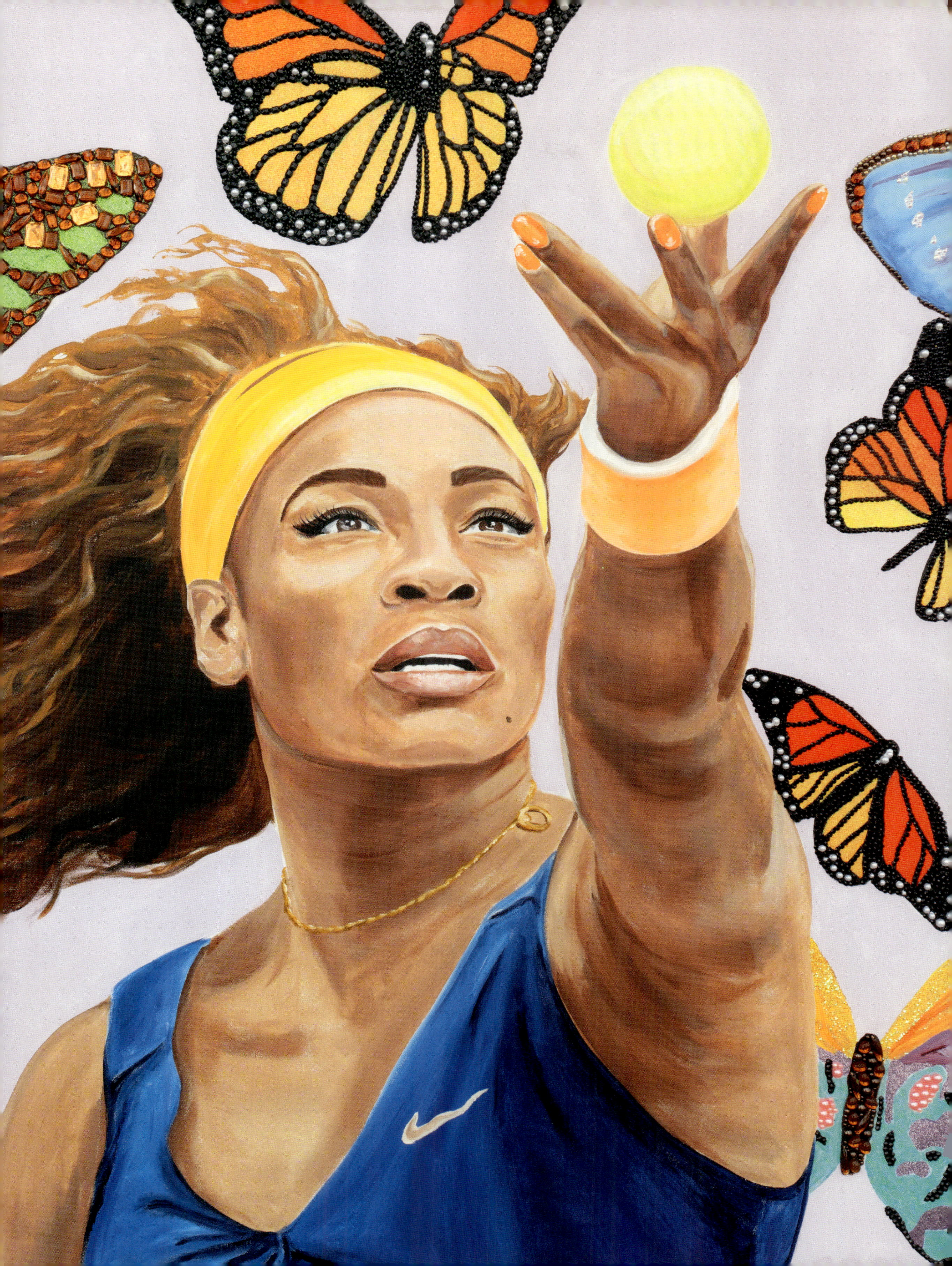

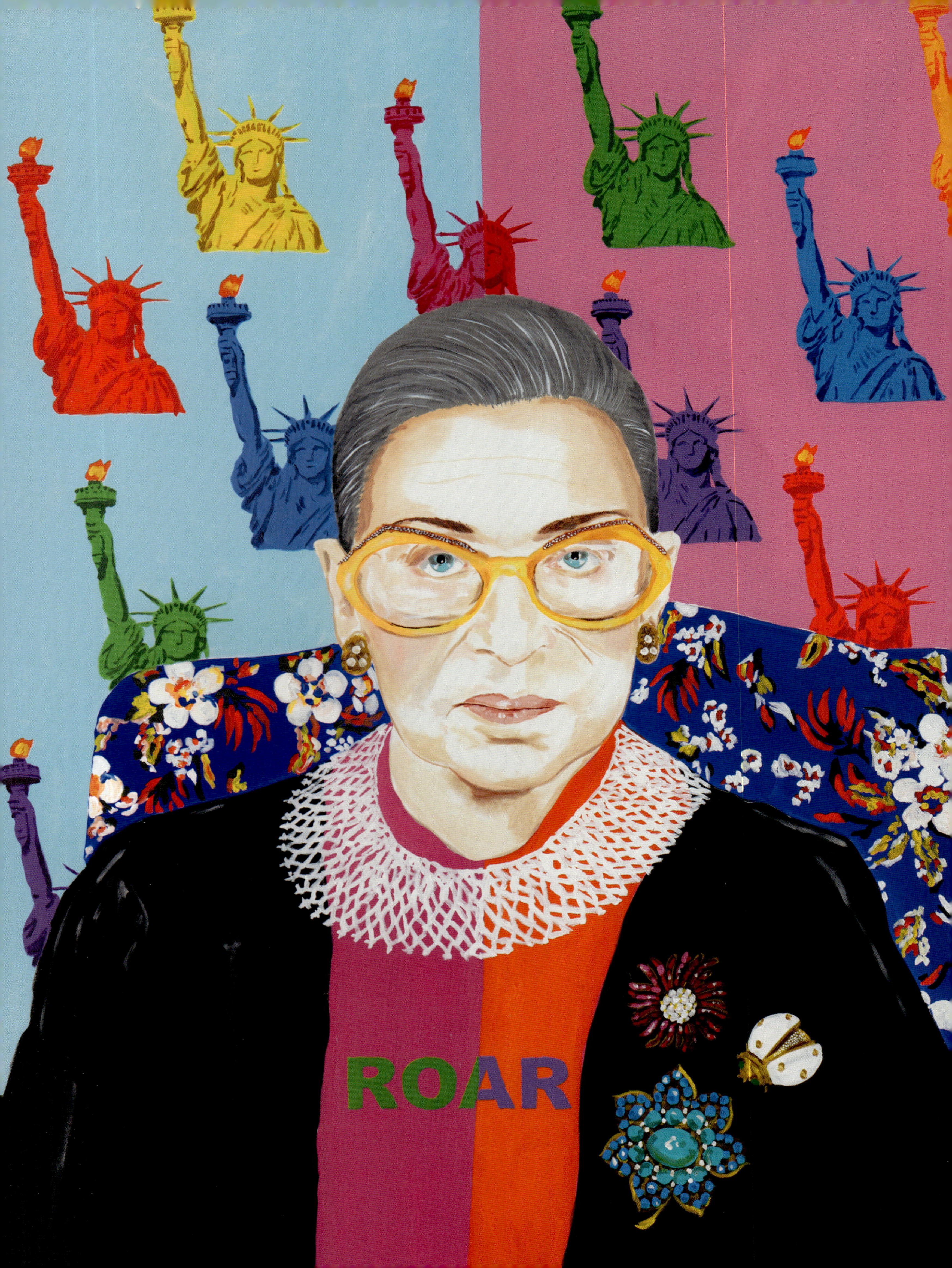
ROAR

Ruth Bader Ginsburg

Because she showed us how capable we all are.

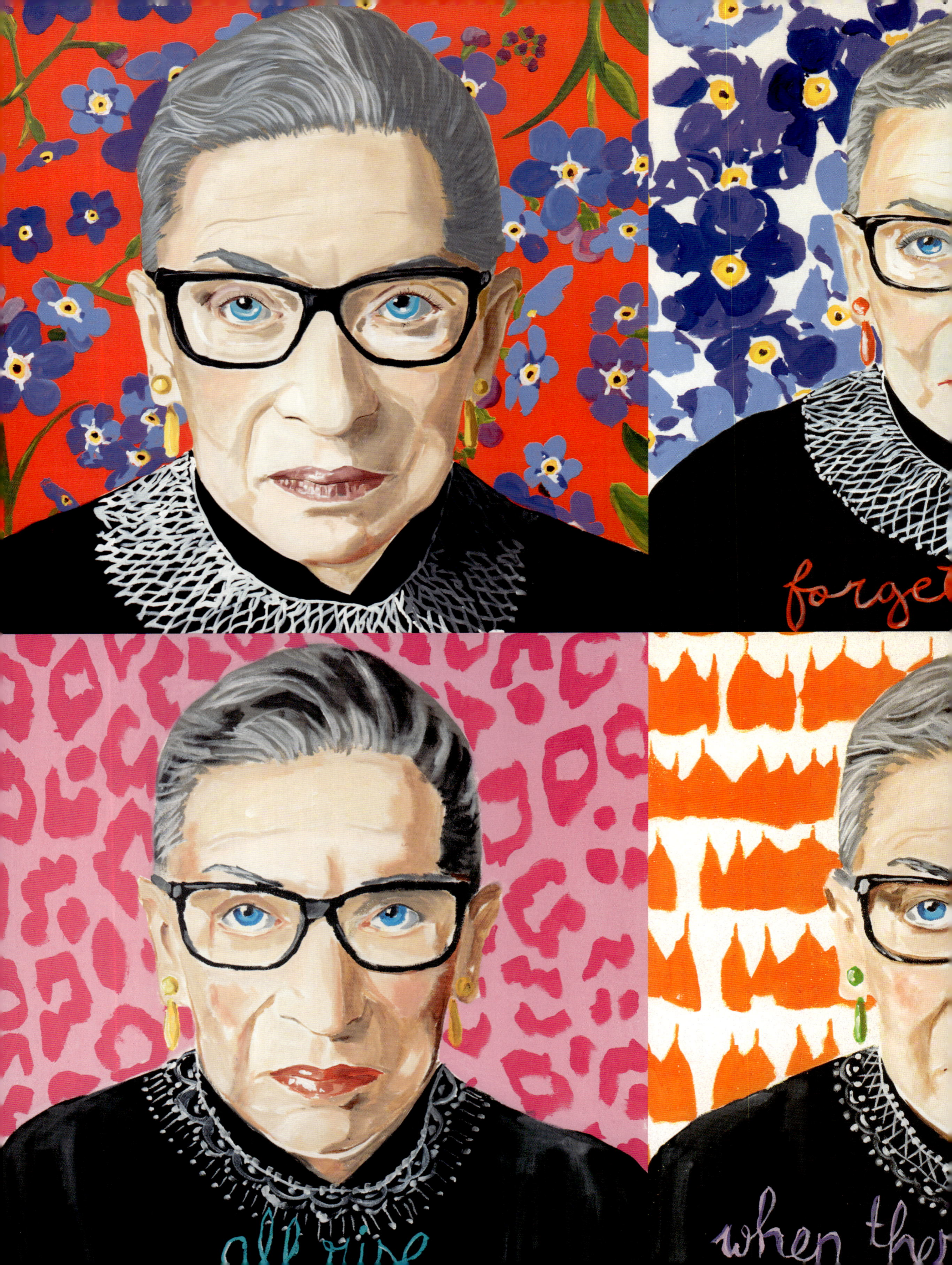
forget
when the
all rise

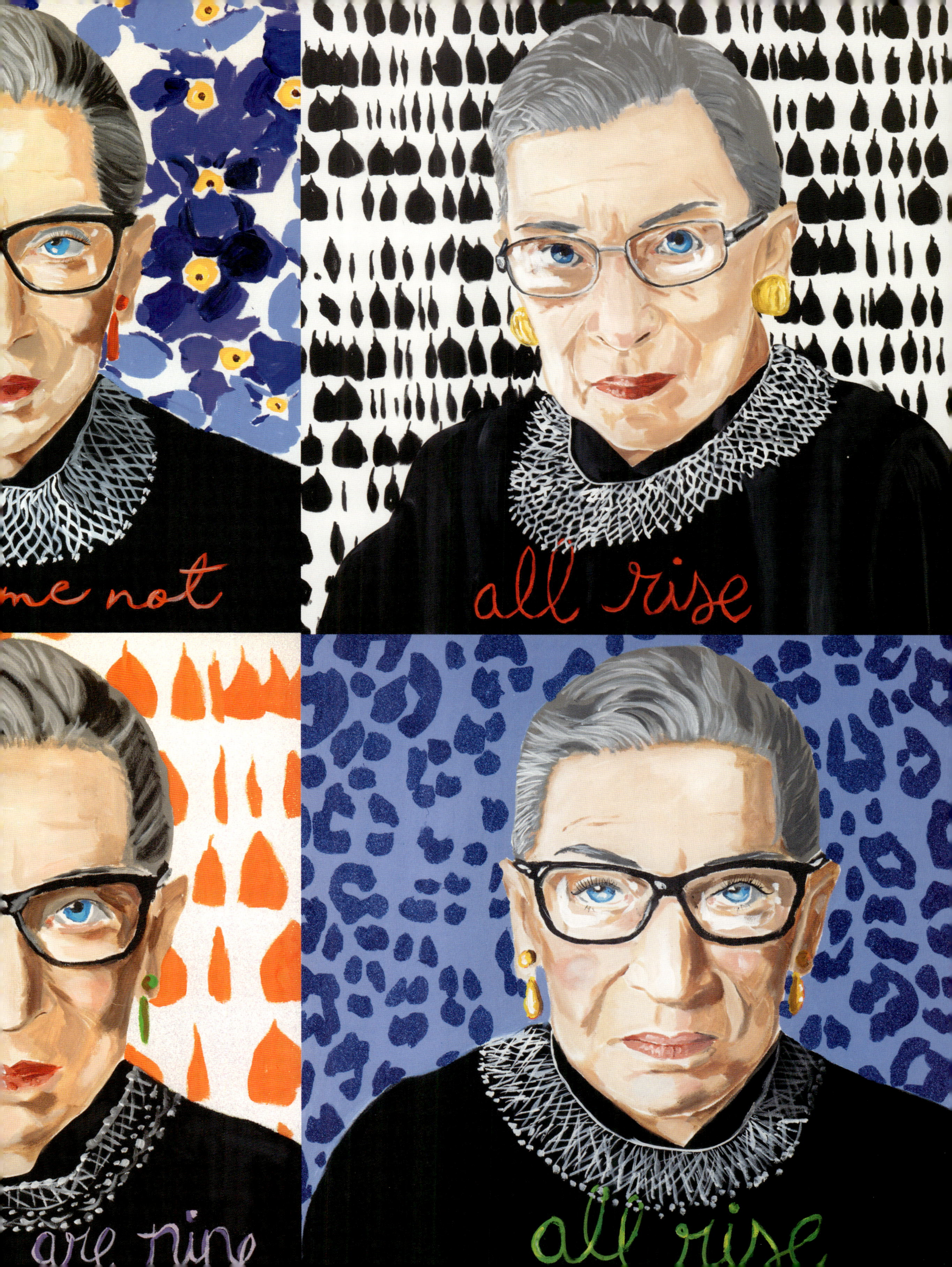
me not
all rise
are nine
all rise

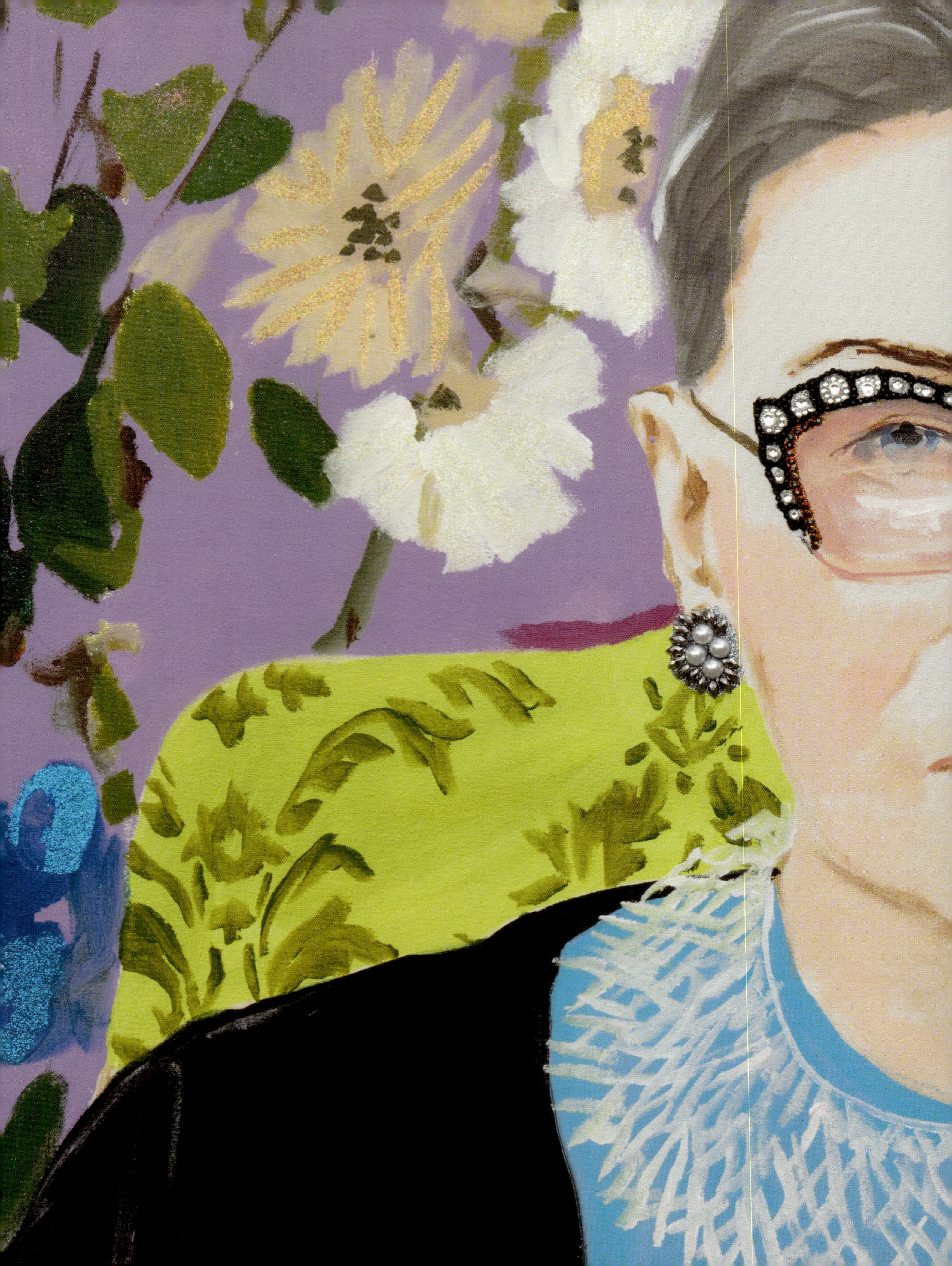

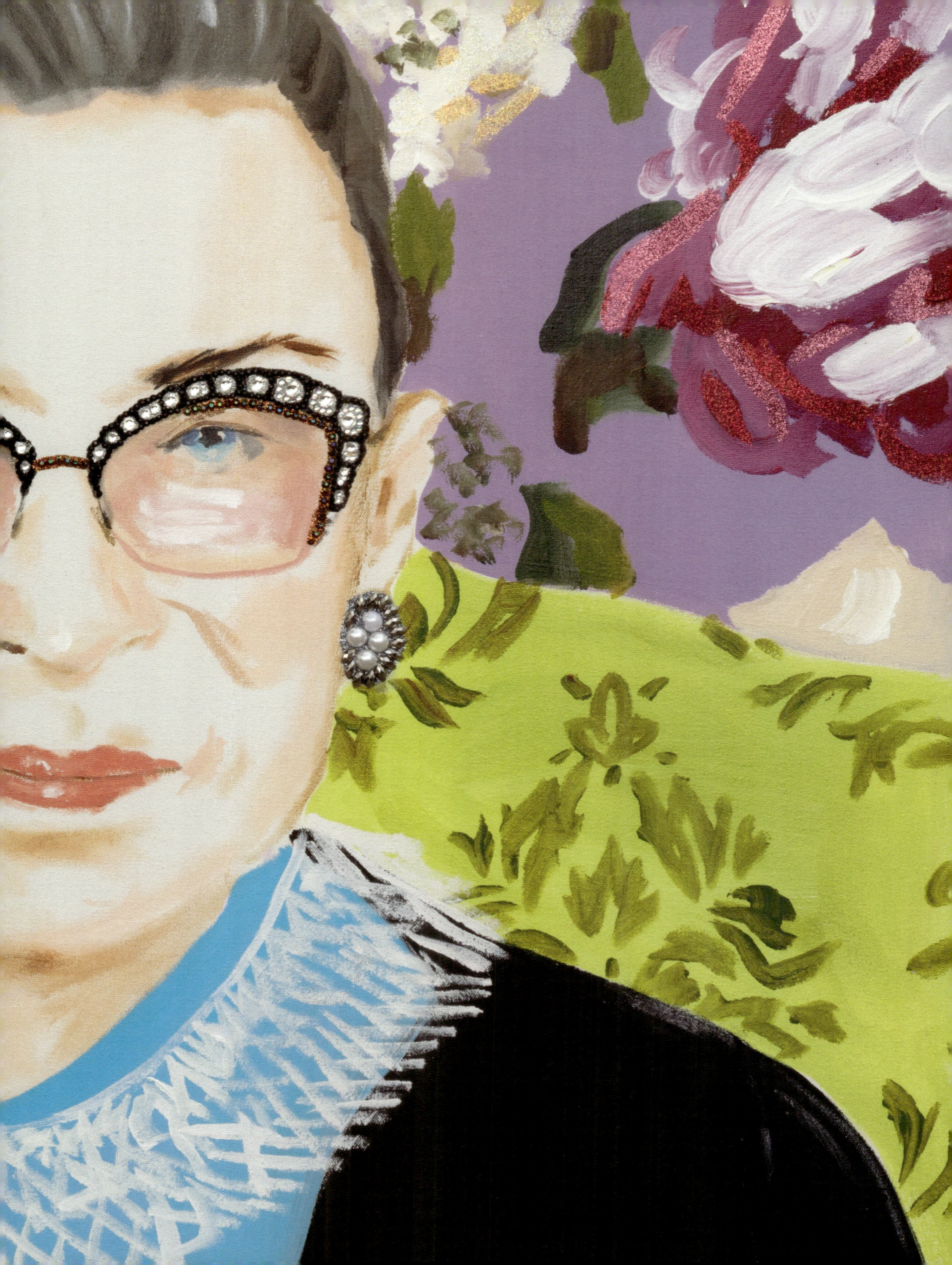

Mother Teresa

Because she taught us selfless sacrifice.

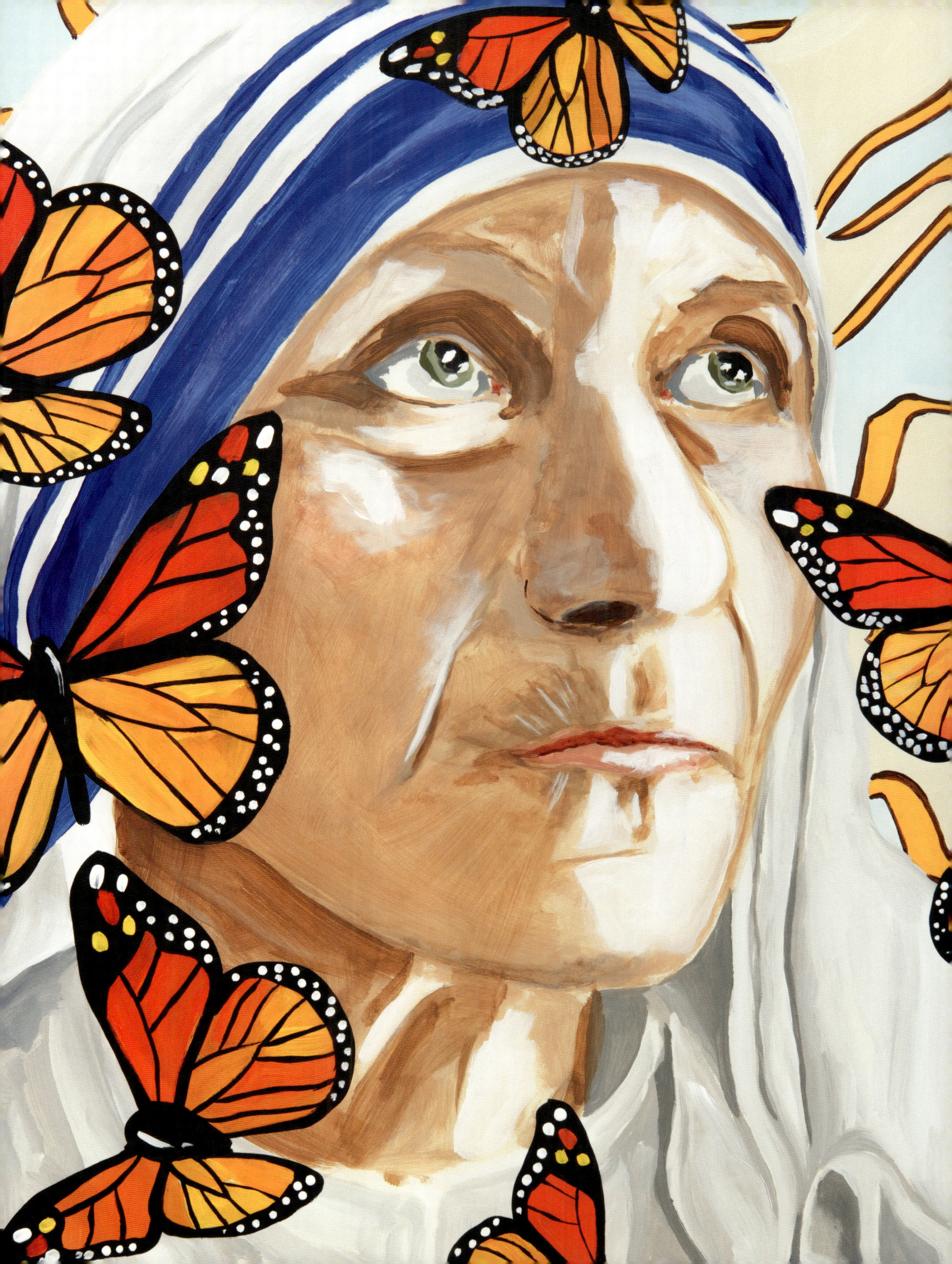

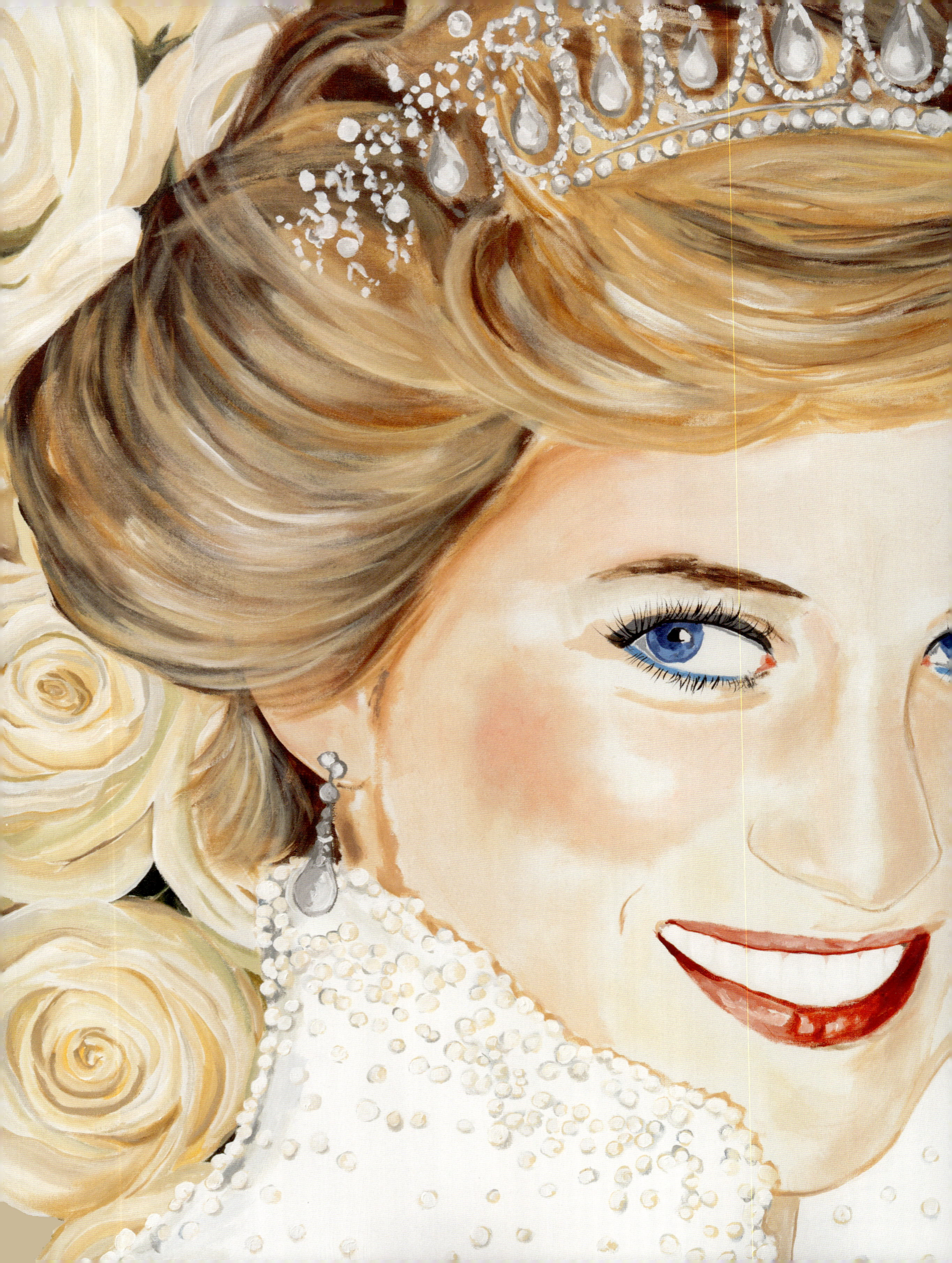

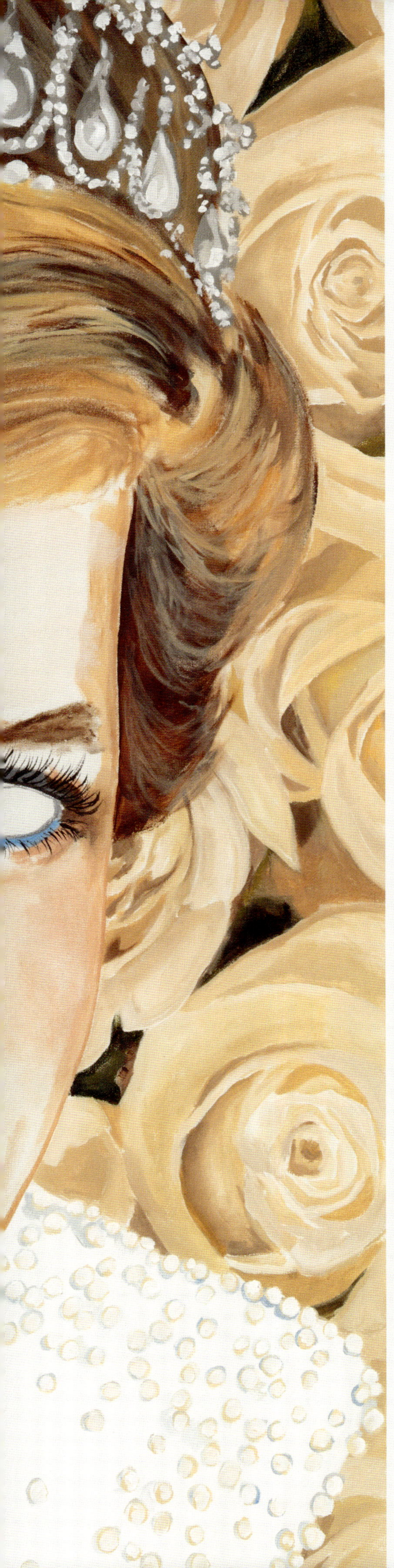

Diana, Princess of Wales

Because she was a rare, beautiful jewel among a handful of diamonds. She was a loving mother and the tallest wildflower in a rose garden.

Elizabeth II

Because she demonstrated that a woman can wear a very heavy crown with conviction, grace, and honor.

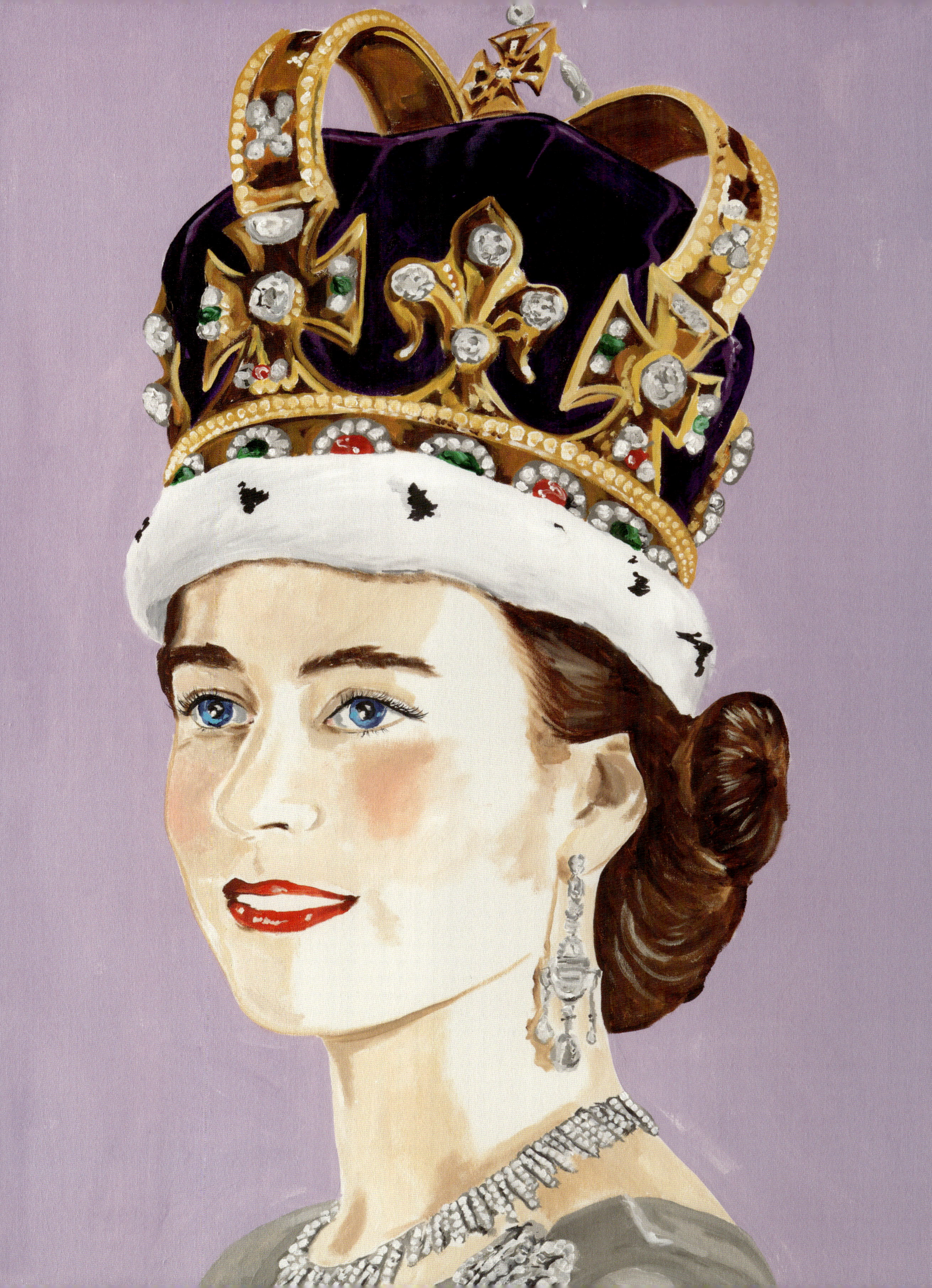

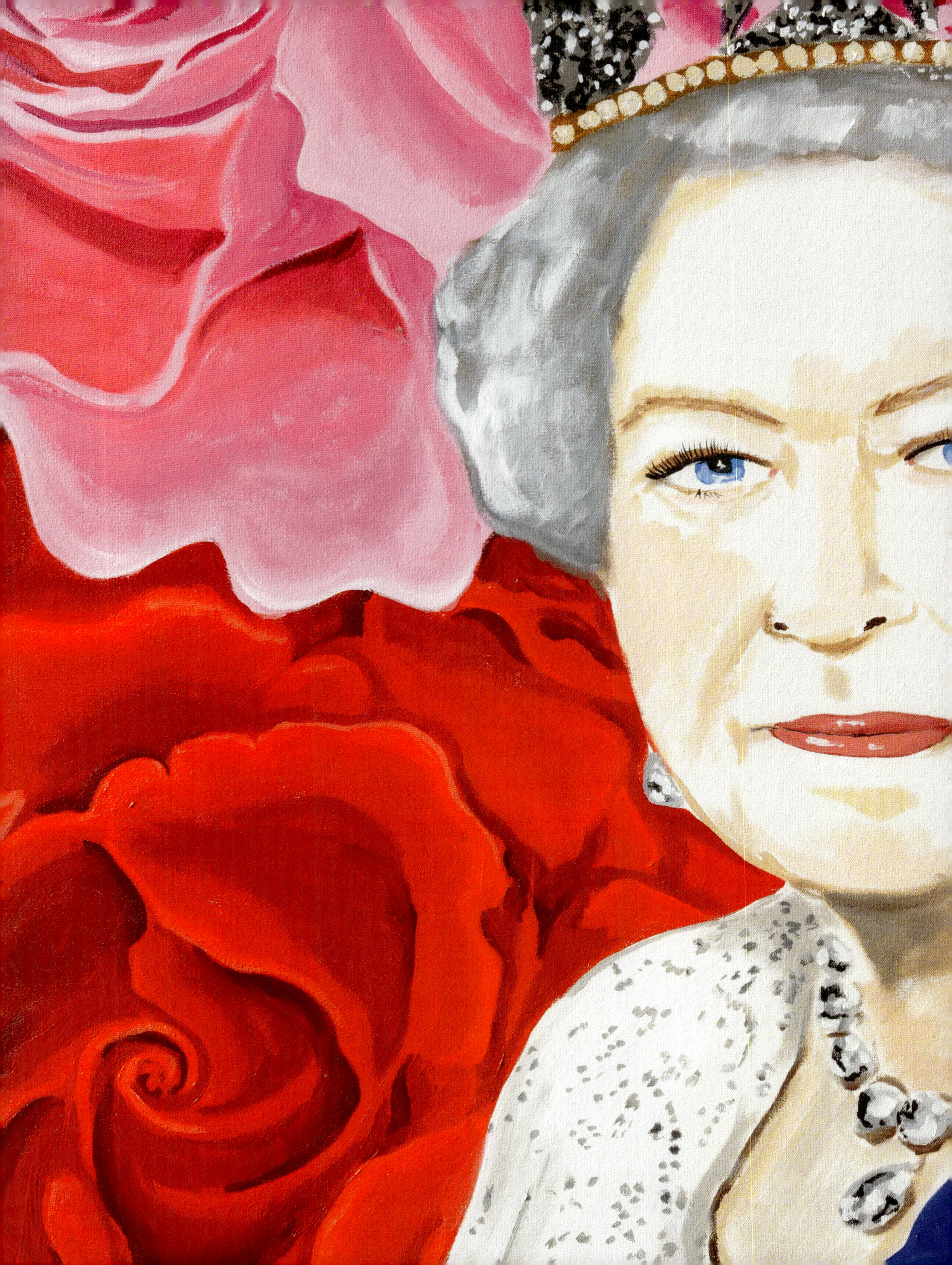

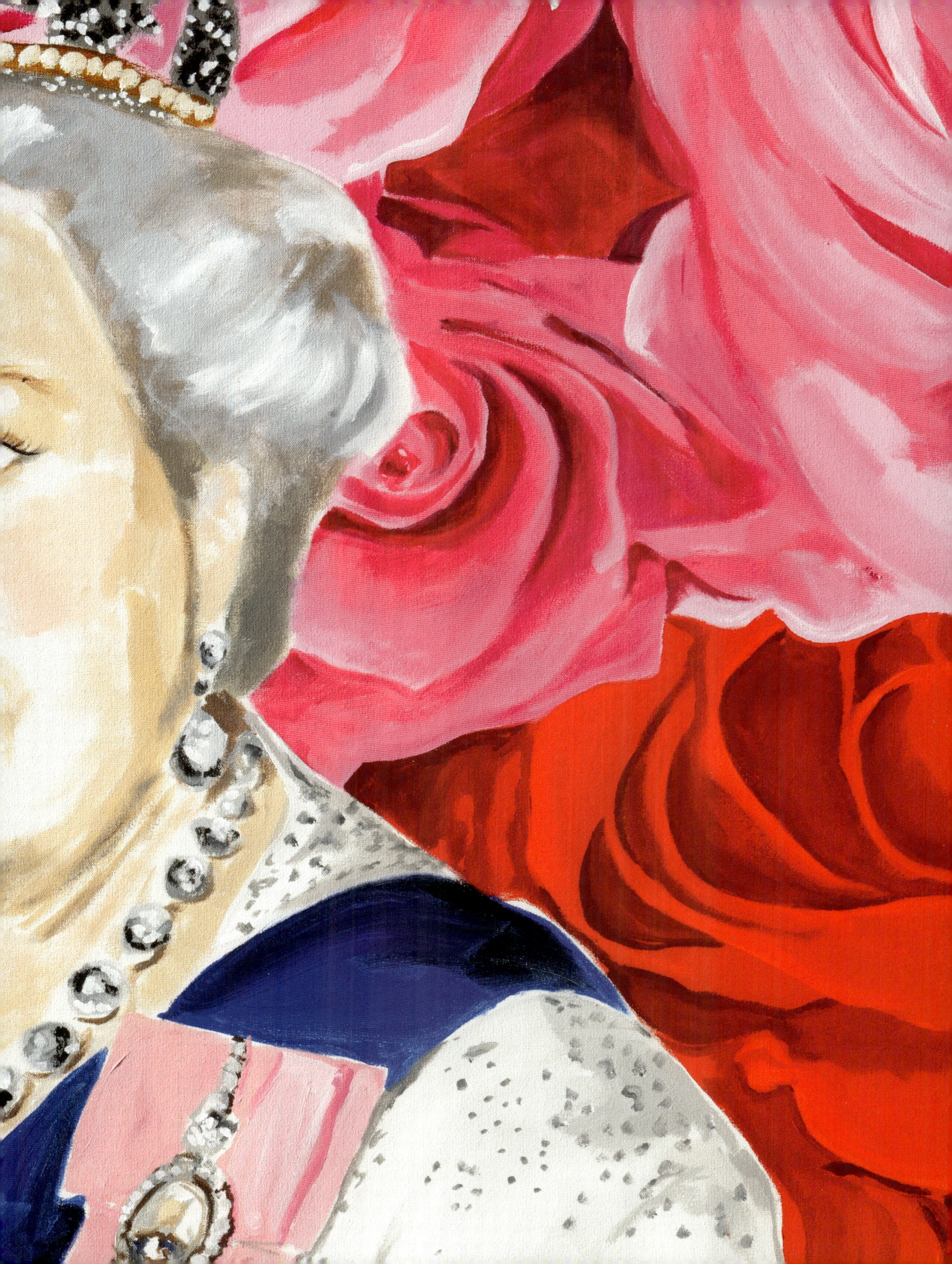

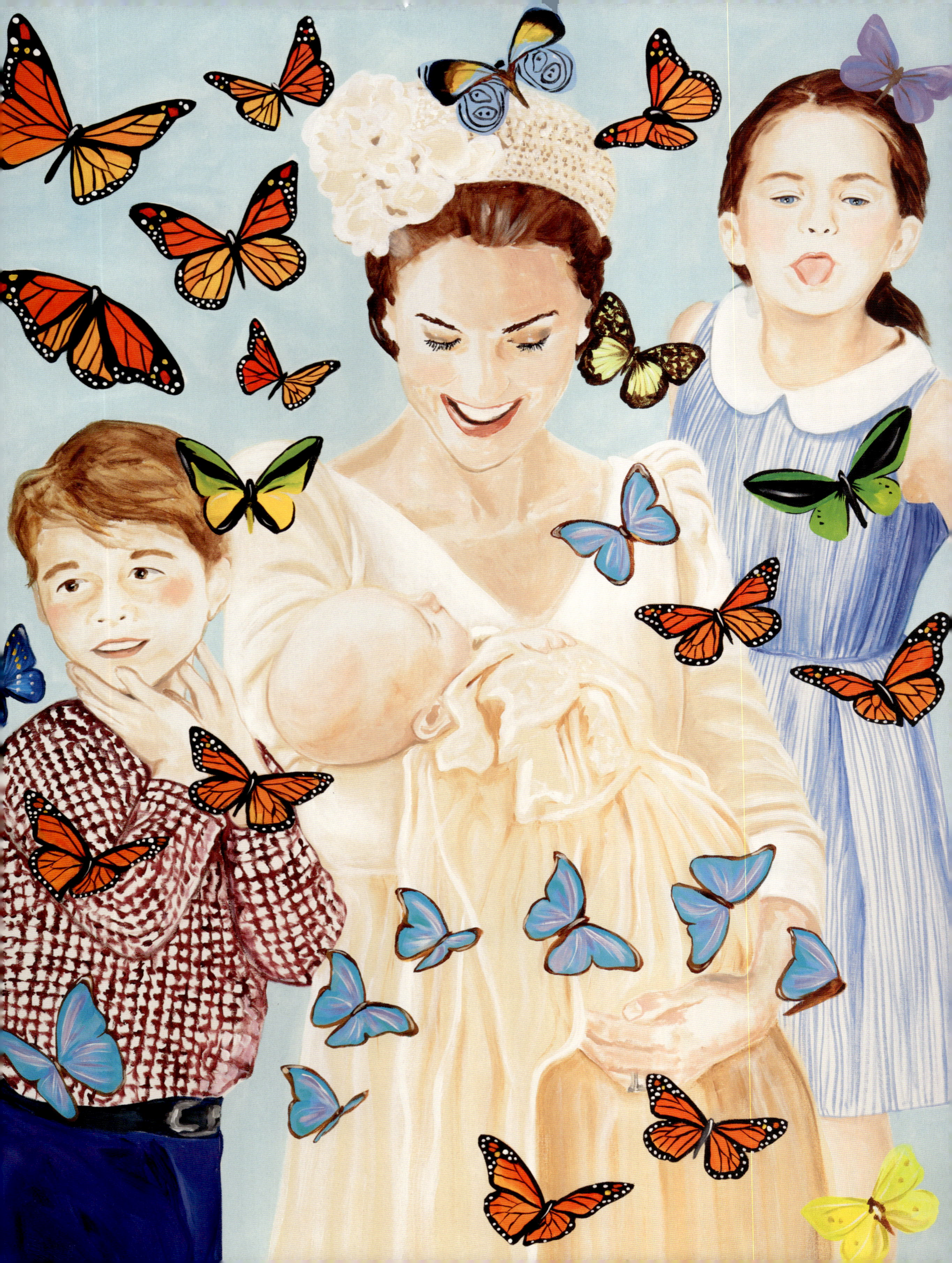

Kate Middleton

Because she is poised, elegant, and makes it look easy under a global microscope.

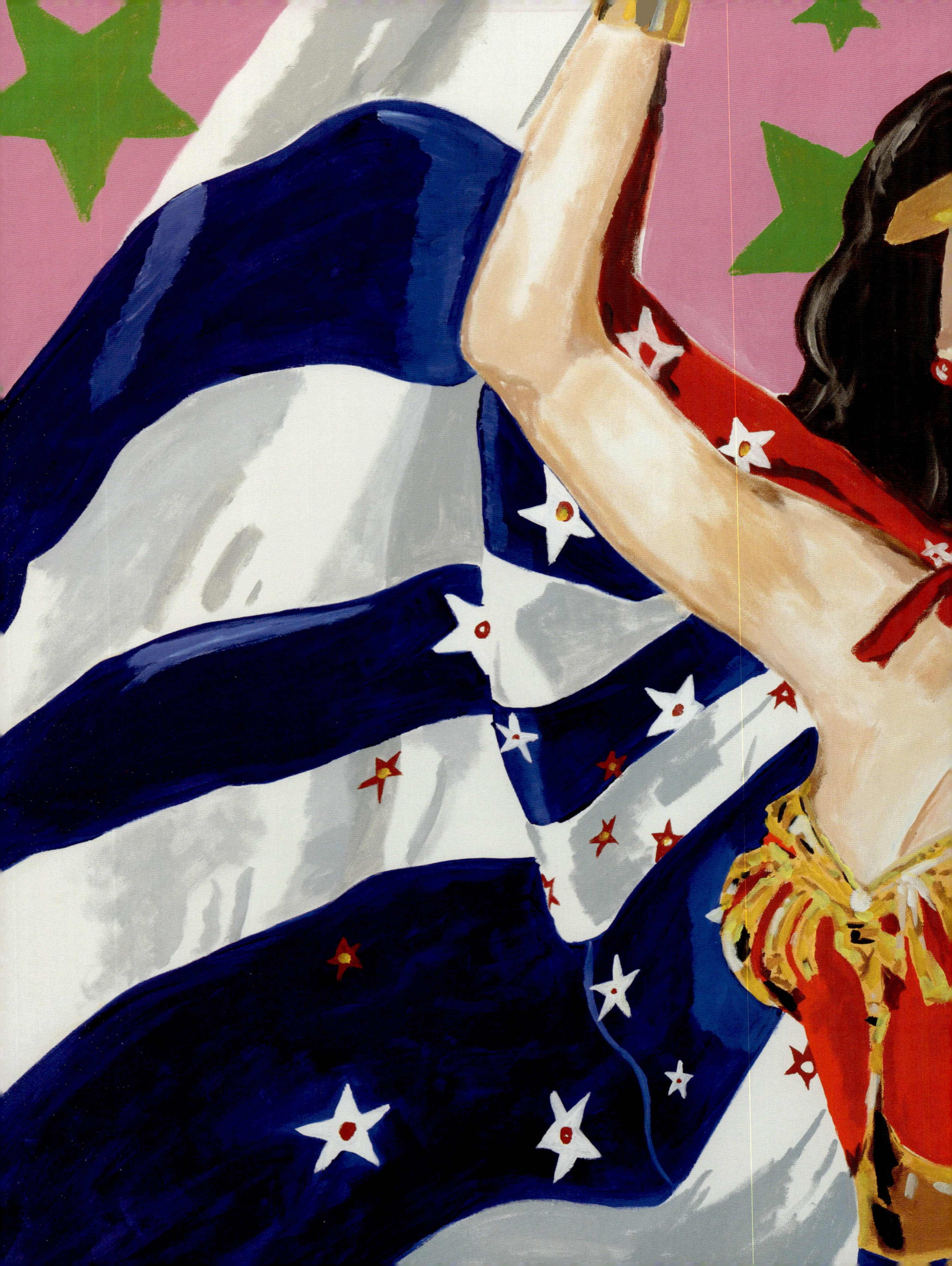

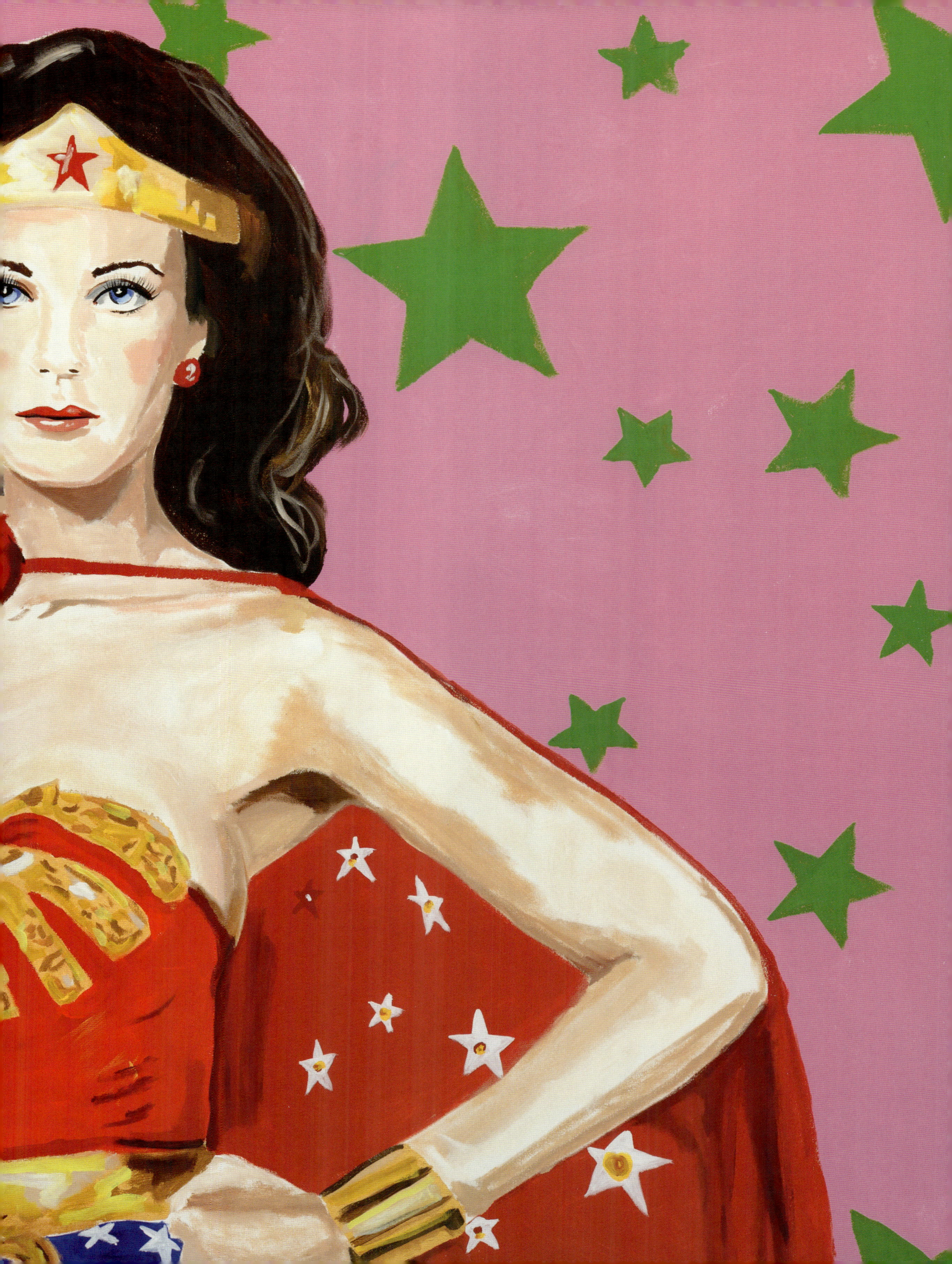

Meghan Markle

Because she stands up for herself and for love, no matter the cost.

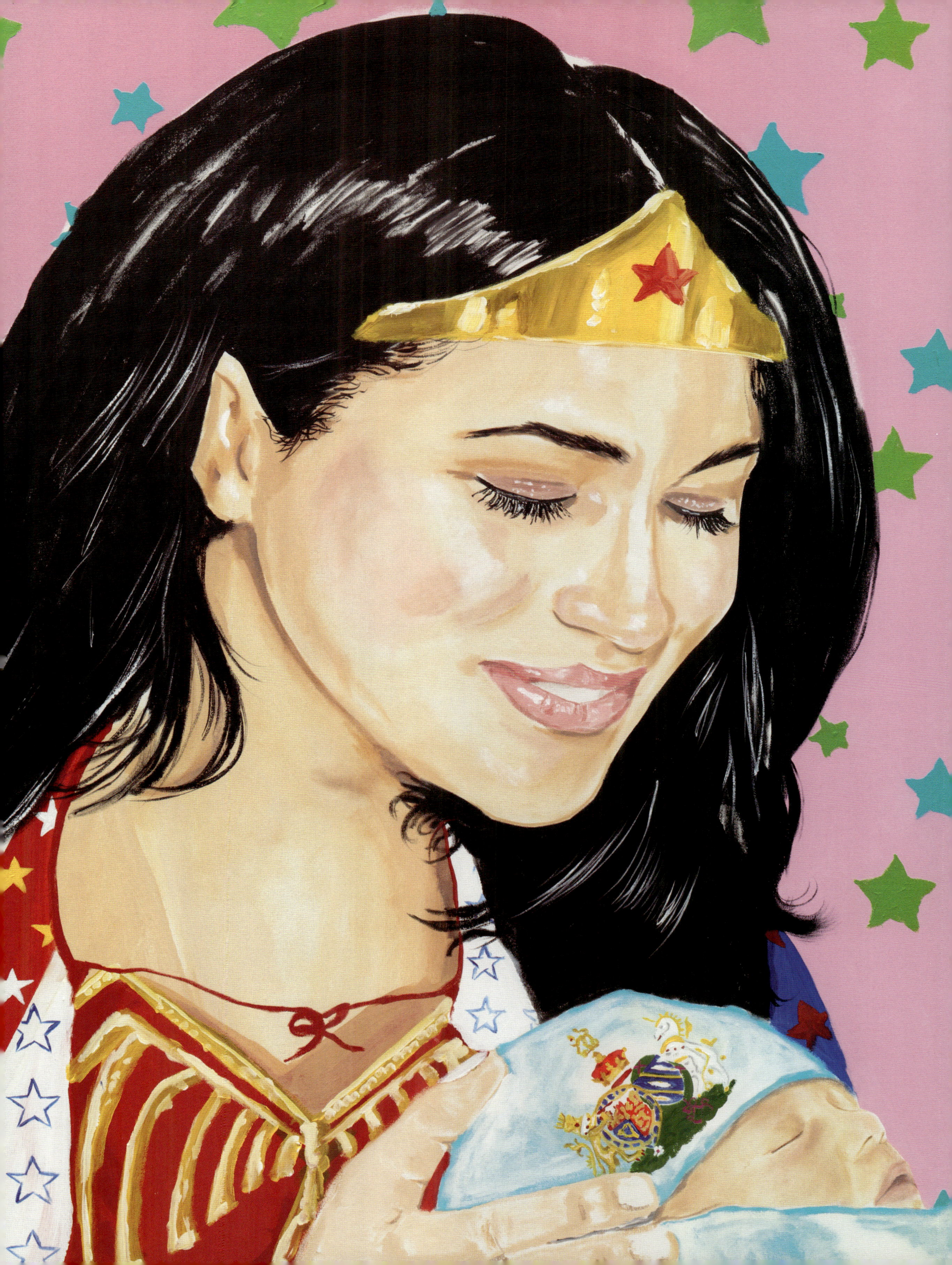

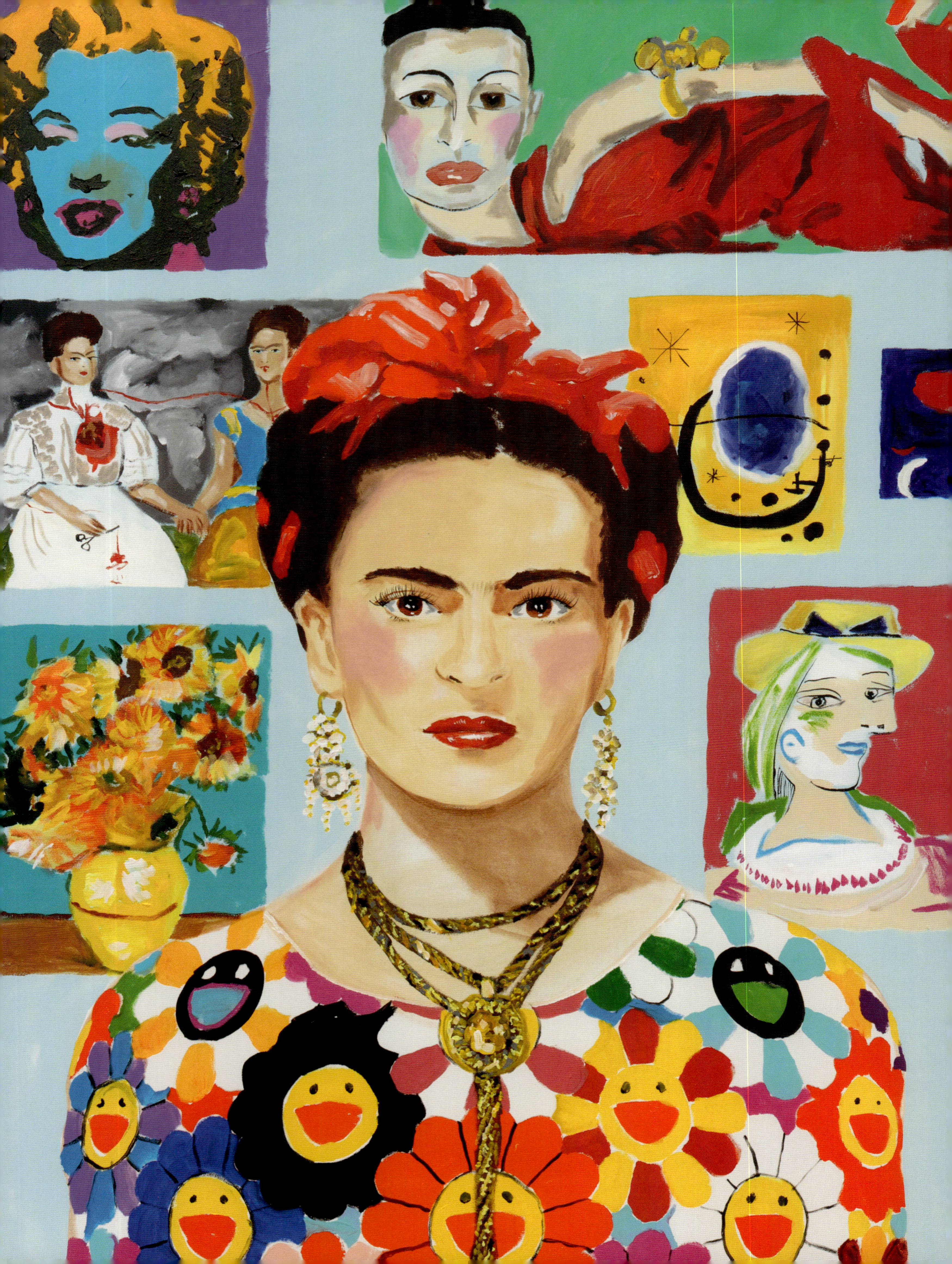

Frida Kahlo

Because she was endlessly authentic and true to herself.

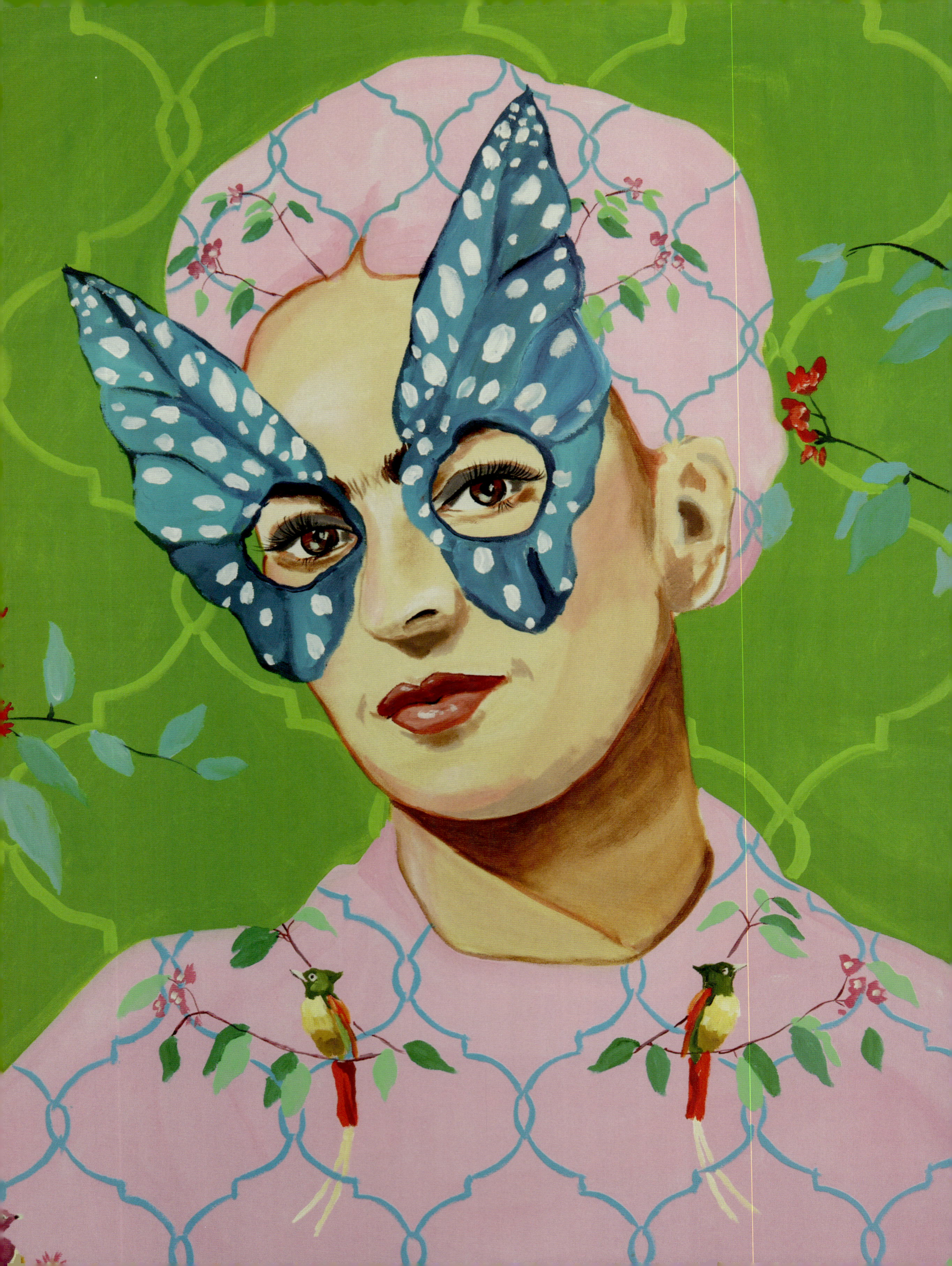

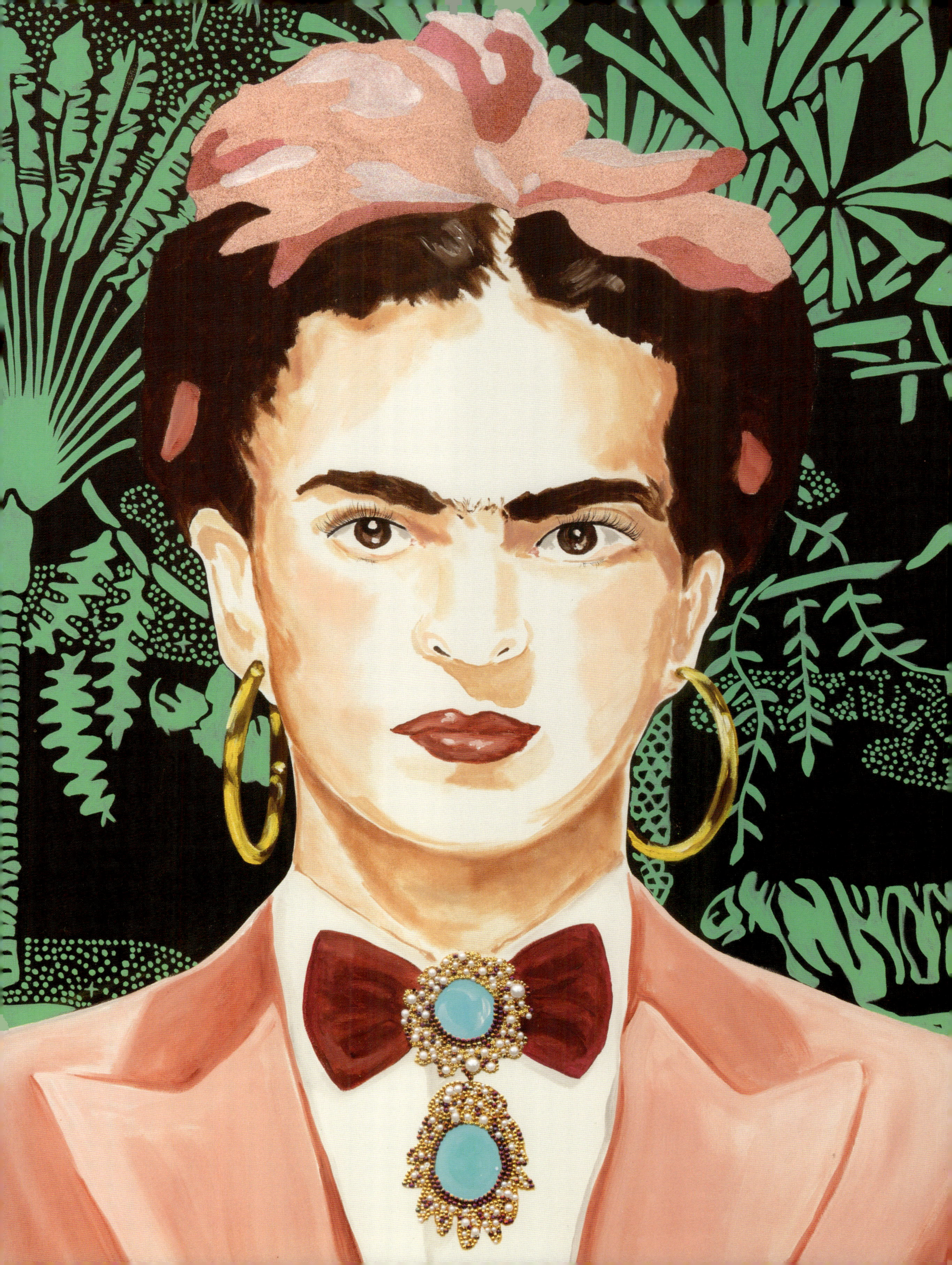

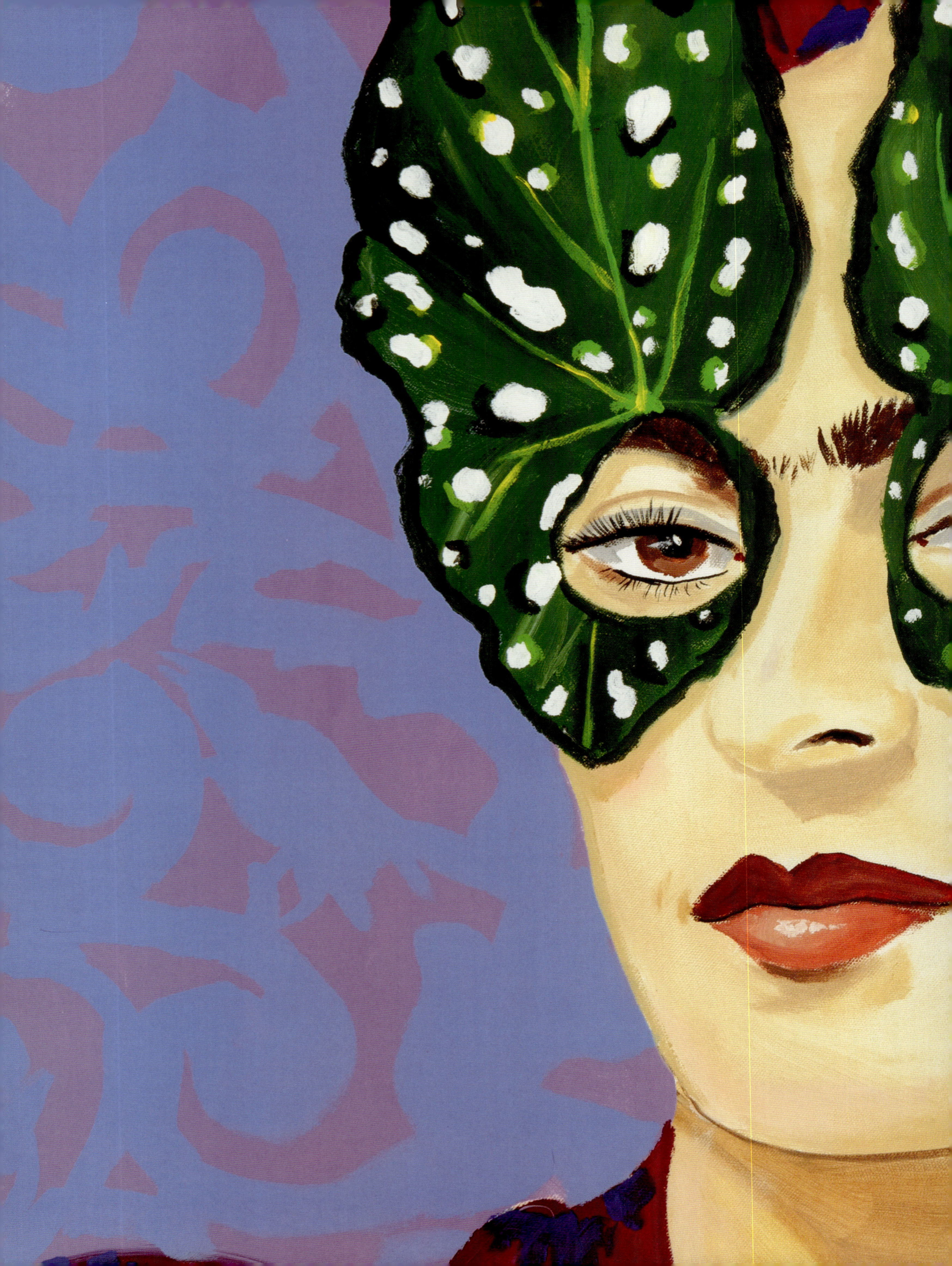

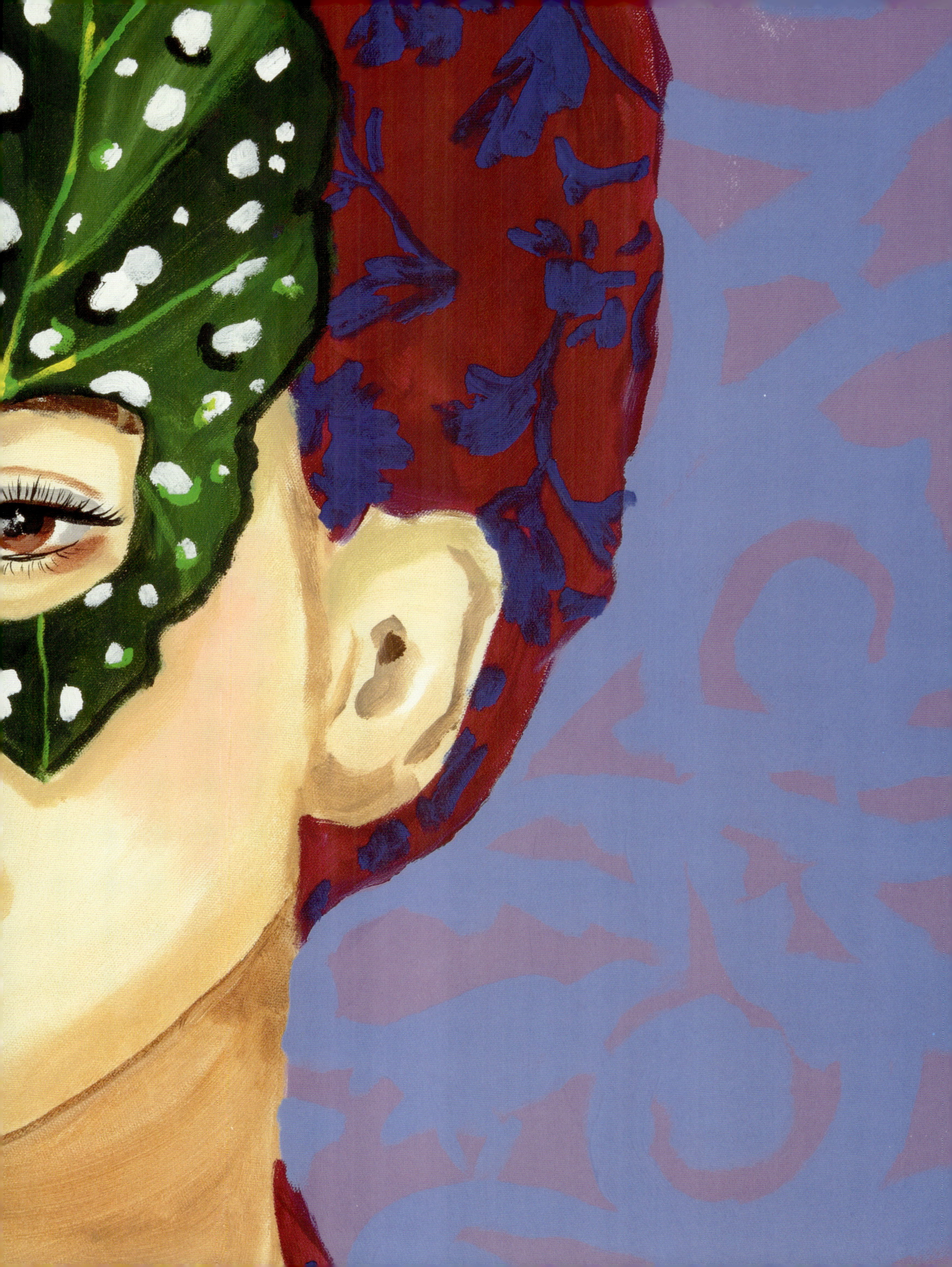

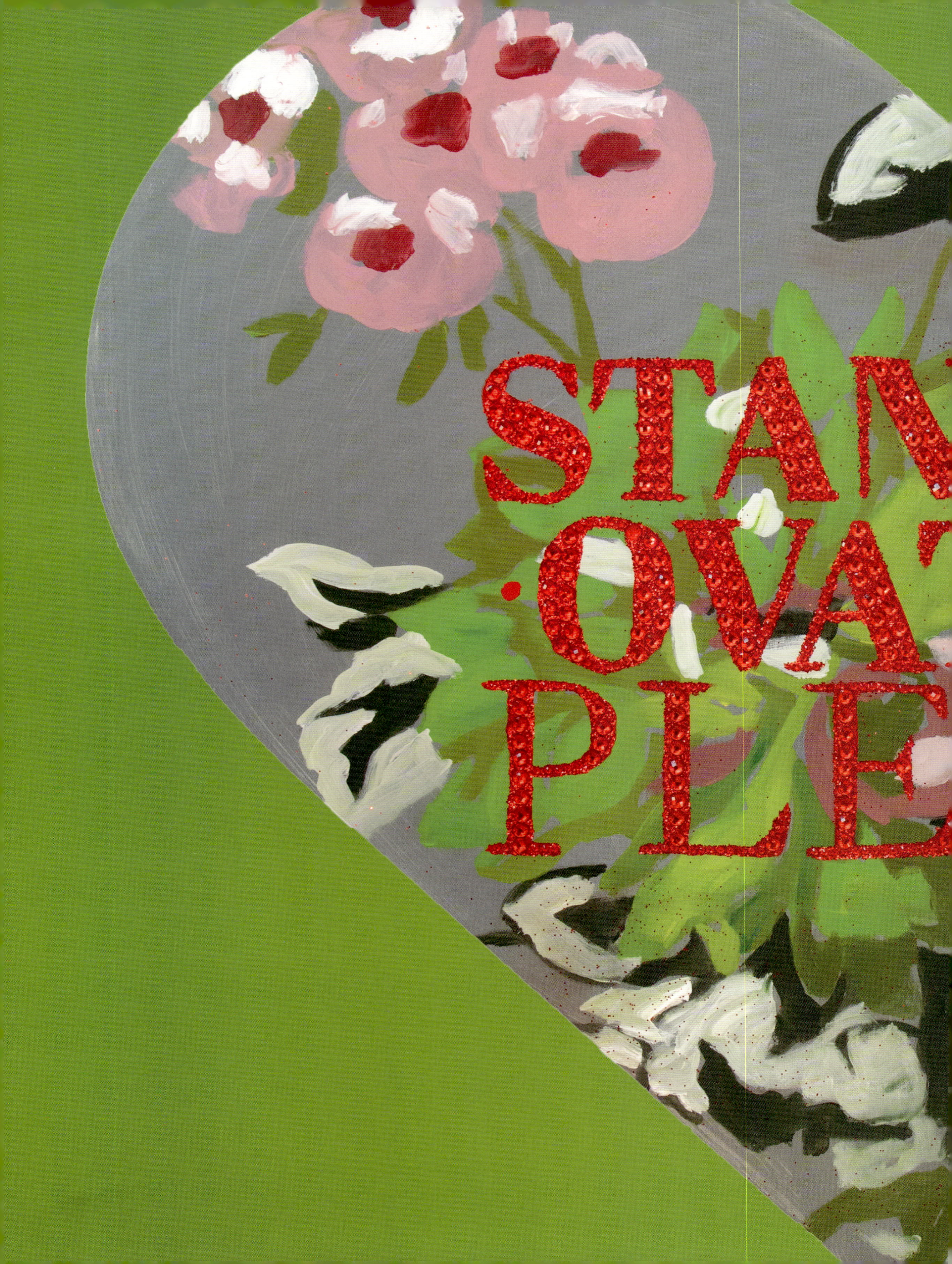

STAN
OVA
PLE

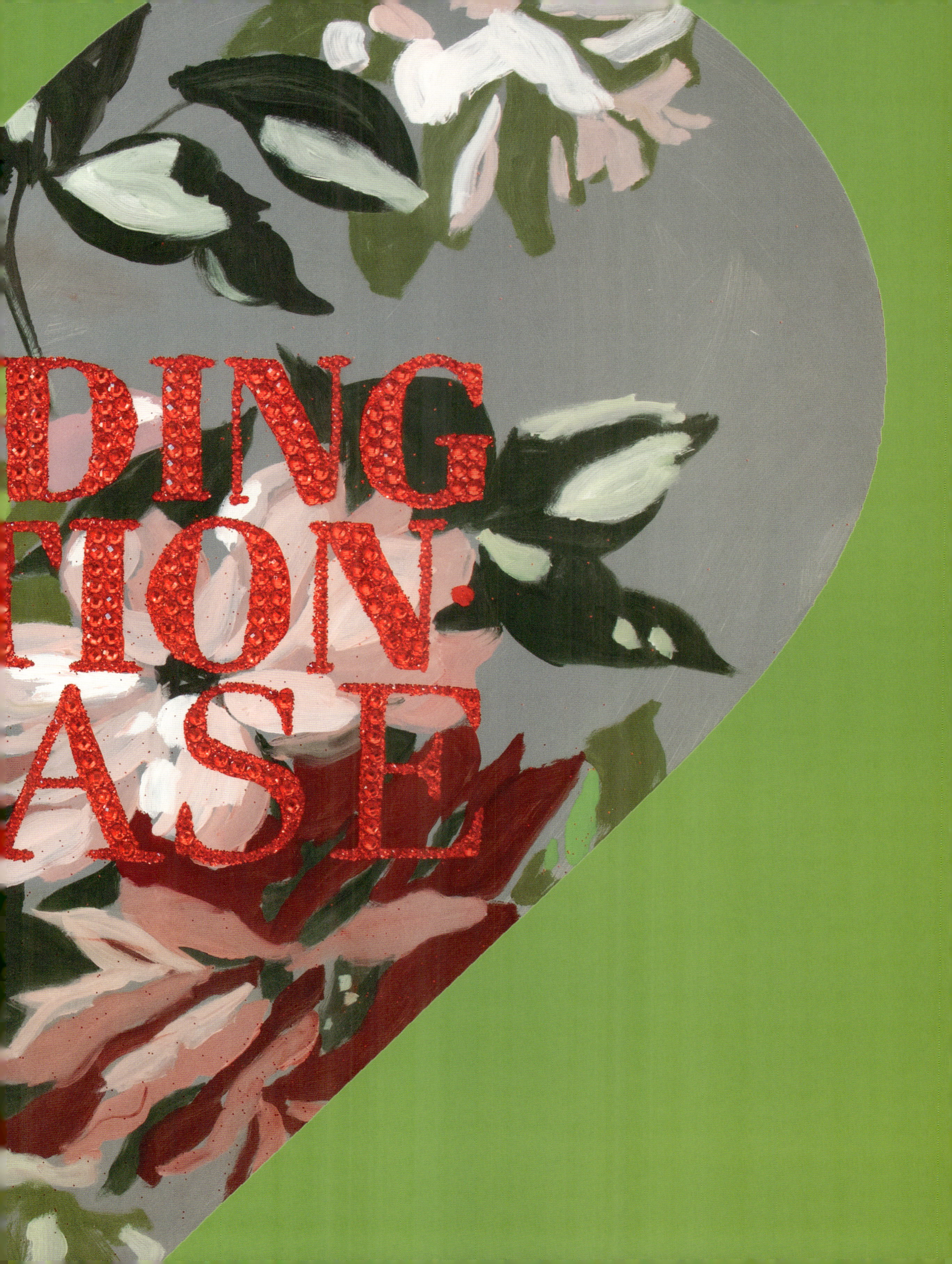
DING
TION.
ASE

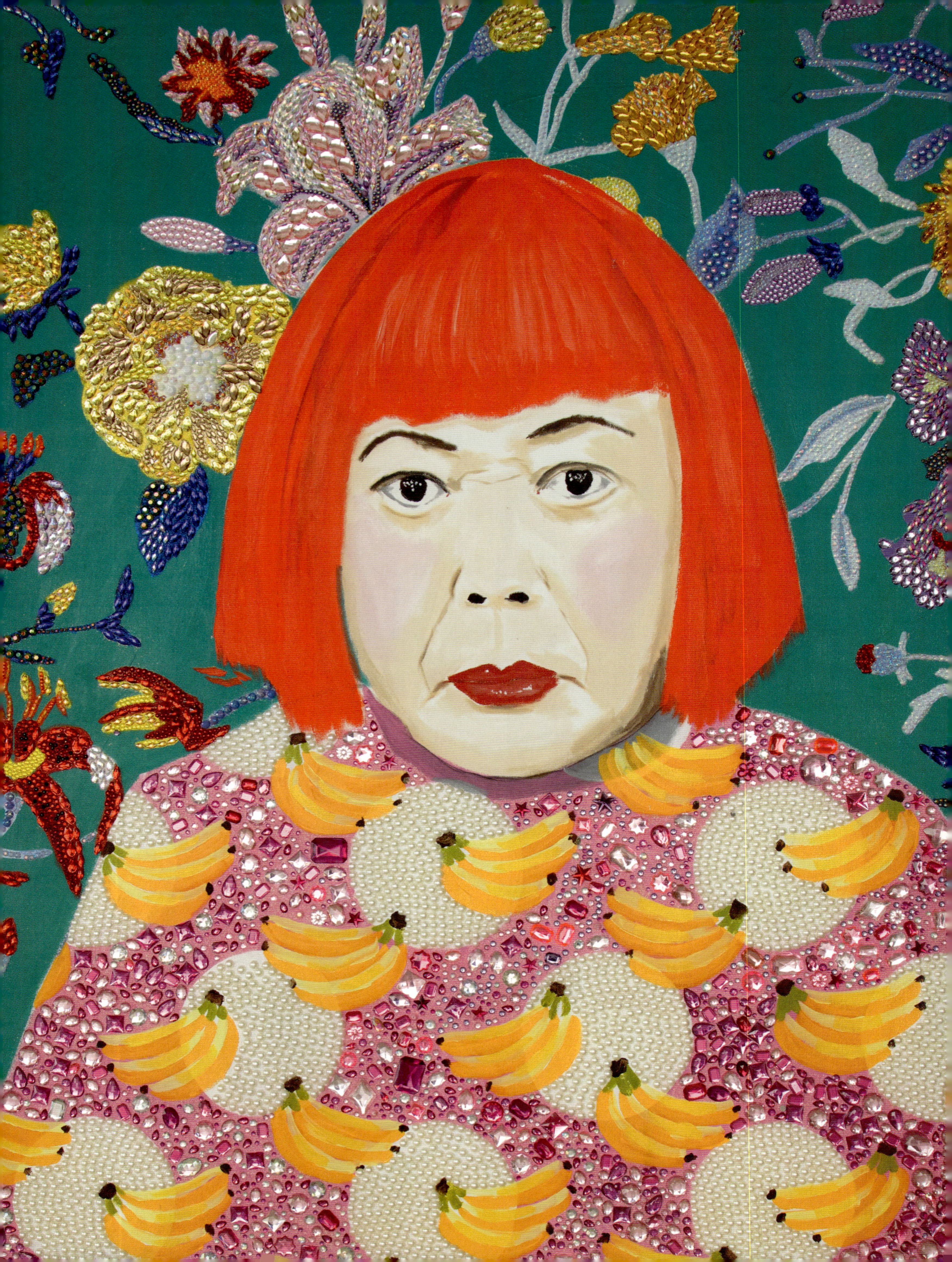

Yayoi Kusama

Because she is so brave to share her world with us. She lets us into the world she sees. She is a precious gift to the world.

Jacqueline Kennedy Onassis

Because she showed us what grace and beauty look like. She was such a lady even under the greatest duress.

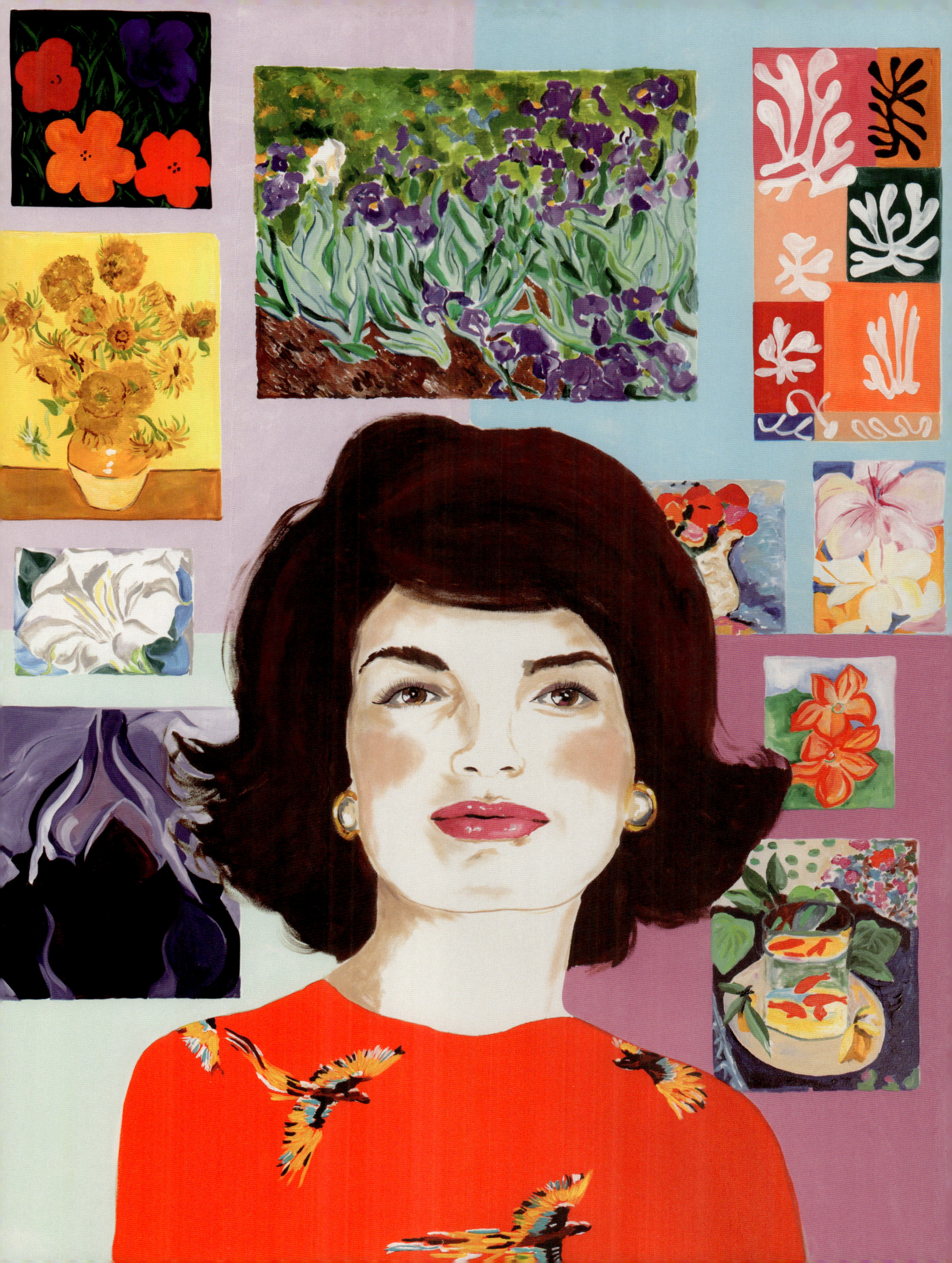

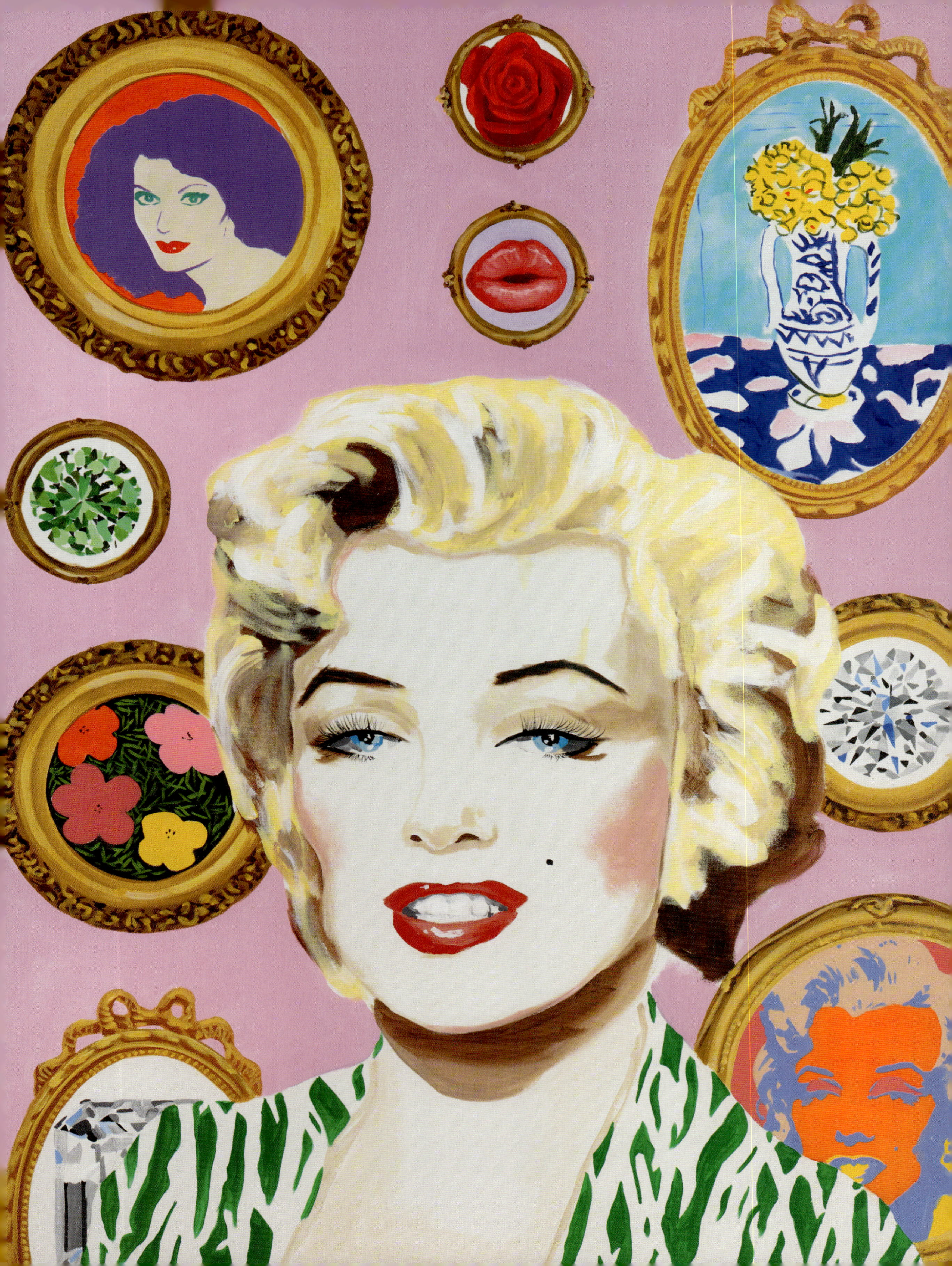

Marilyn Monroe

Because she gave us her heart, both on and off the big screen, and we loved her to death.

Peggy Guggenheim

Because her love of the arts and her passion to support artists is a massive inspiration to me. I want to leave a legacy like Peggy's. I love her.

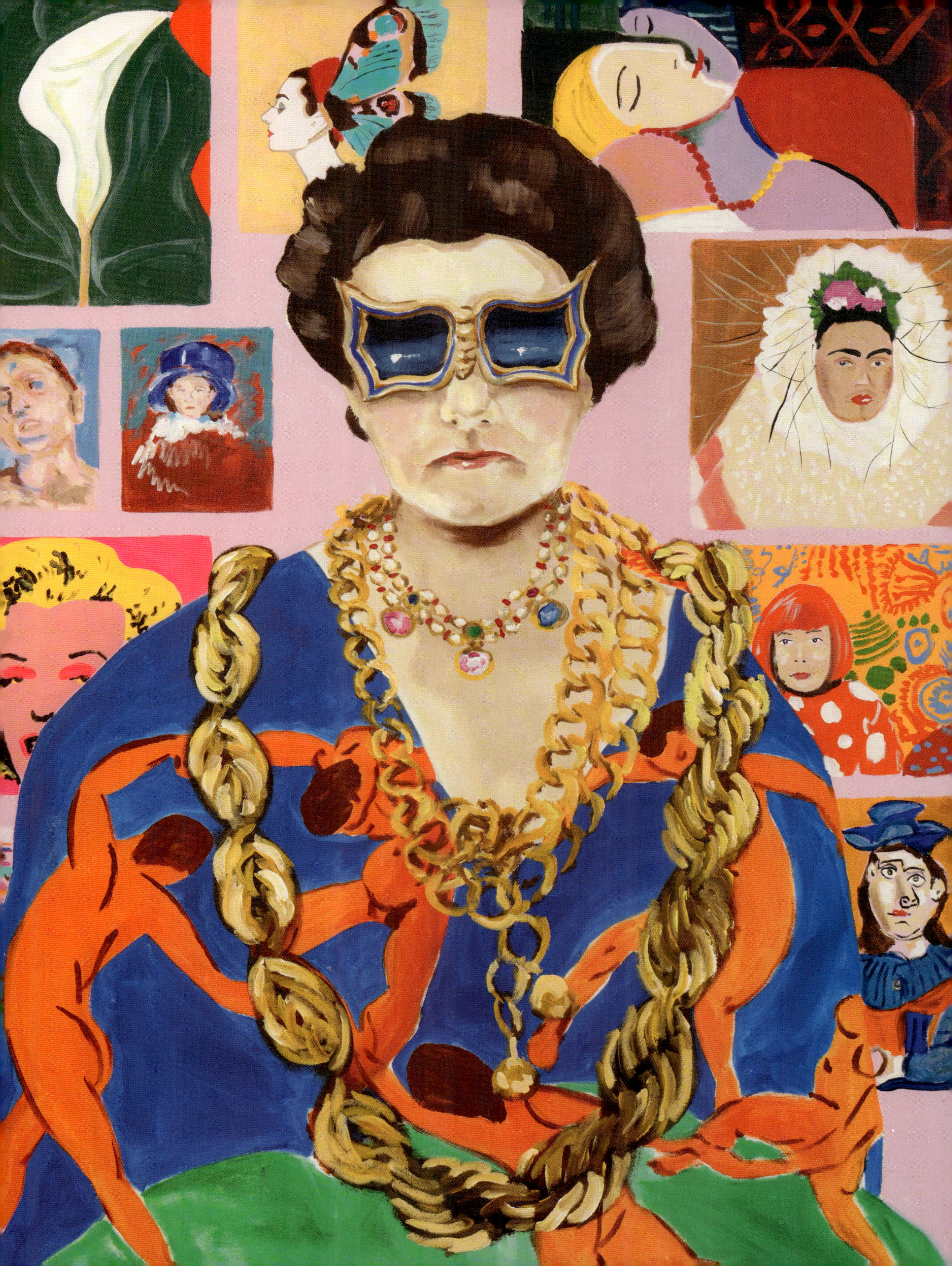

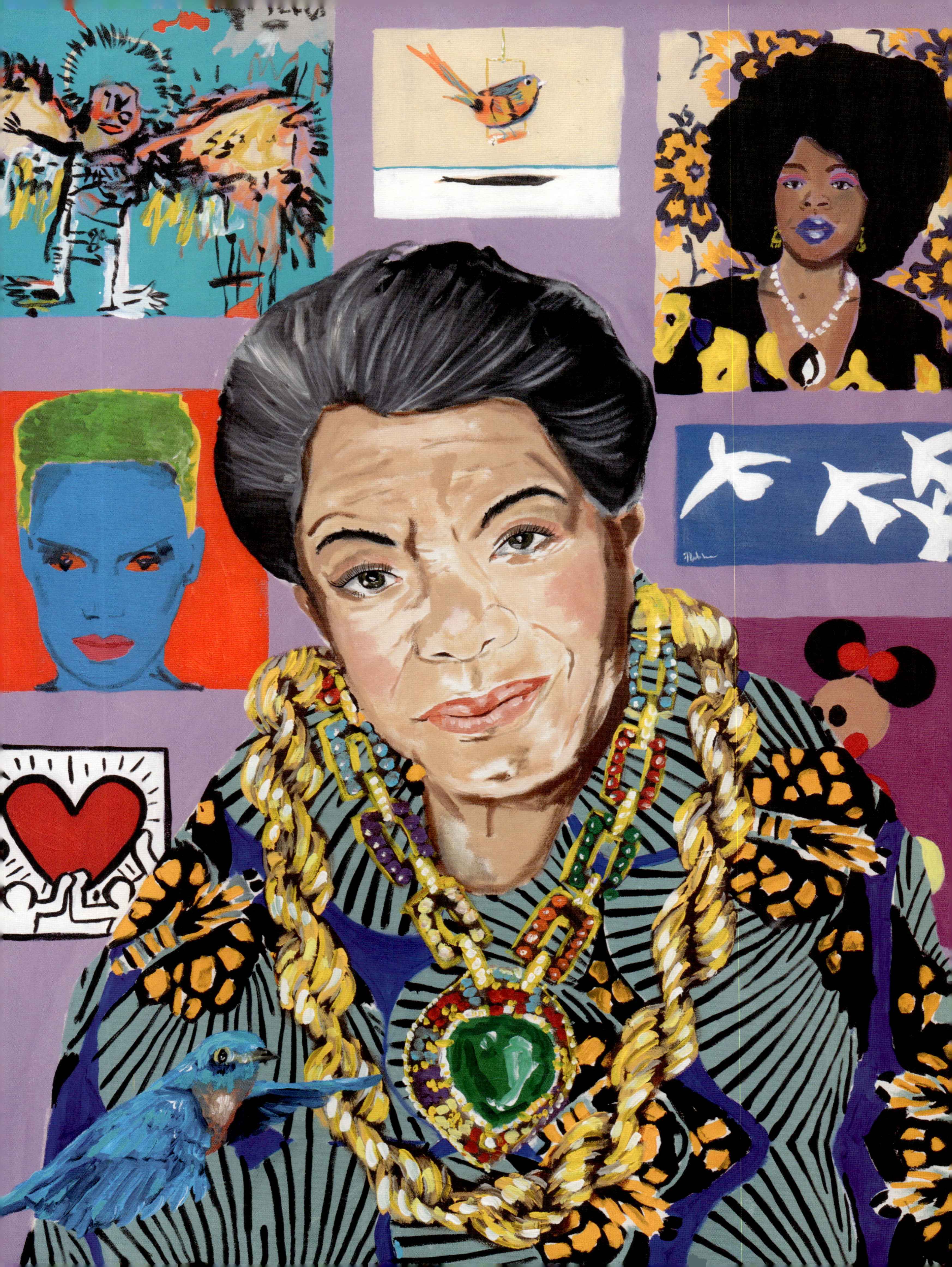

Maya Angelou

Because although she was afraid to use her voice for years, she became the voice and sound of truth, beauty, and the most mellifluous love imagined.

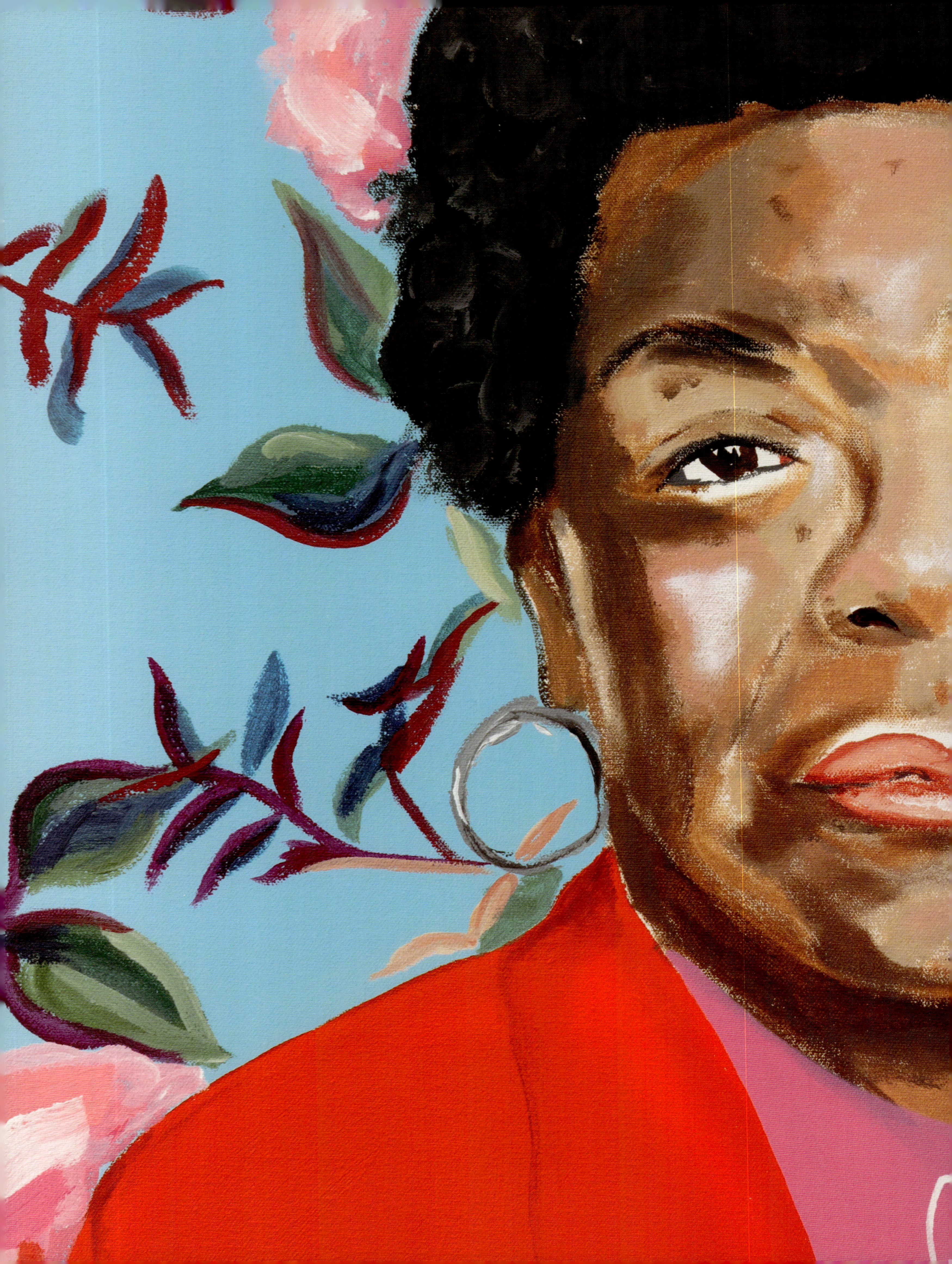

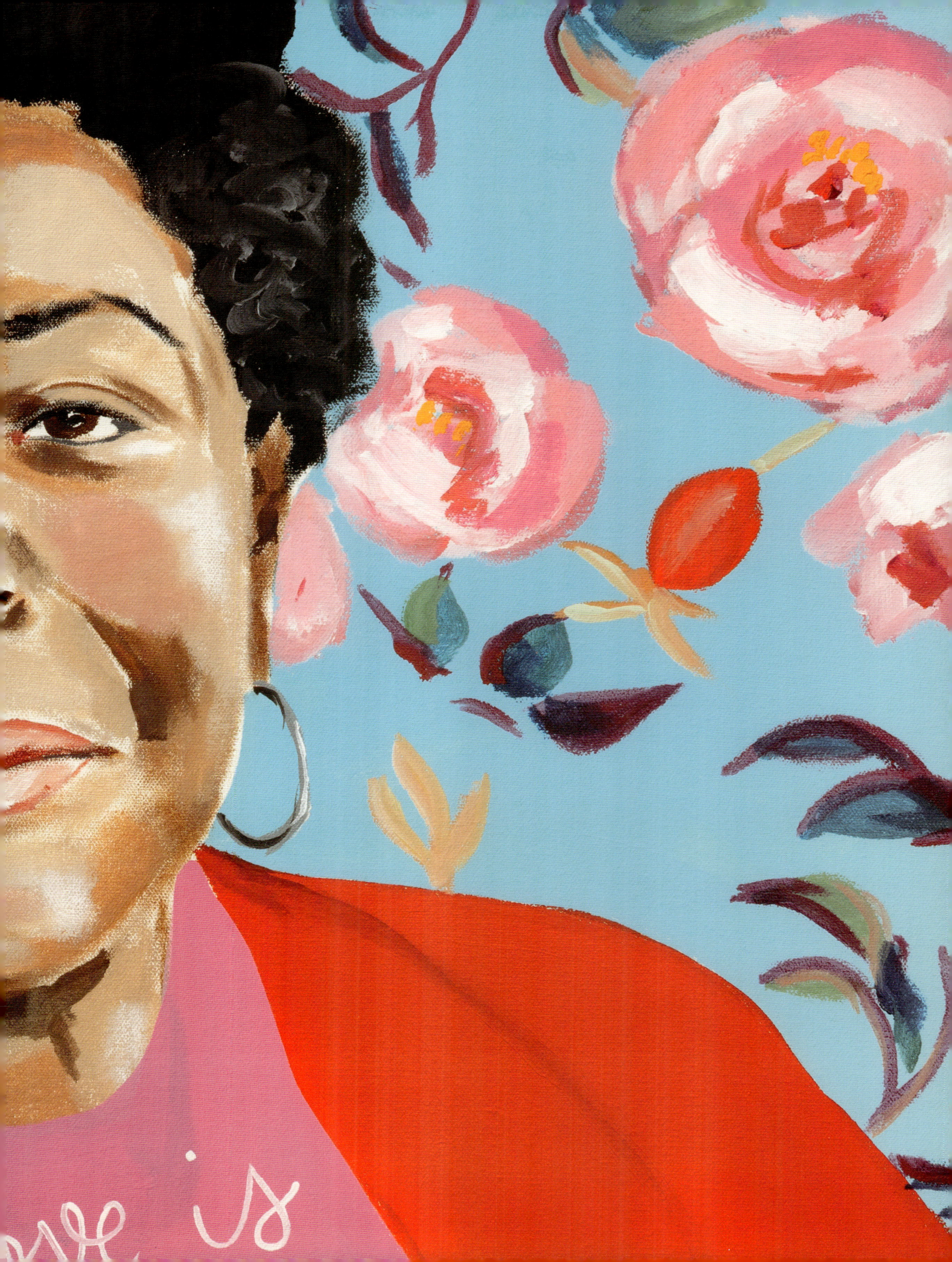
...ve is

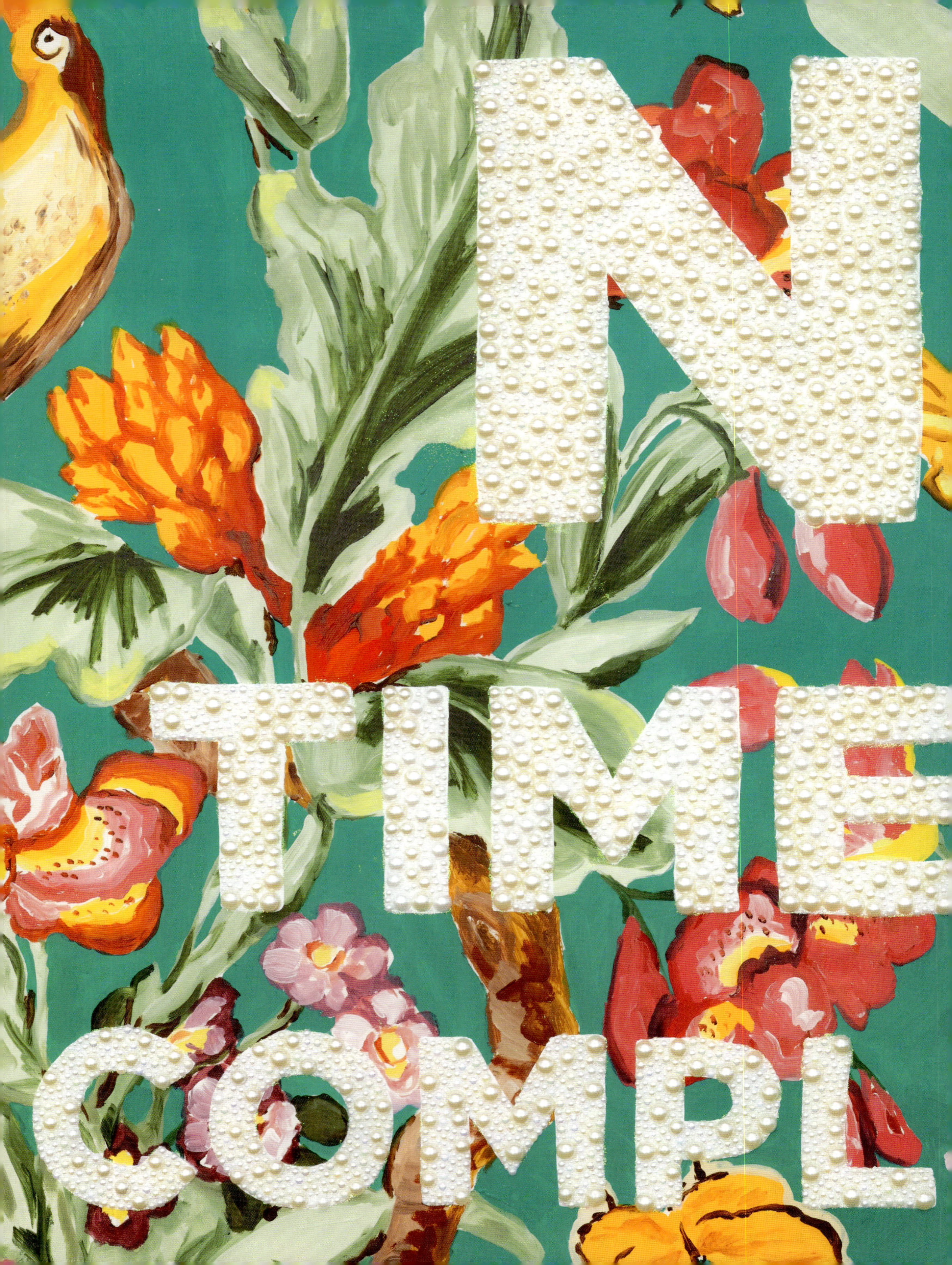
N
TIME
COMPL

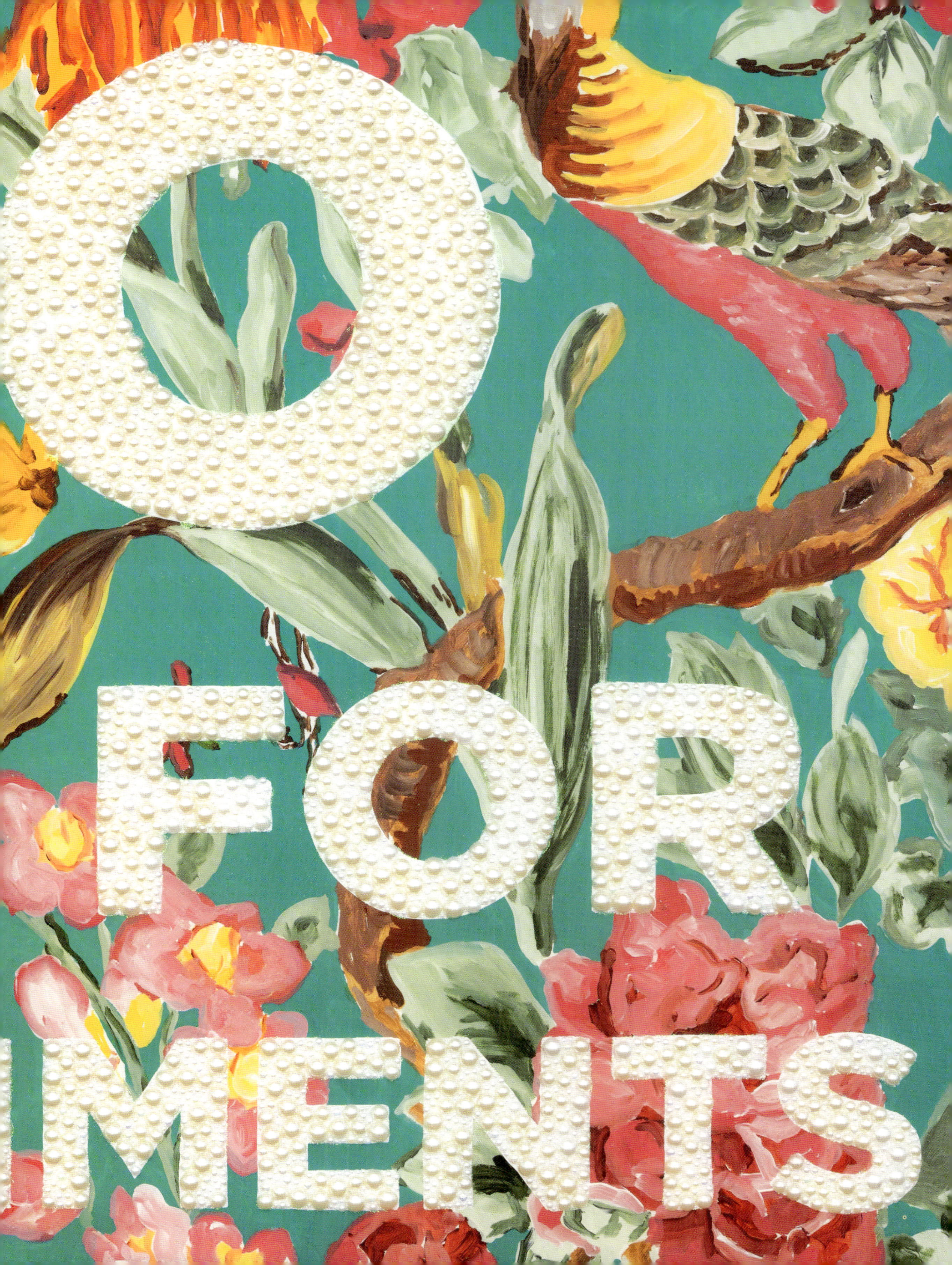
O
FOR
IMENTS

Elizabeth Taylor

Because it wasn't her massive diamonds or her film career that made her grand. It was her heart that made her the grandest of all jewels.

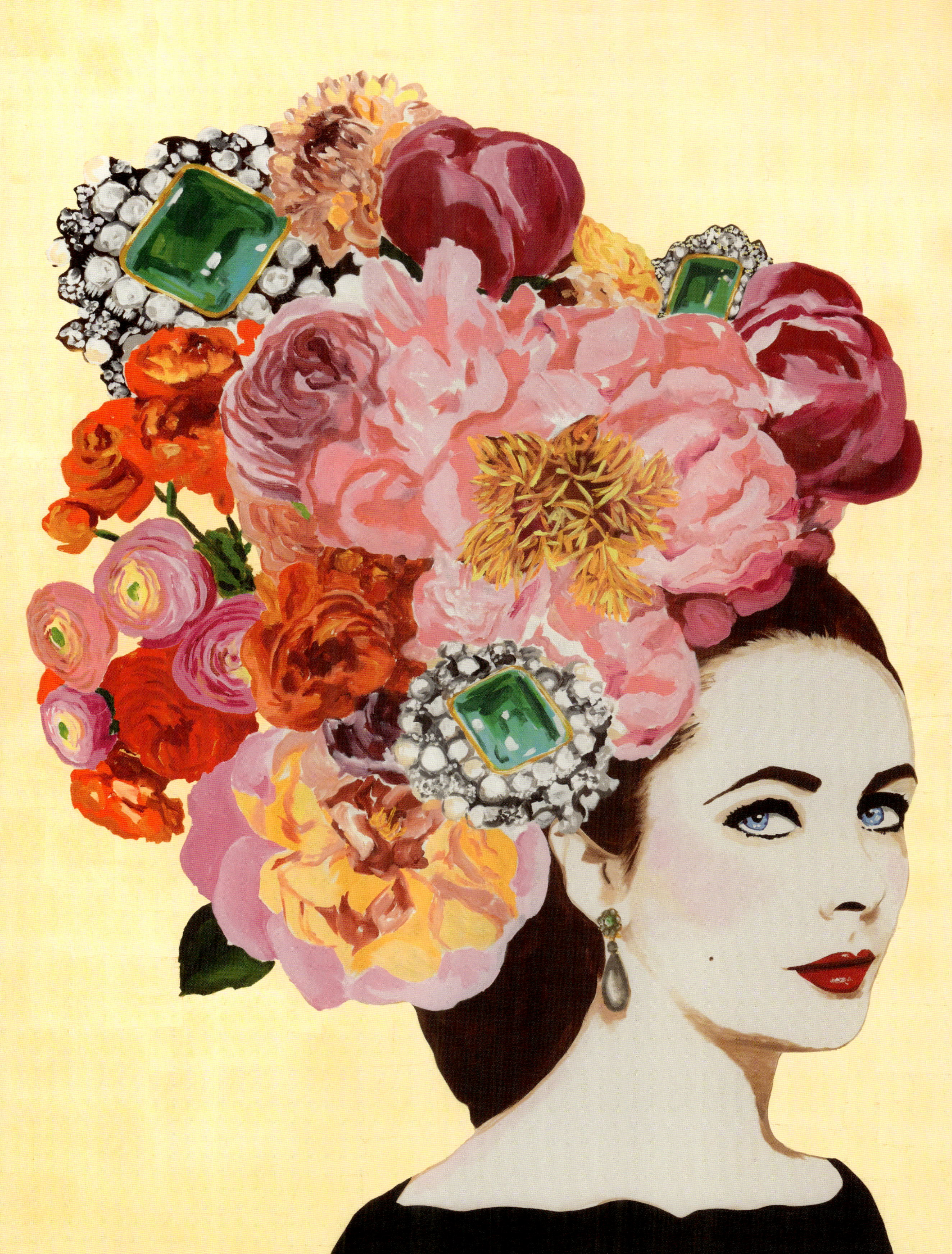

Diana
Ross

Because her style, voice, and radiance always make me smile. She and her music are joy.

Dolly Parton

Because her voice, self-worth, and sparkle have always been in my life. She exudes love and talent. She is a light in the world.

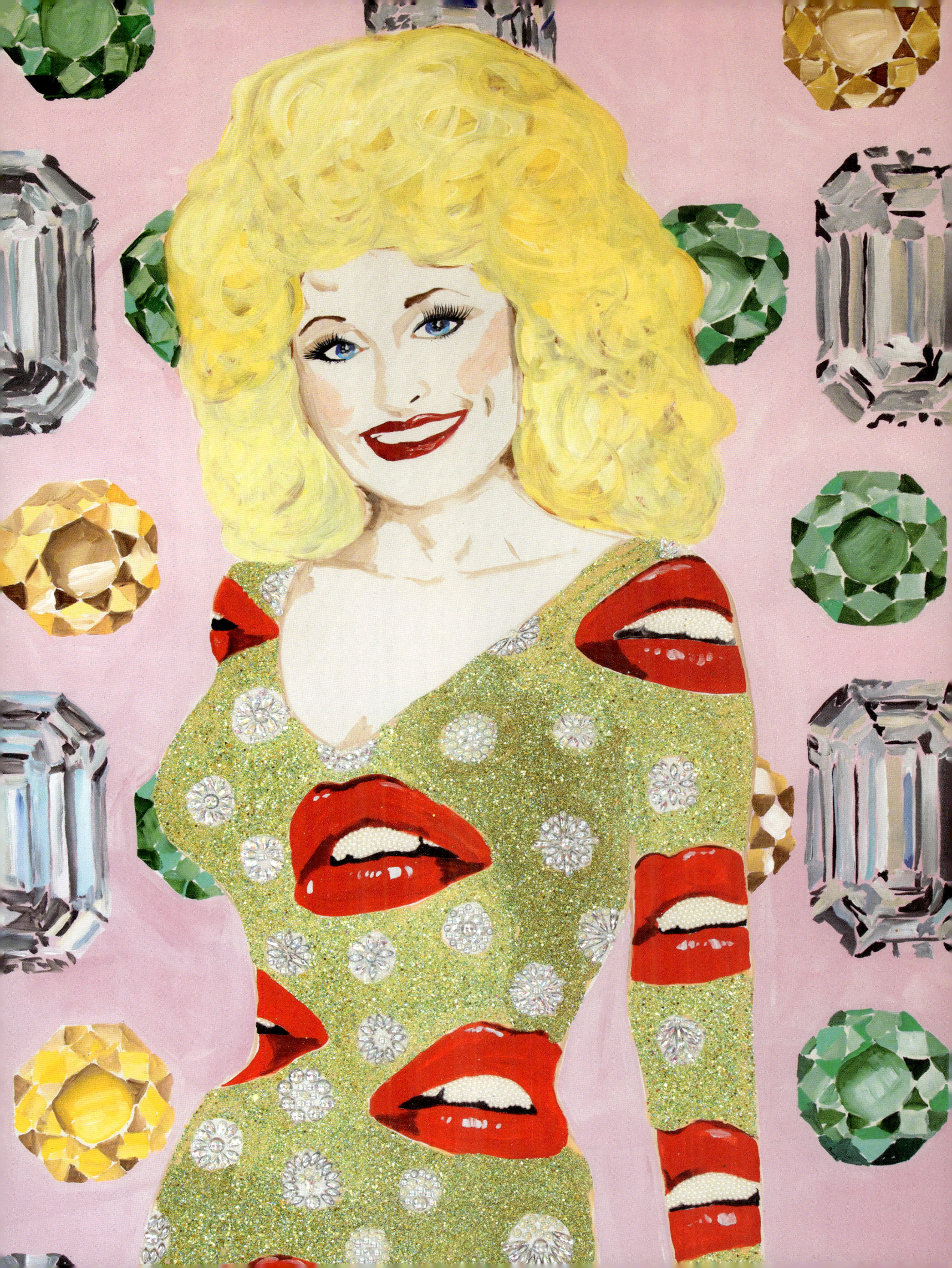

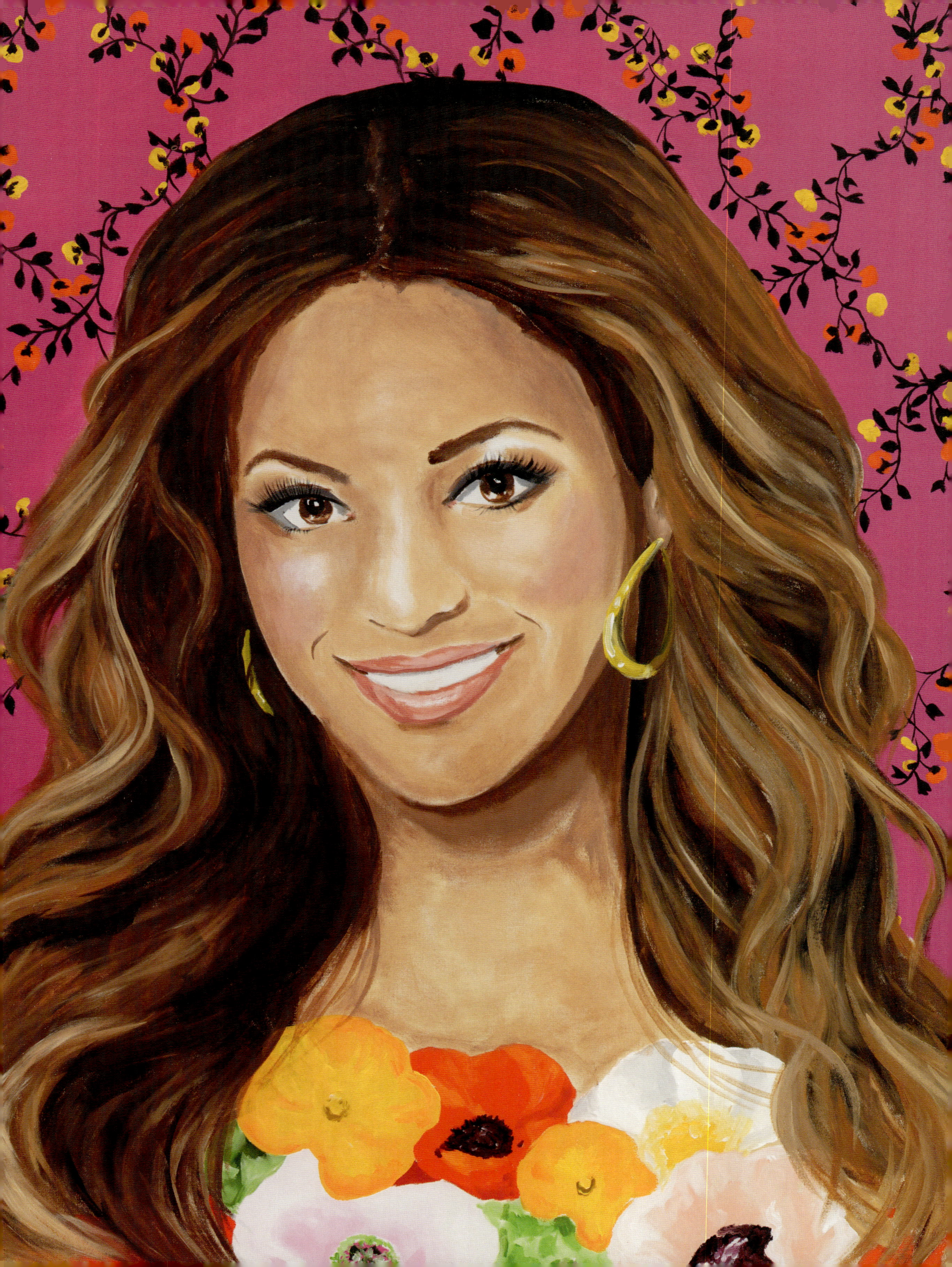

Beyoncé Knowles

Because her work ethic and commitment to her craft are unmatched. She is a role model and an incredible woman, and her voice has played on repeat on the soundtrack of my life.

Barbra Streisand

Because she has an angel's voice, an incomparable talent, and a work ethic and career like no other.

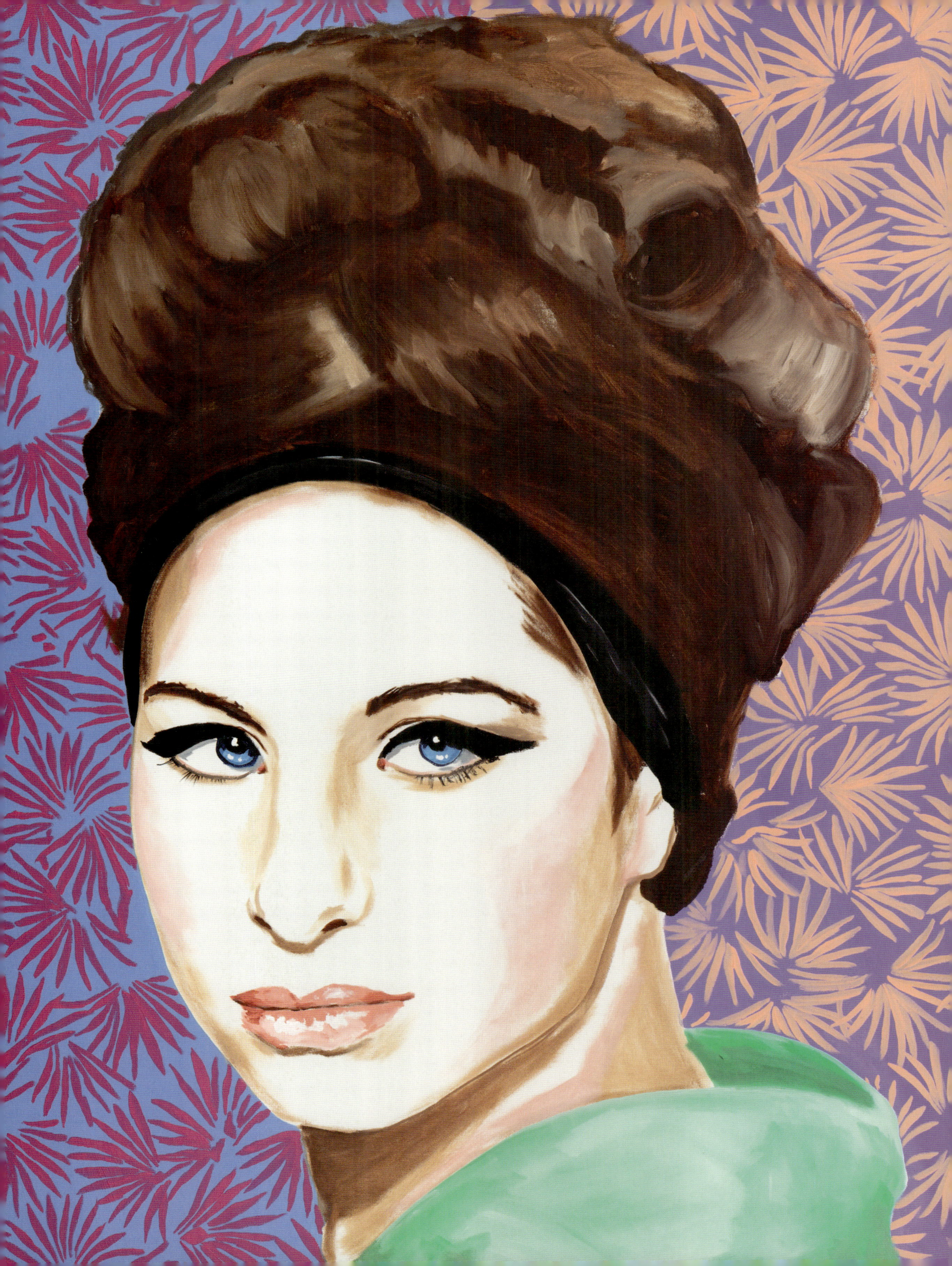

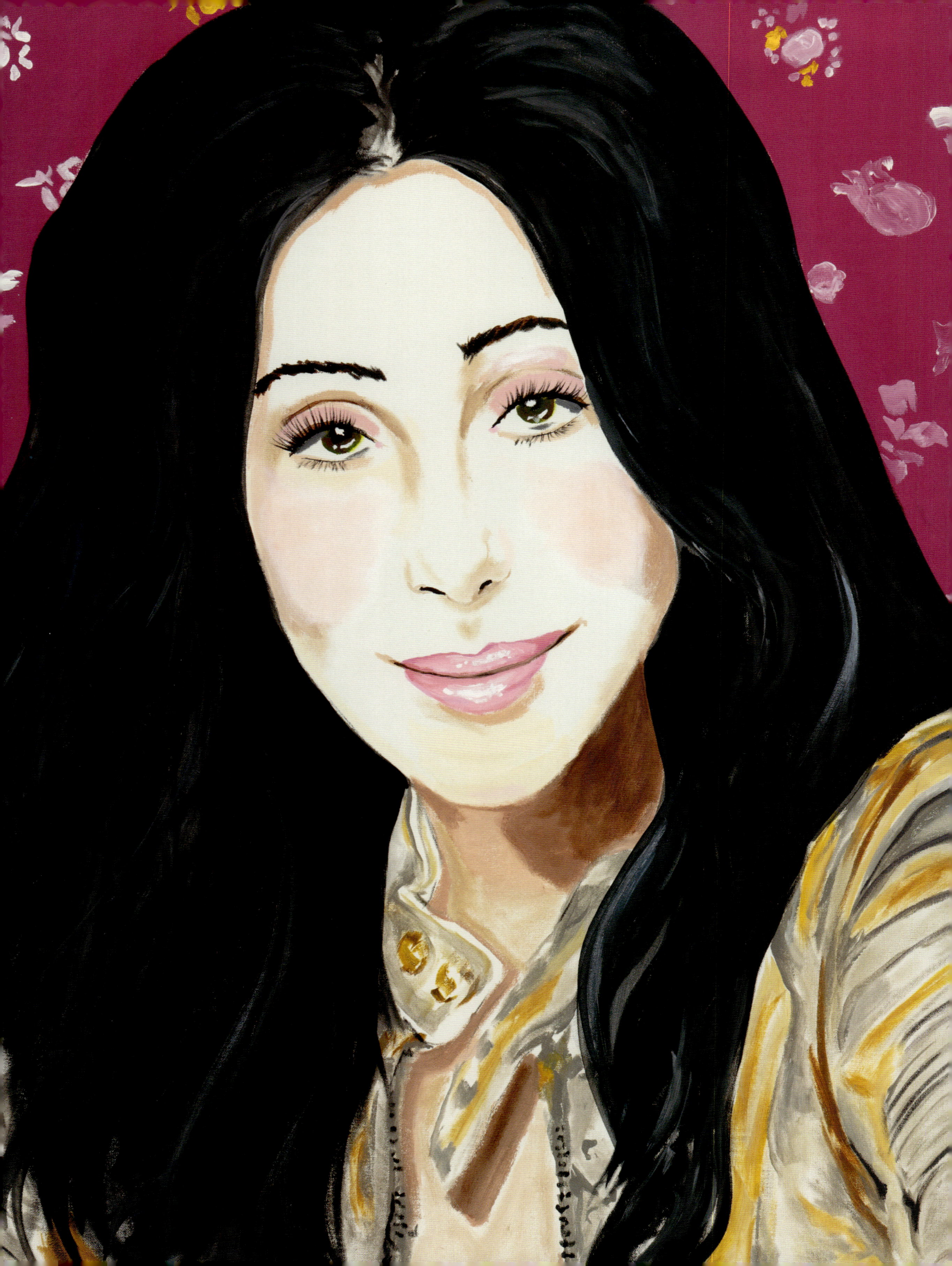

Cher

Because she unapologetically loves herself through every part of her incredible career. She is a global icon. My favorite story about Cher is when her mother told her to marry a rich man, she said, "Mom, I am a rich man." Boom. That's all I needed to hear.

Josephine Baker

Because she was a rainbow and a legendary performer who was the first black woman to star in a major motion picture. She entertained us and showed us how to love fearlessly.

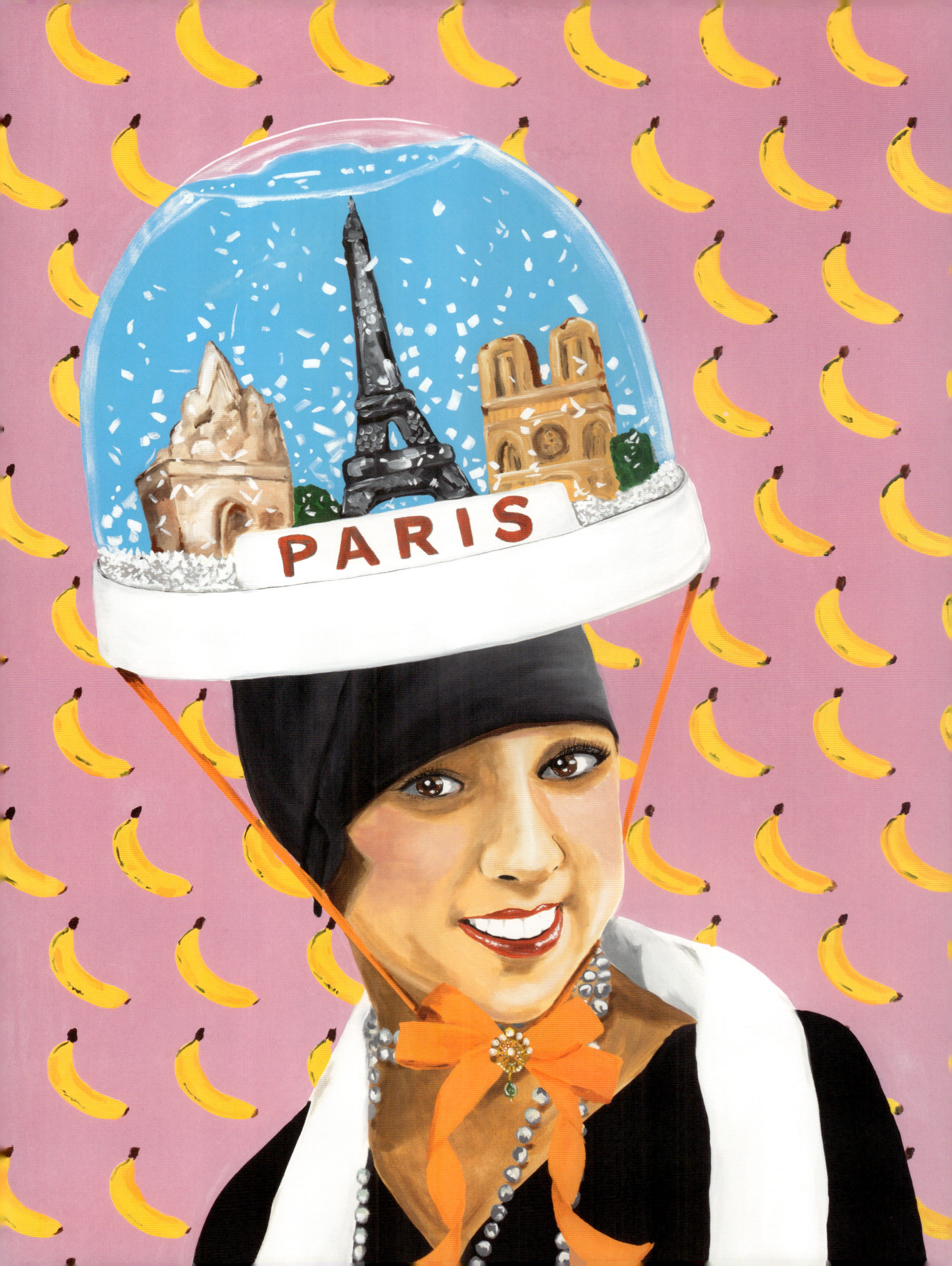
PARIS

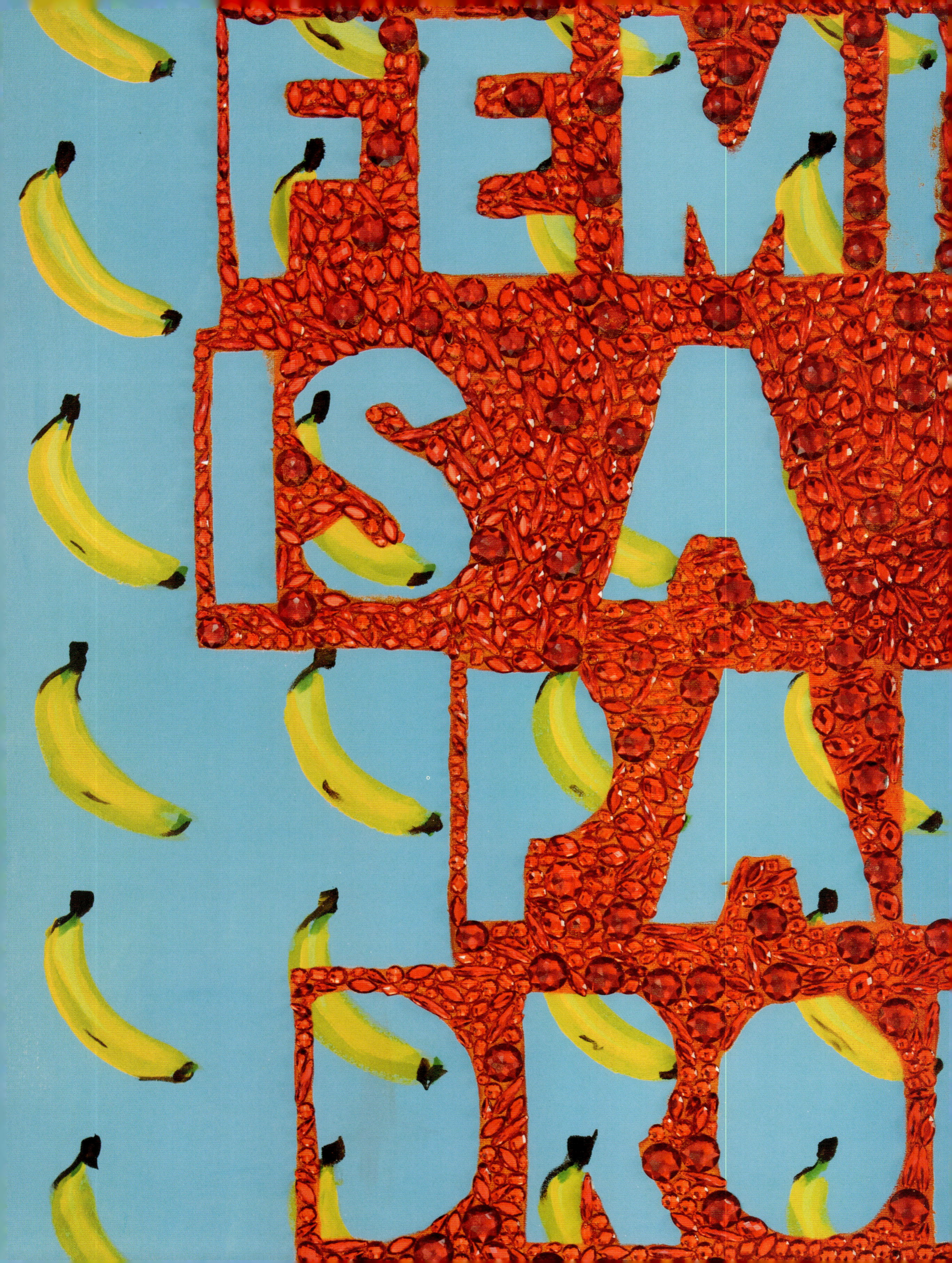
FEMI
ISA
PA
ISA
PA
DR O

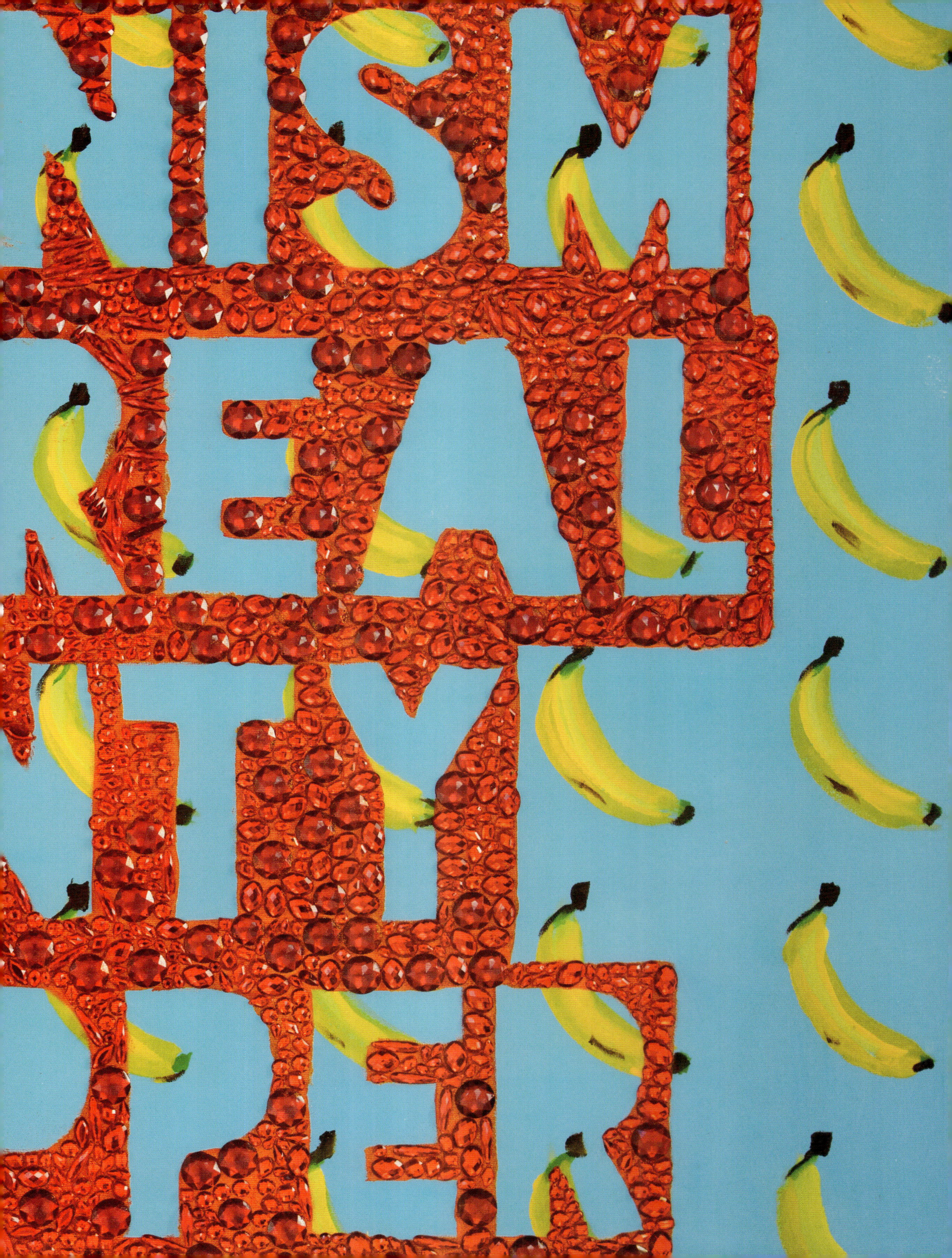
RISM
REAL
ITY
PER

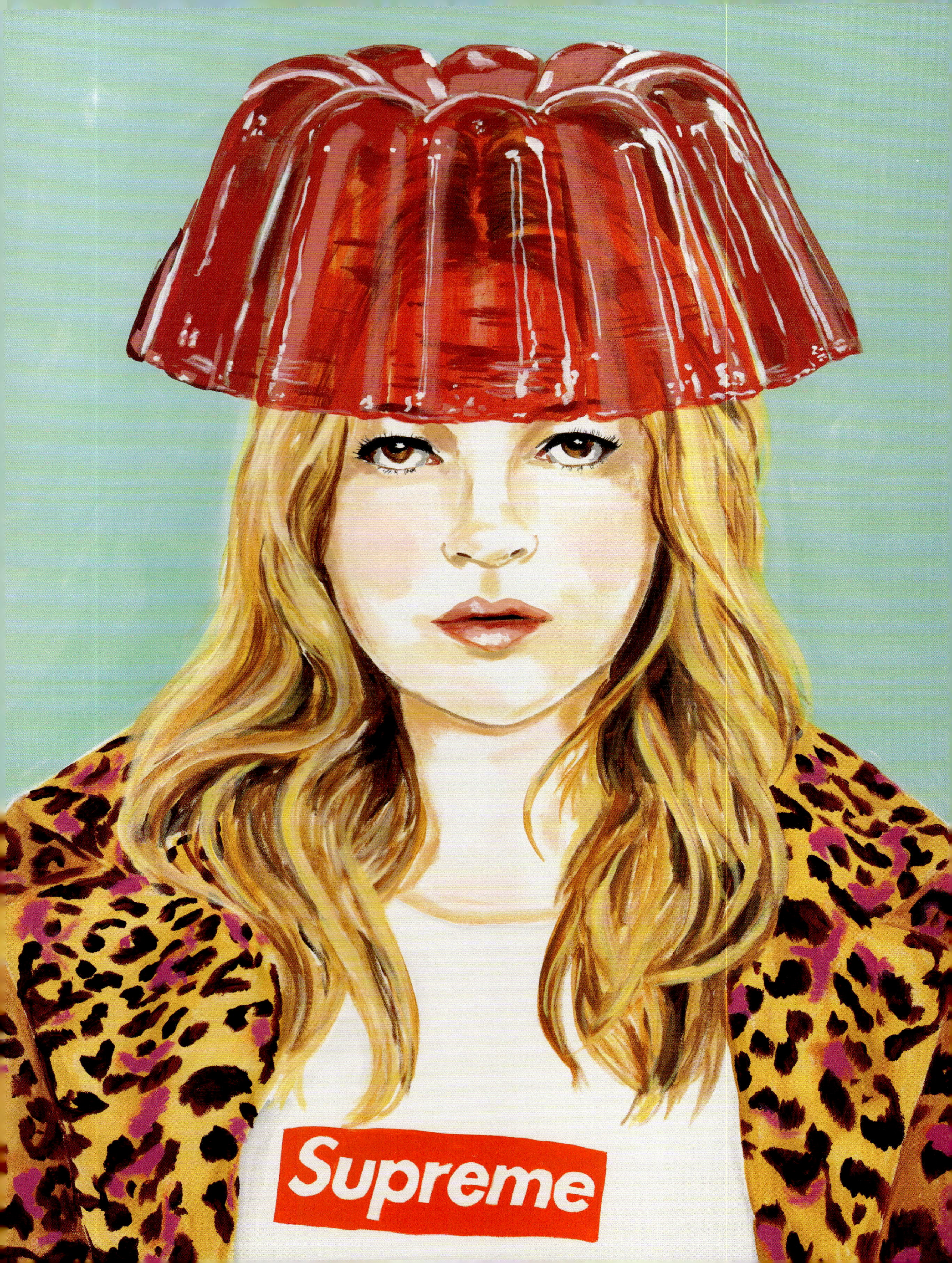
Supreme

Kate Moss

Because she is how you supermodel.

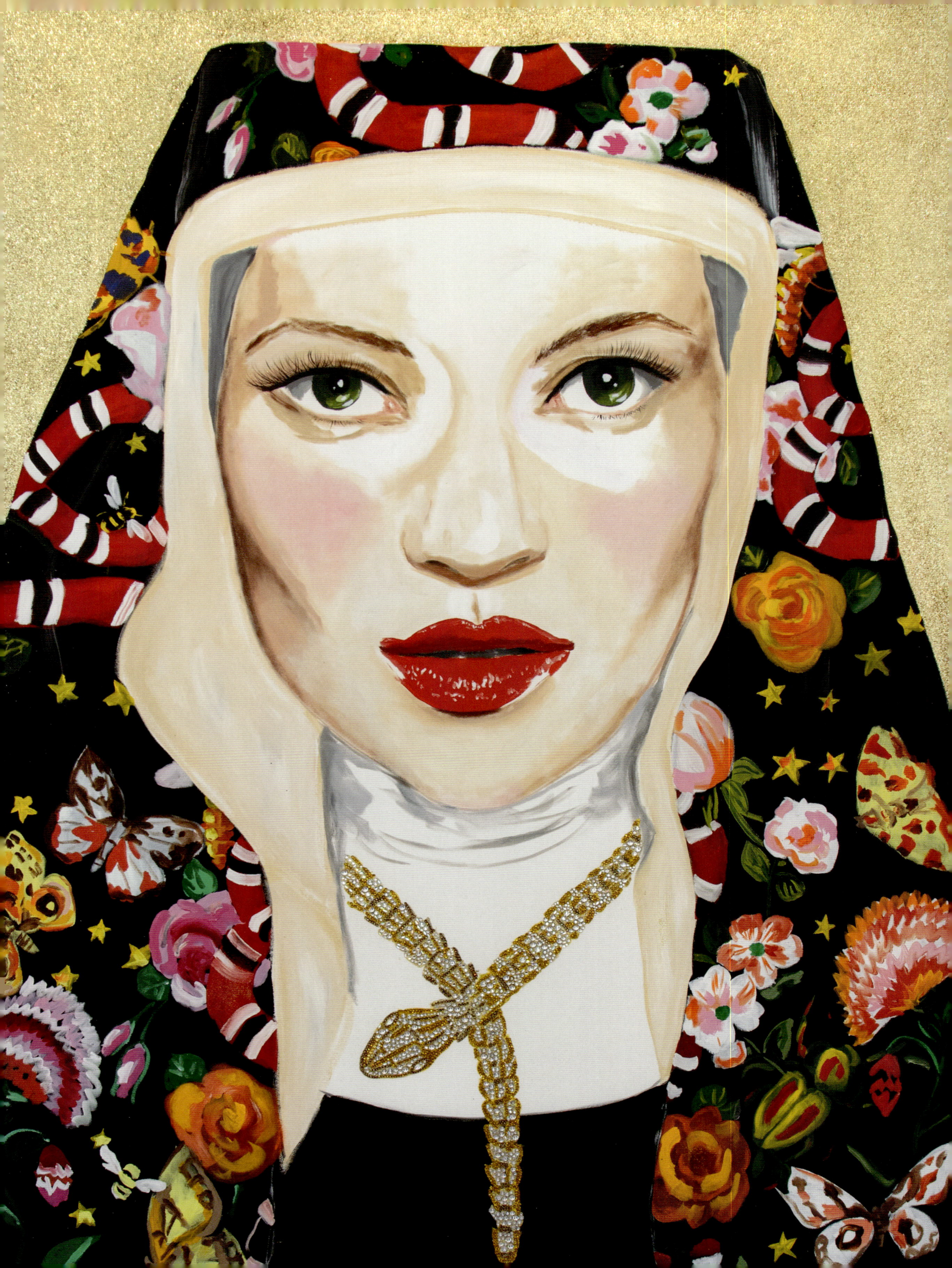

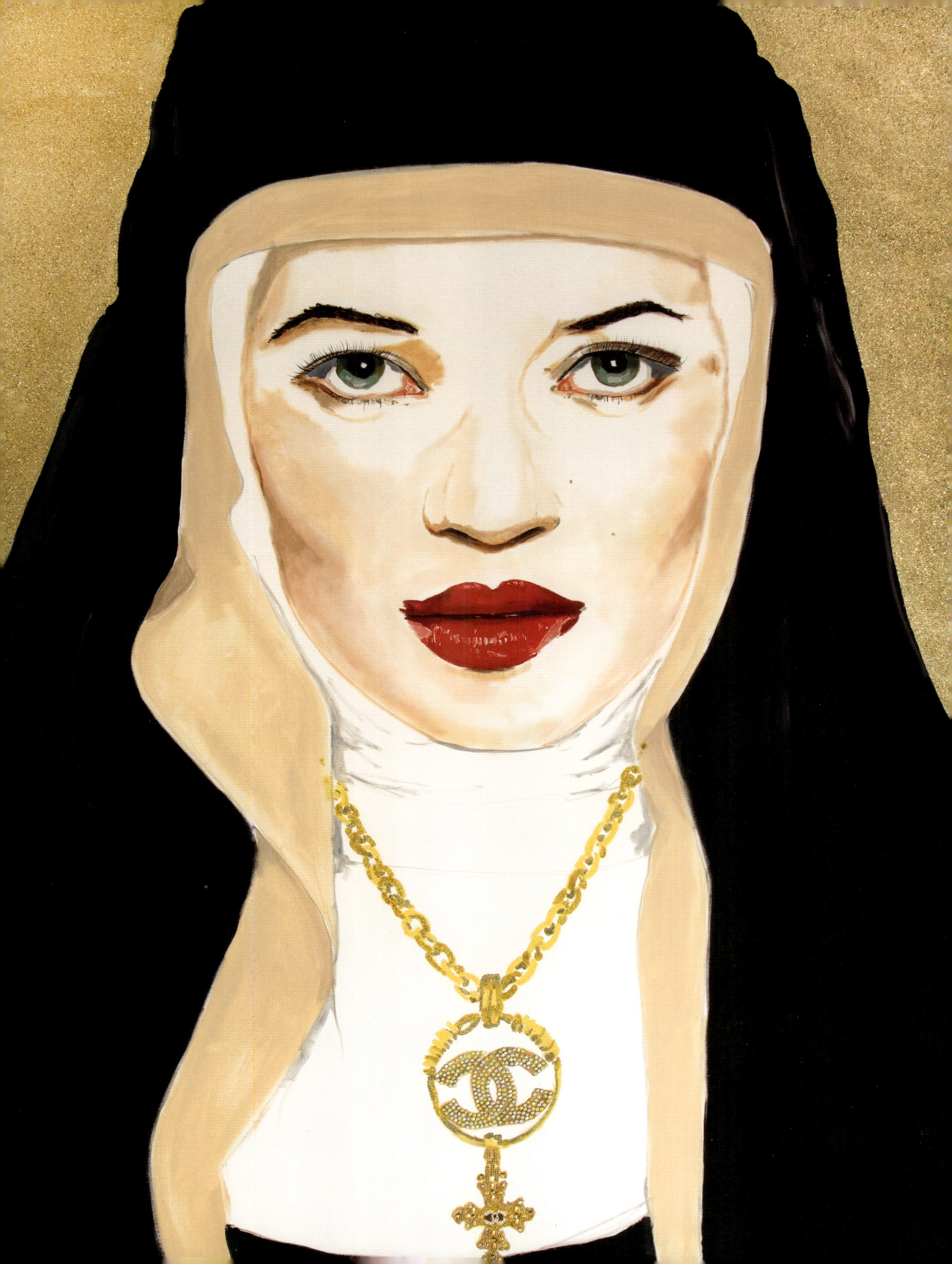

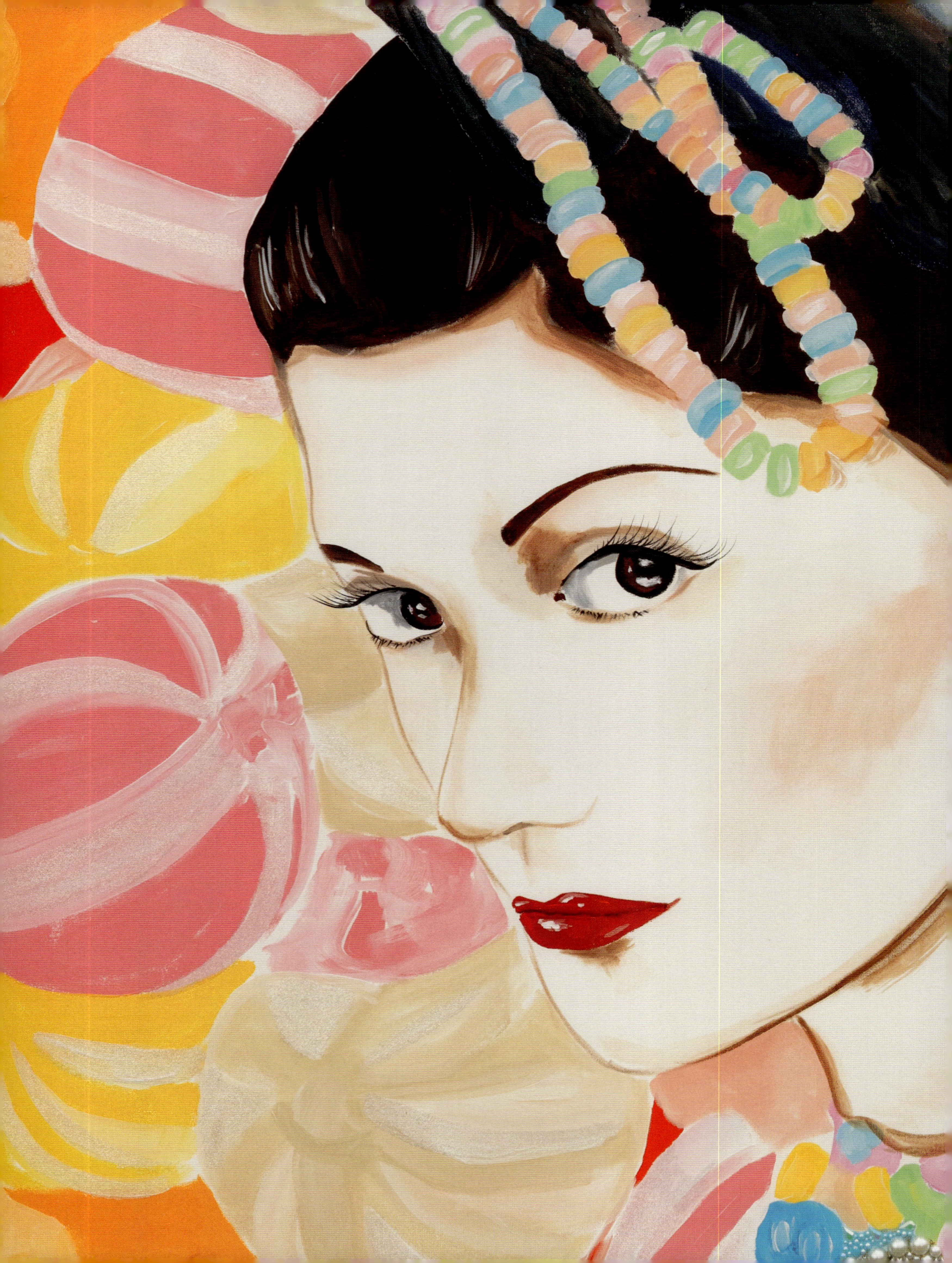

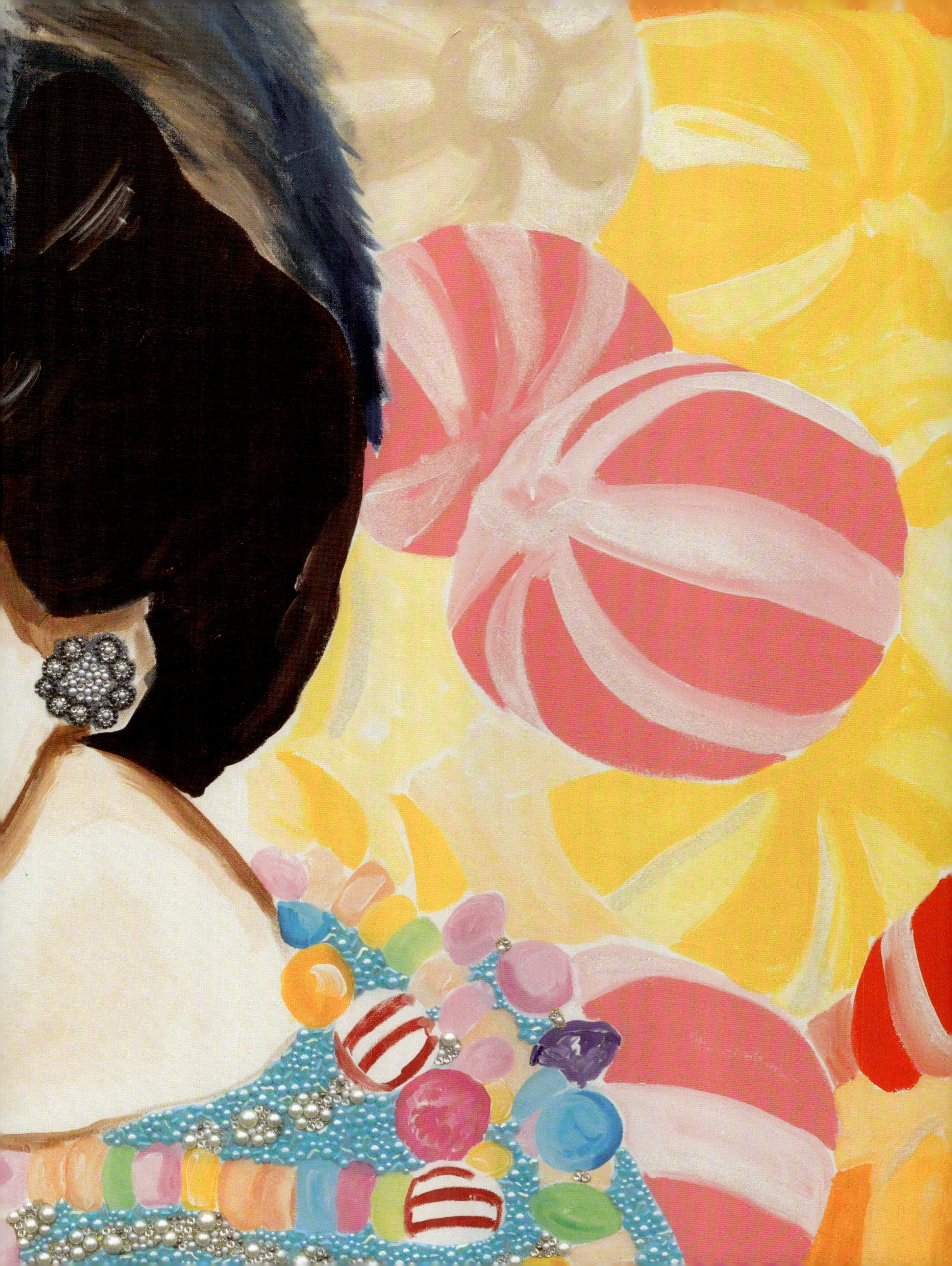

Coco Chanel

Because she was unabashedly authentic, stylish, and iconic. Her logo has become an incomparable emblem of prosperity and style.

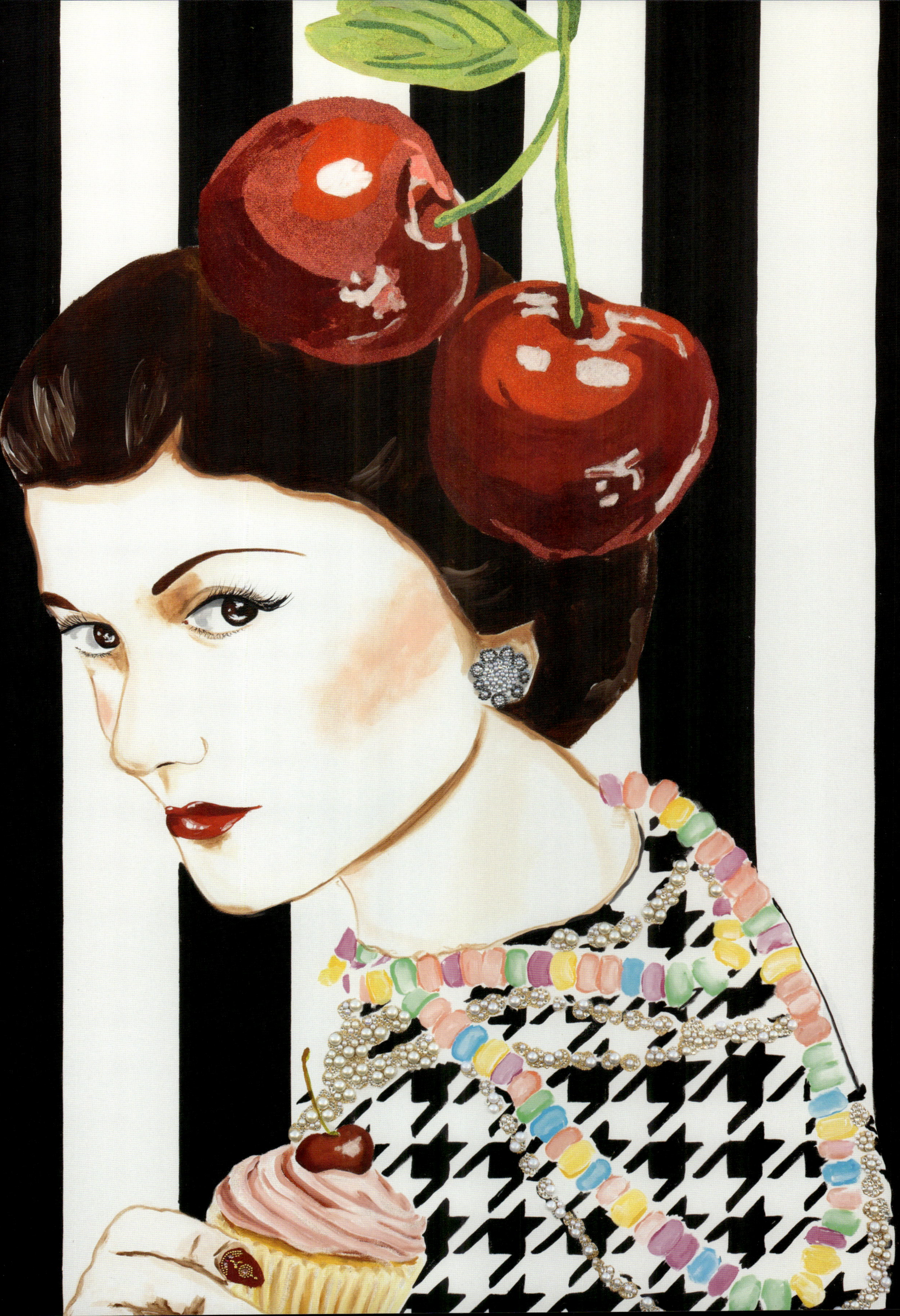

Barbie

Because she has become a symbol of women, now represented with 9 body types, 35 skin tones, and 94 hairstyles. She has evolved to represent all of us. This painting depicts the original Barbie wearing DVF.

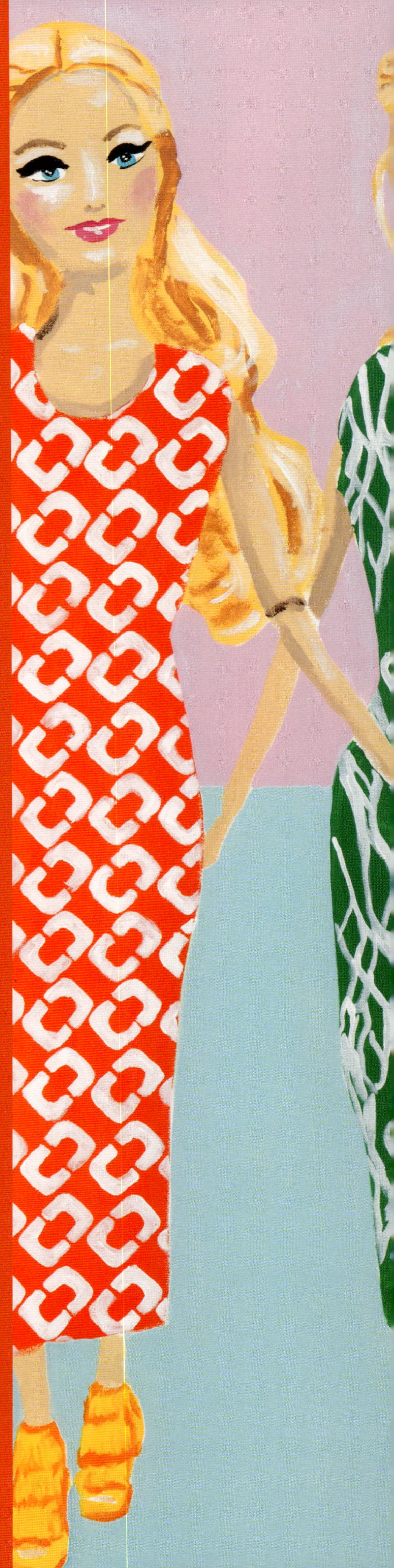

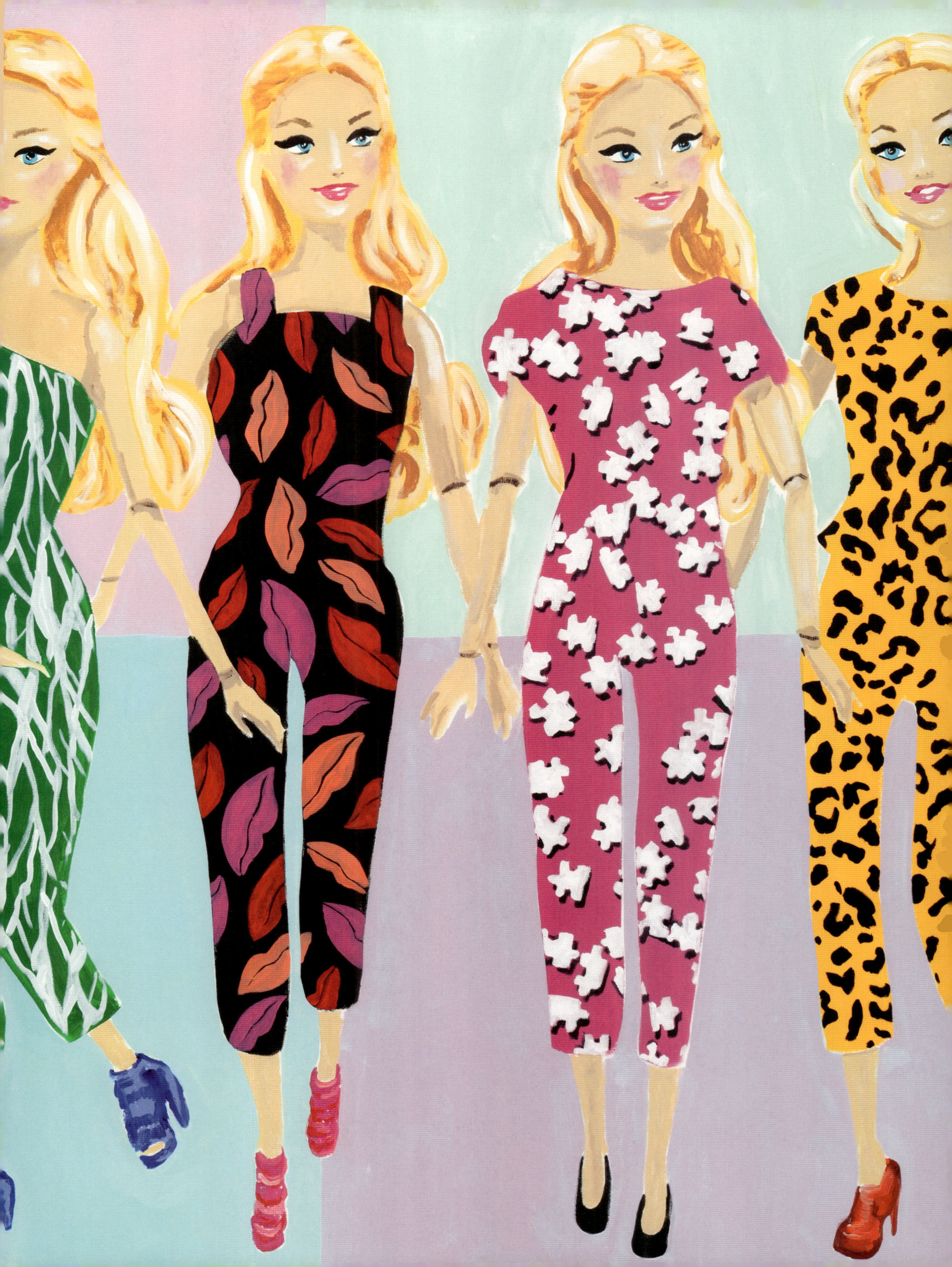

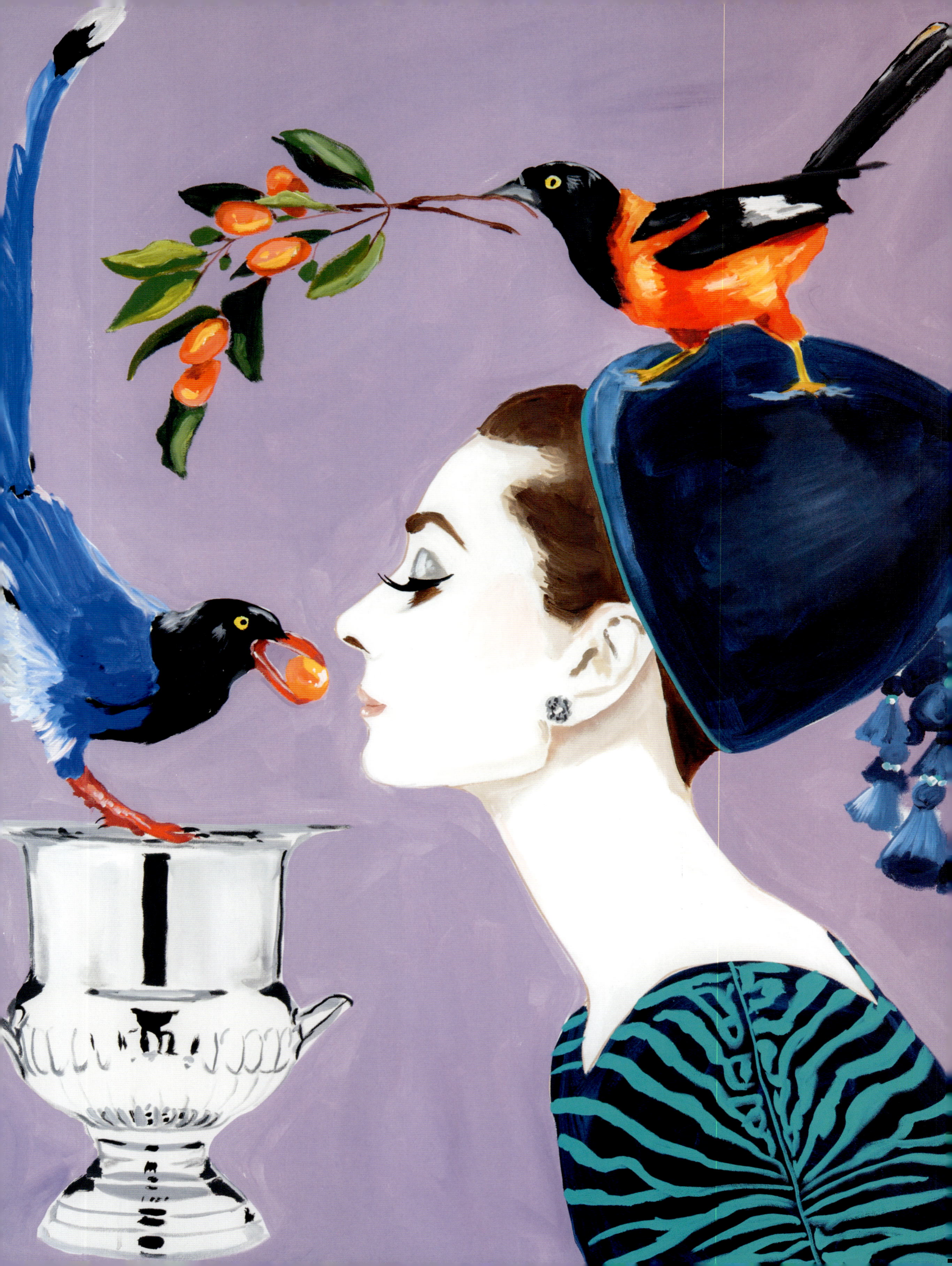

Audrey Hepburn

Because she was philanthropic, loving, talented, and fashionable. Her poise and style are timeless, and her beauty absolutely captivating.

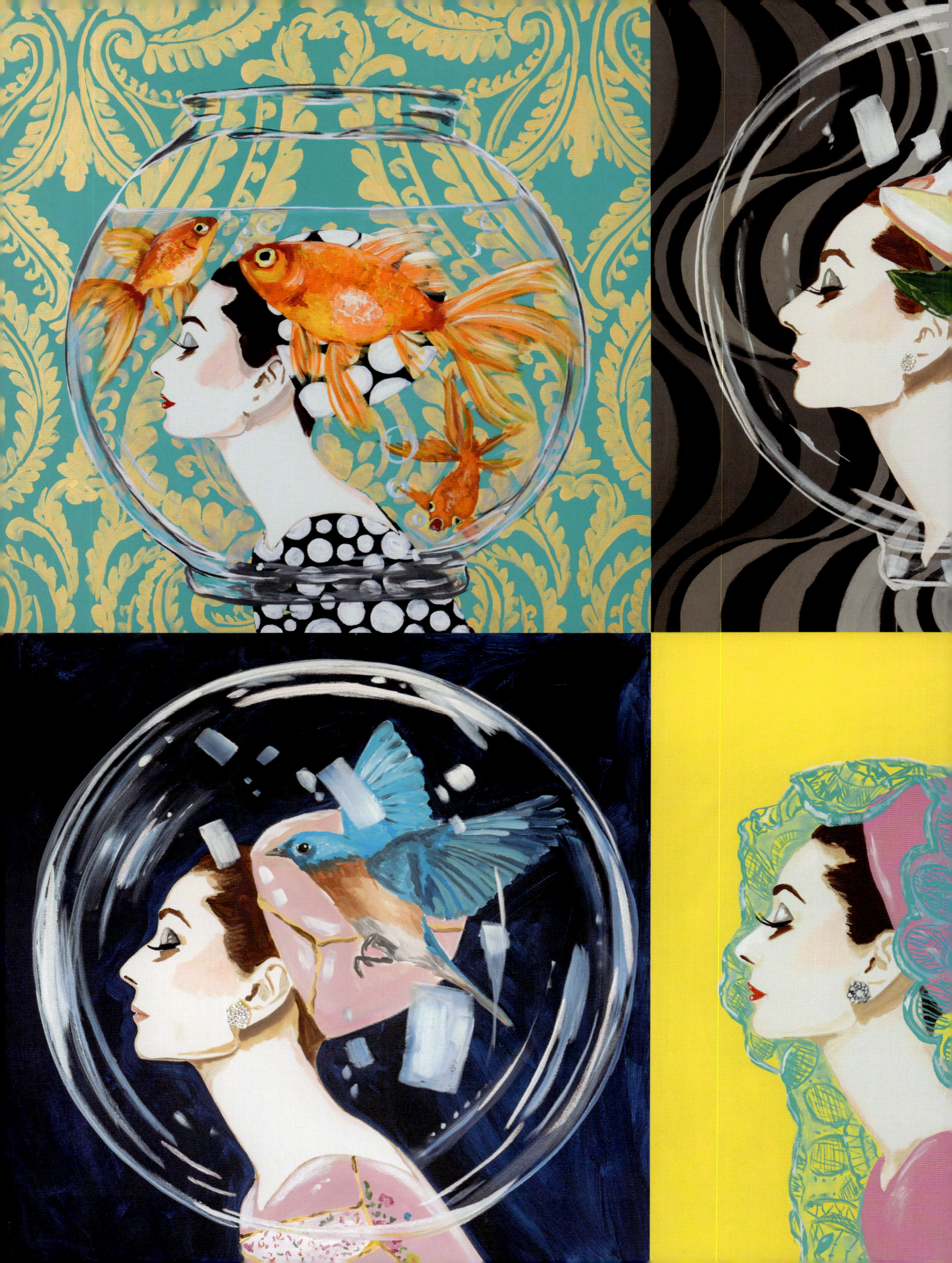

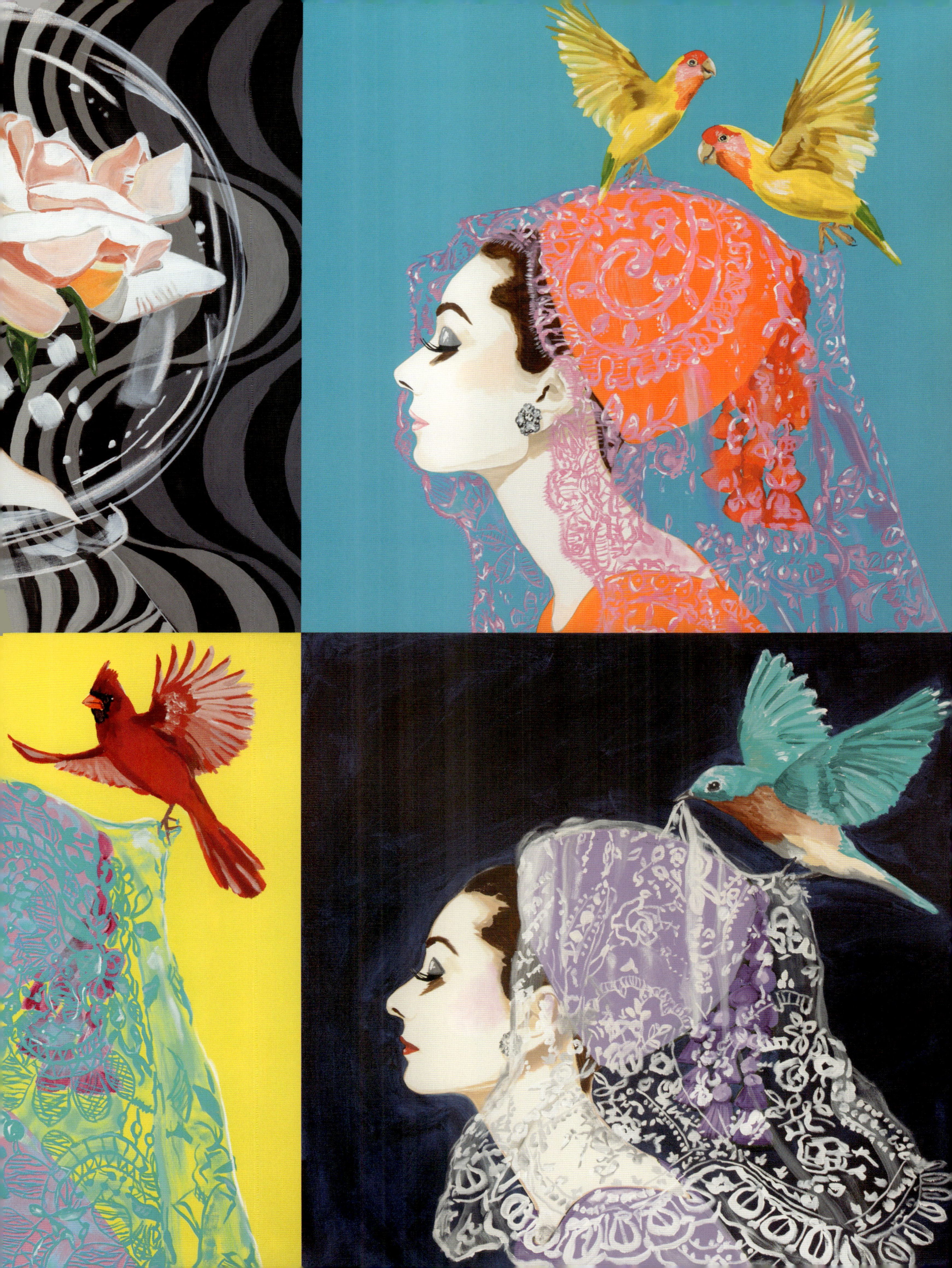

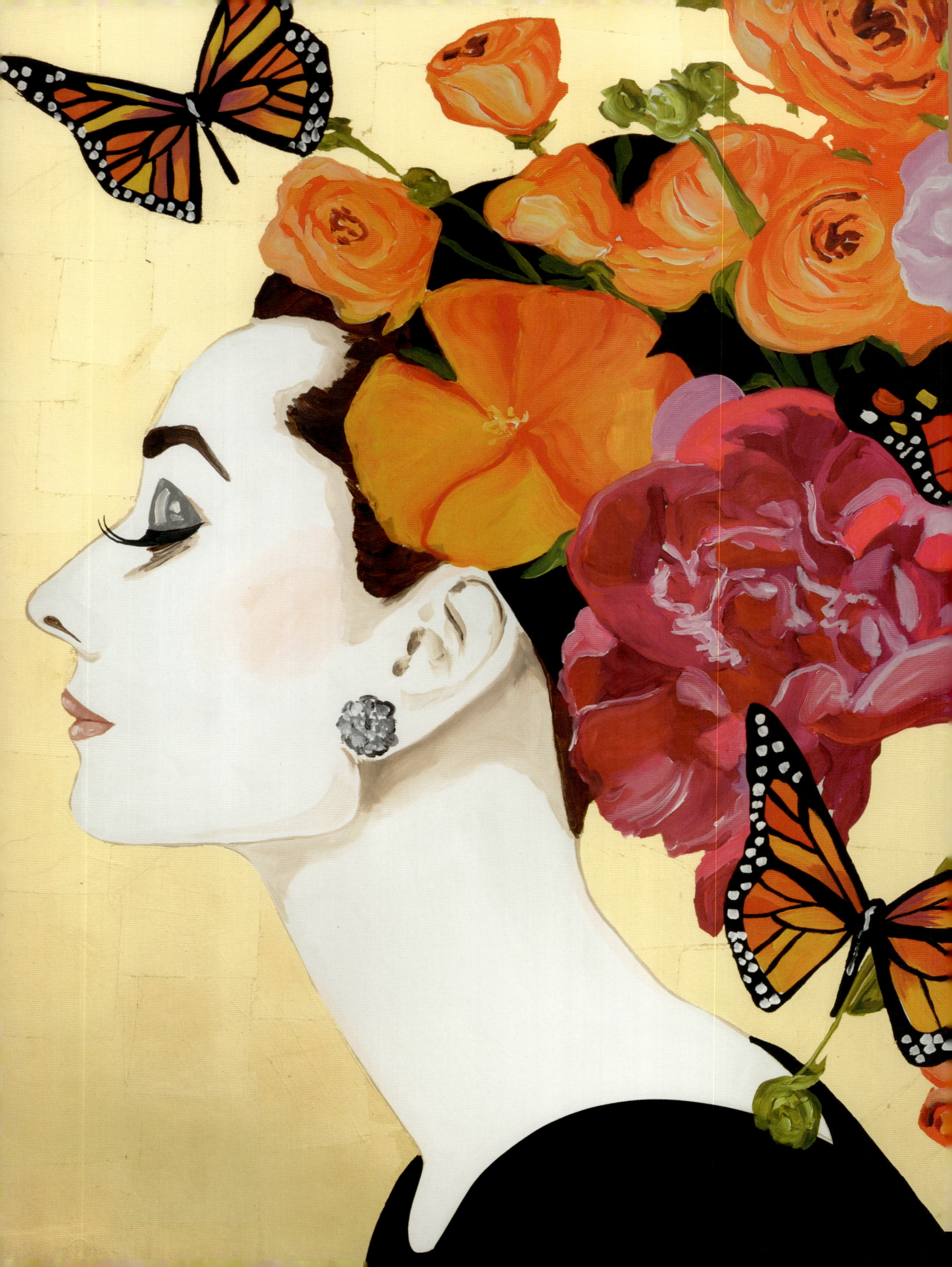

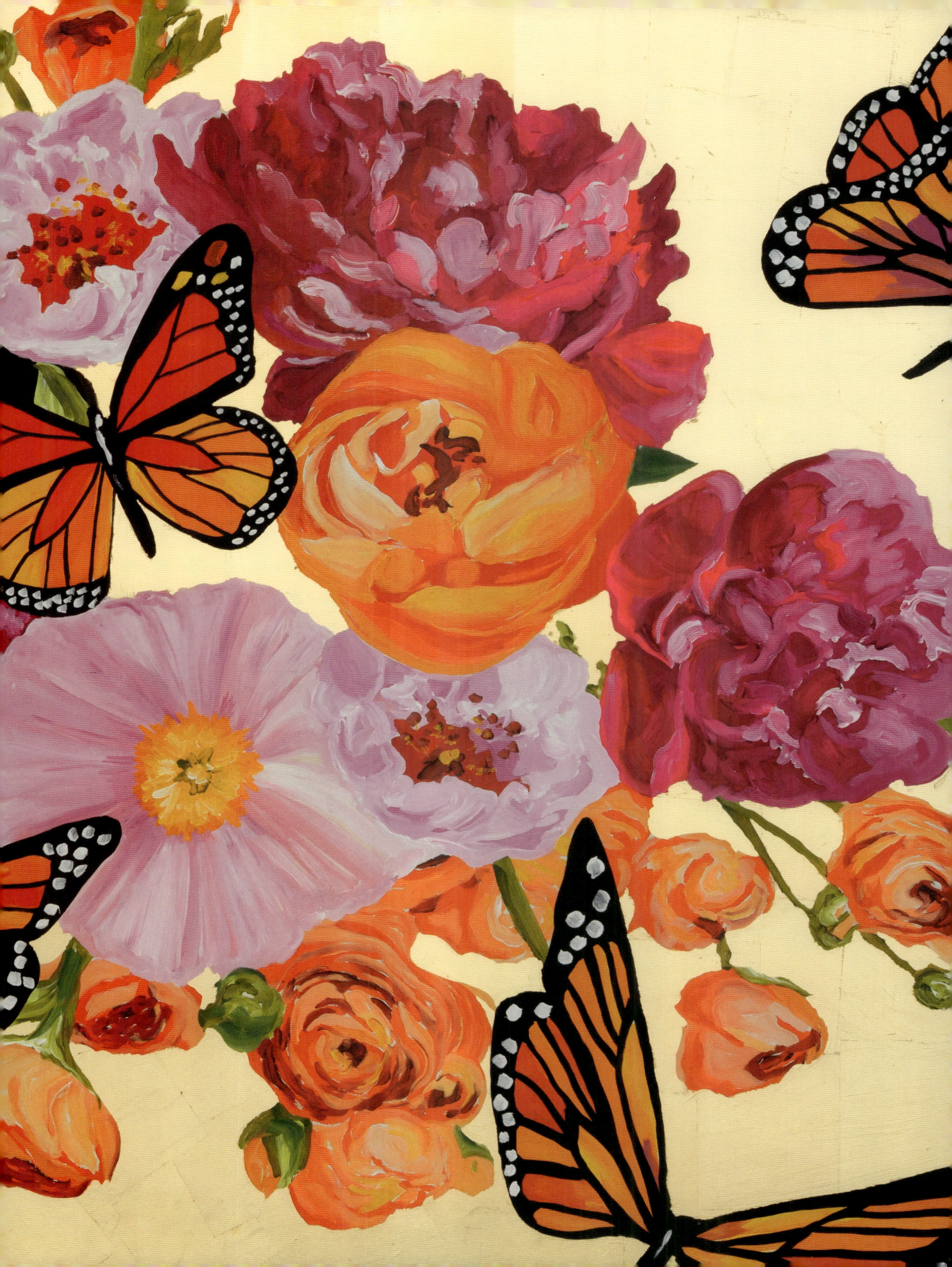

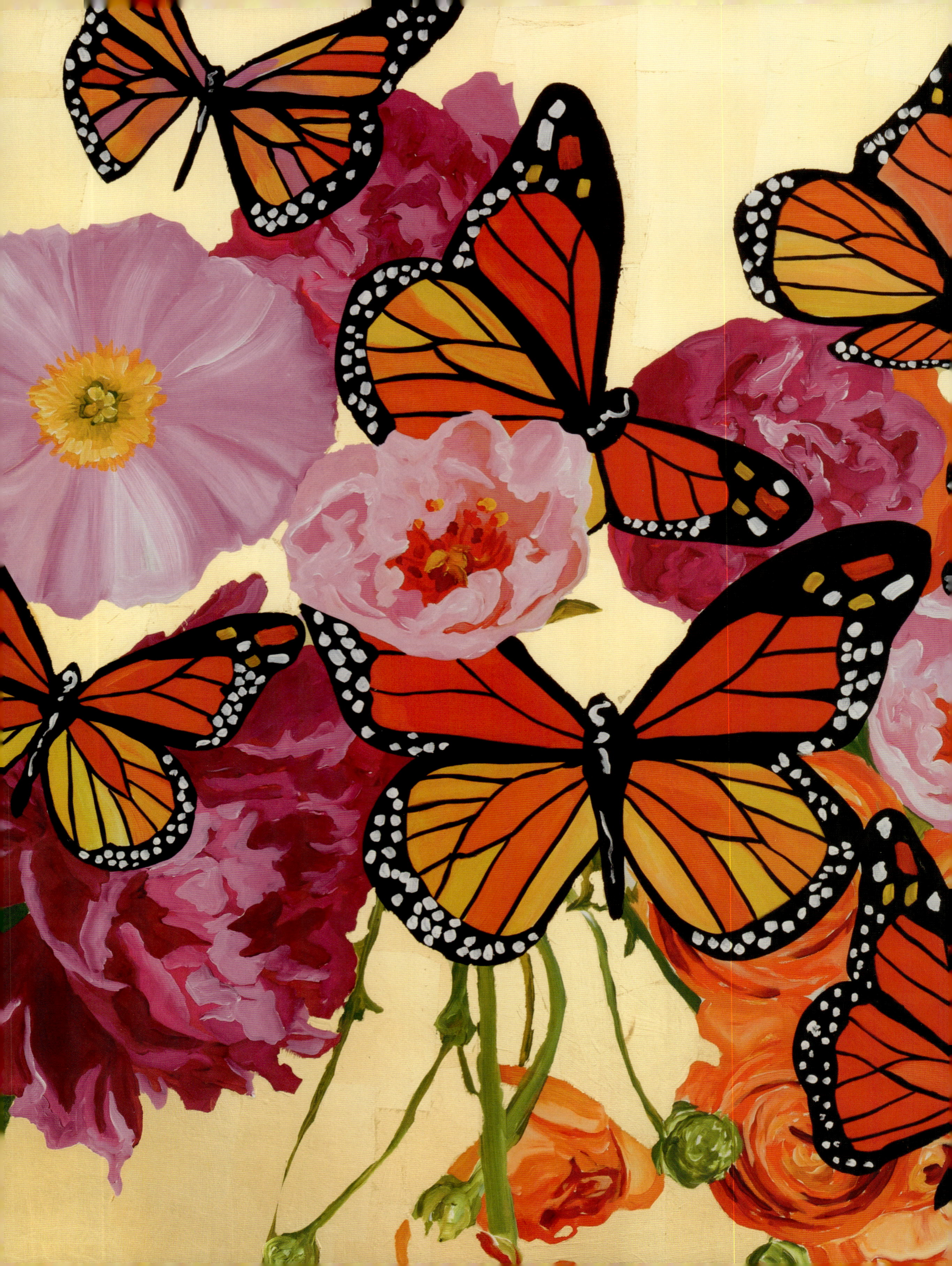

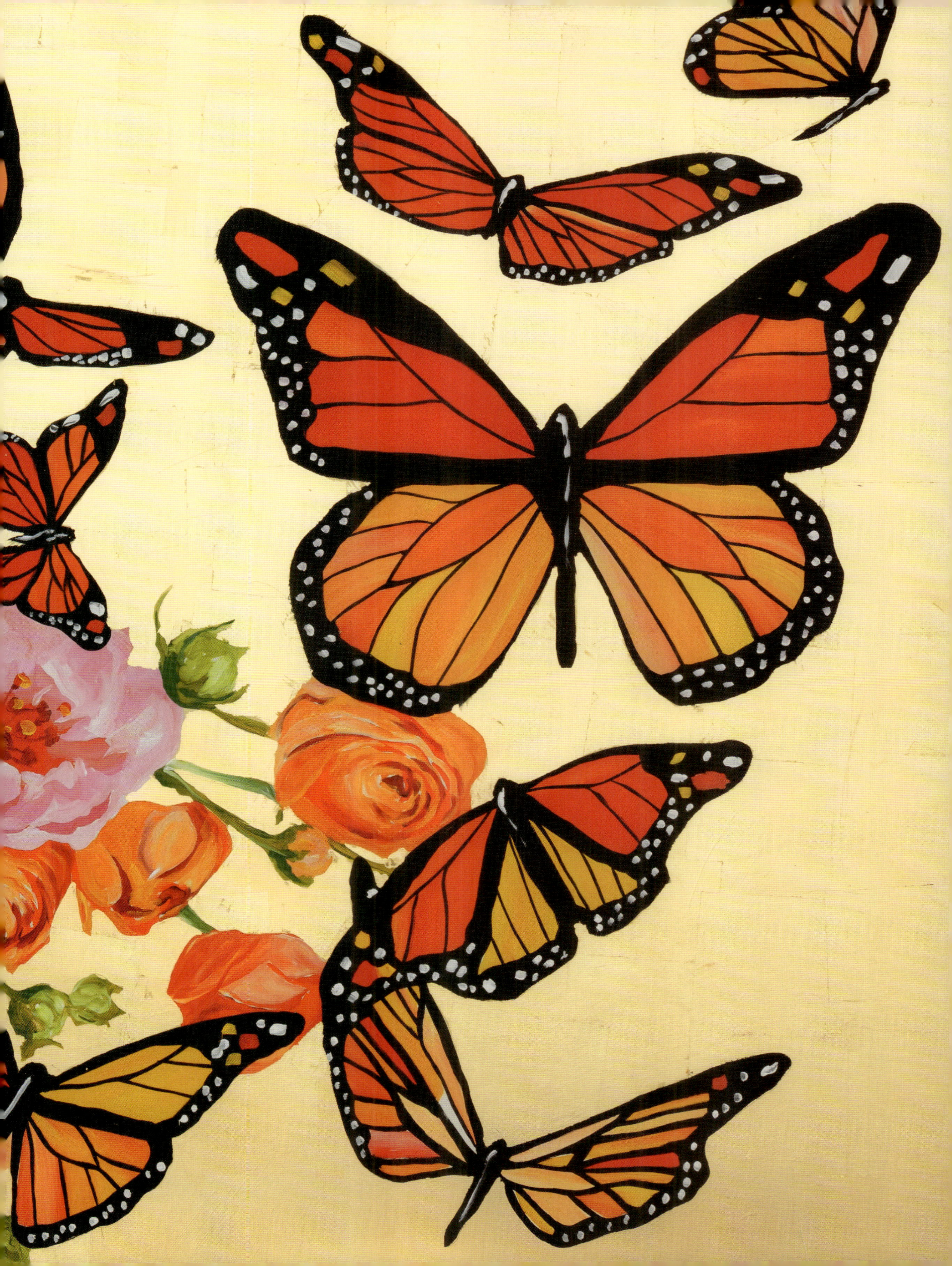

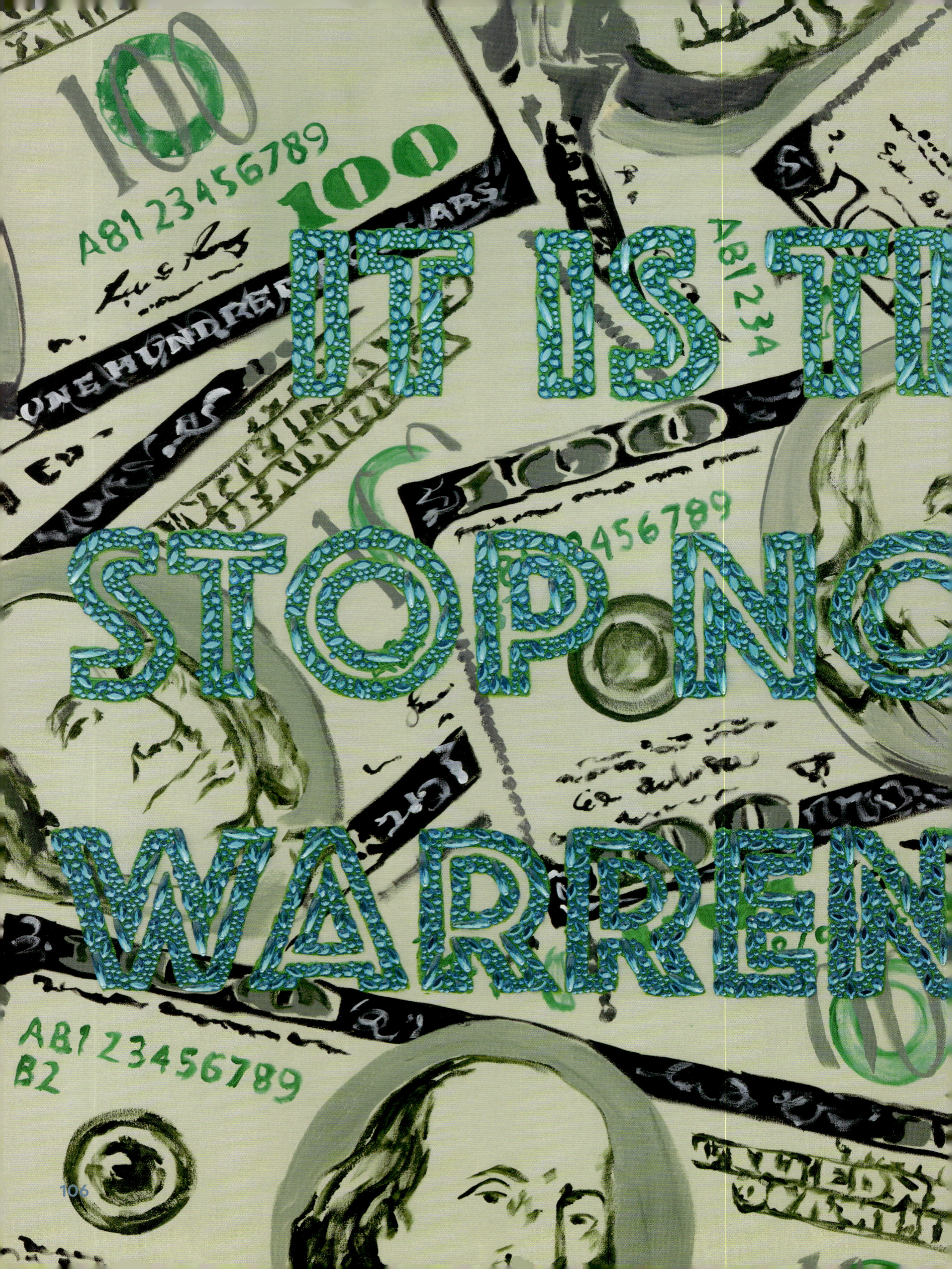
100
A8123456789
100
ONE HUNDRED
A81234
456789
IT IS TH
STOP NO
WARREN
A8123456789
B2
106

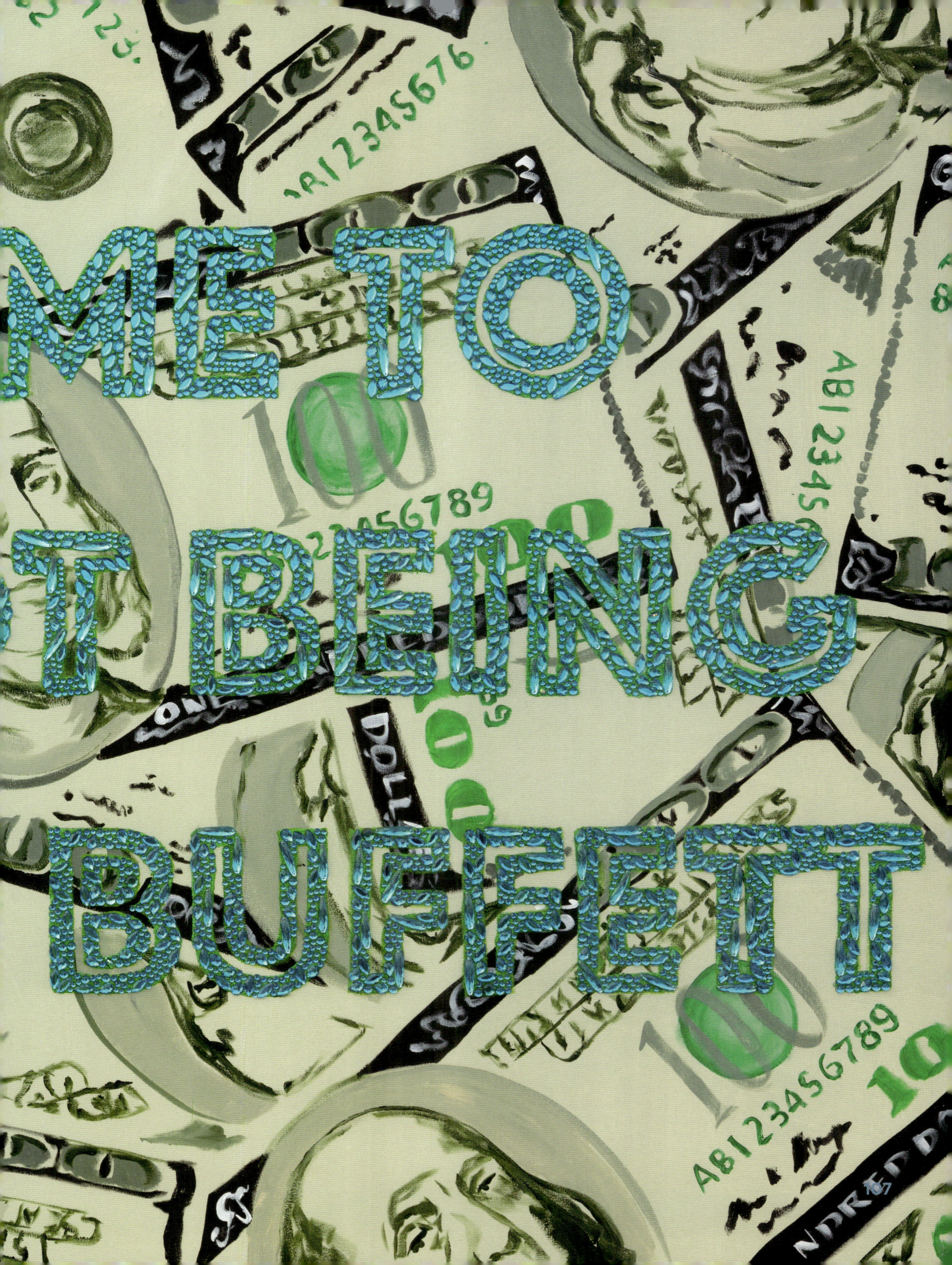
ME TO
T BEING
BUFFETT

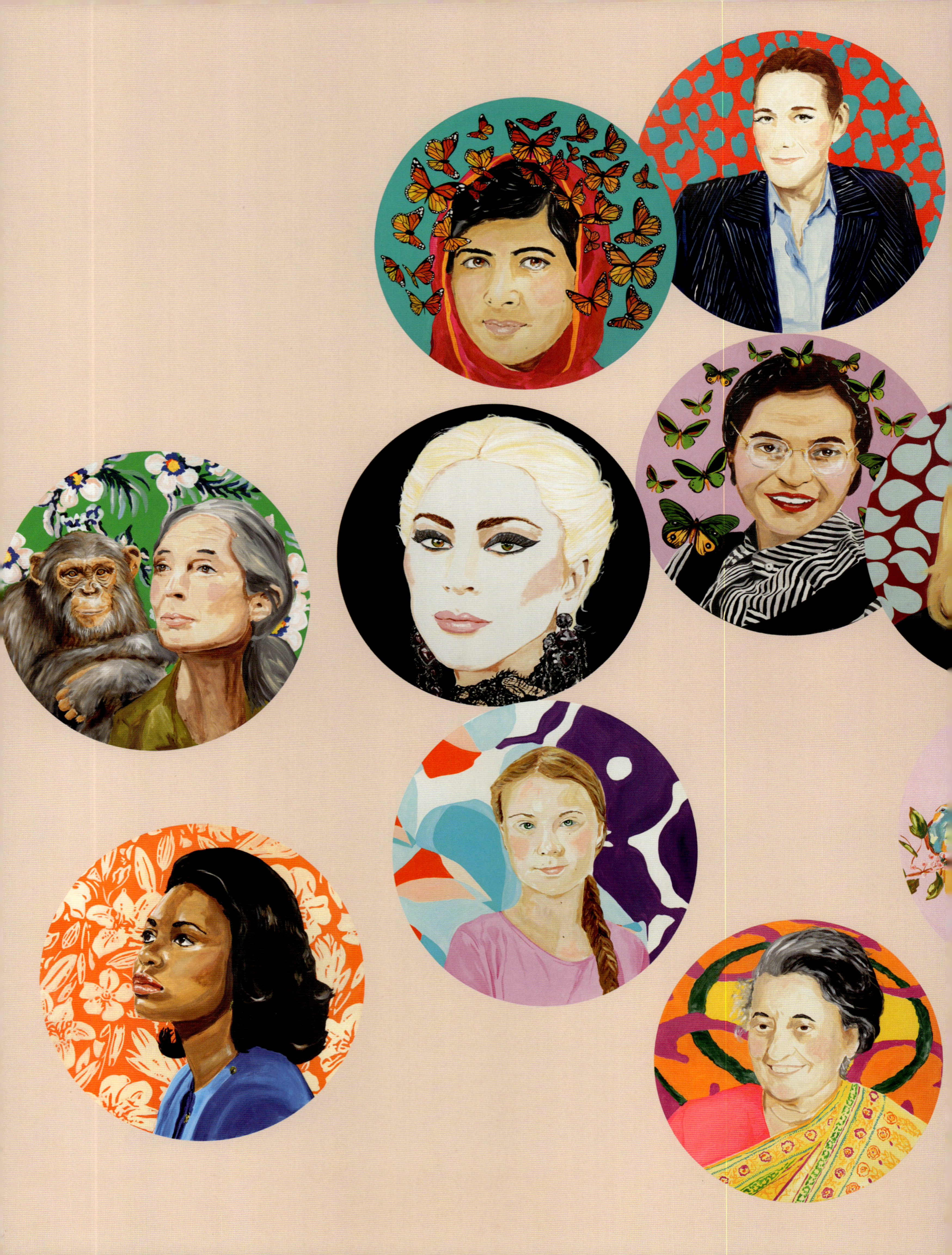

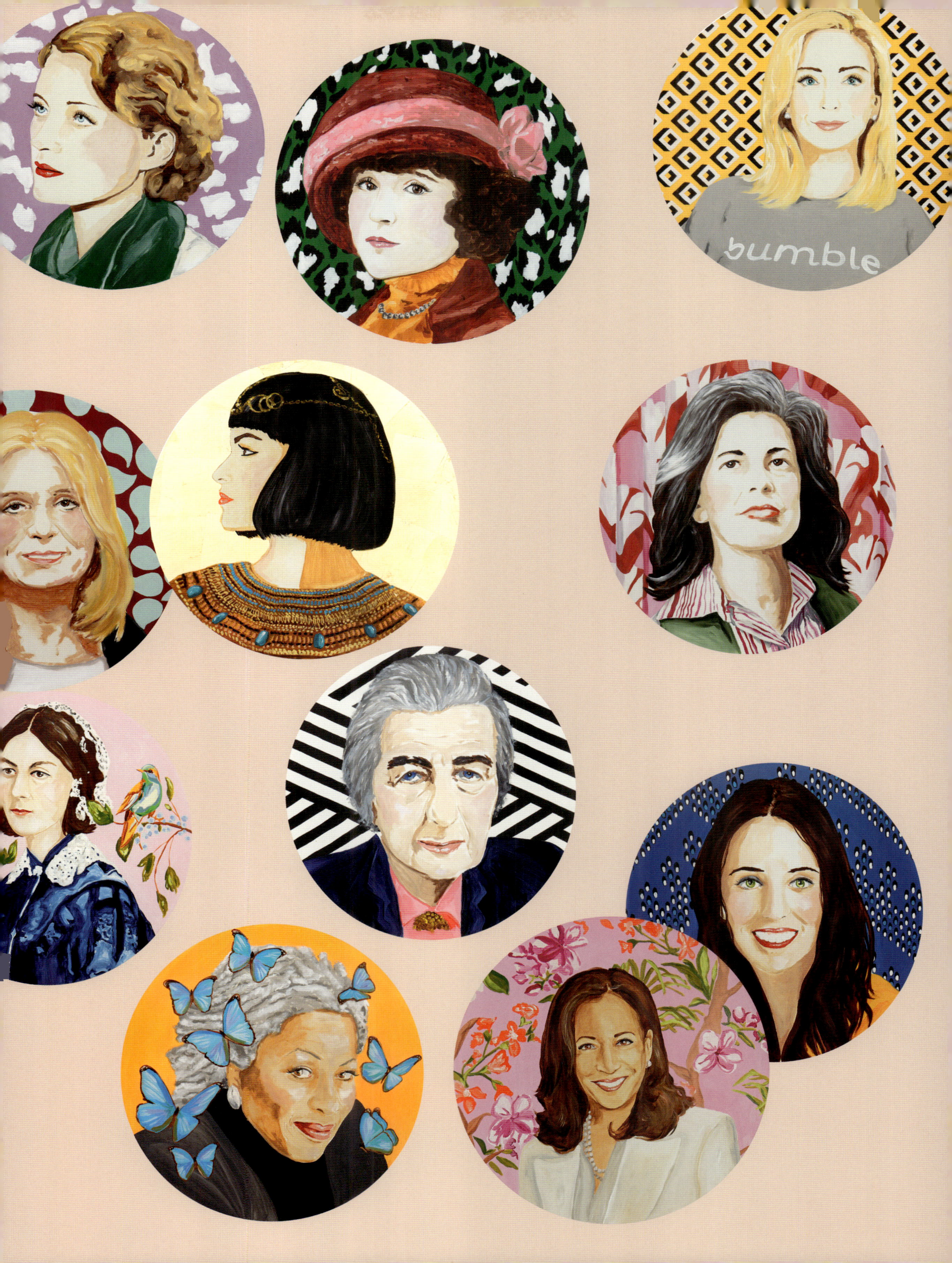

bumble

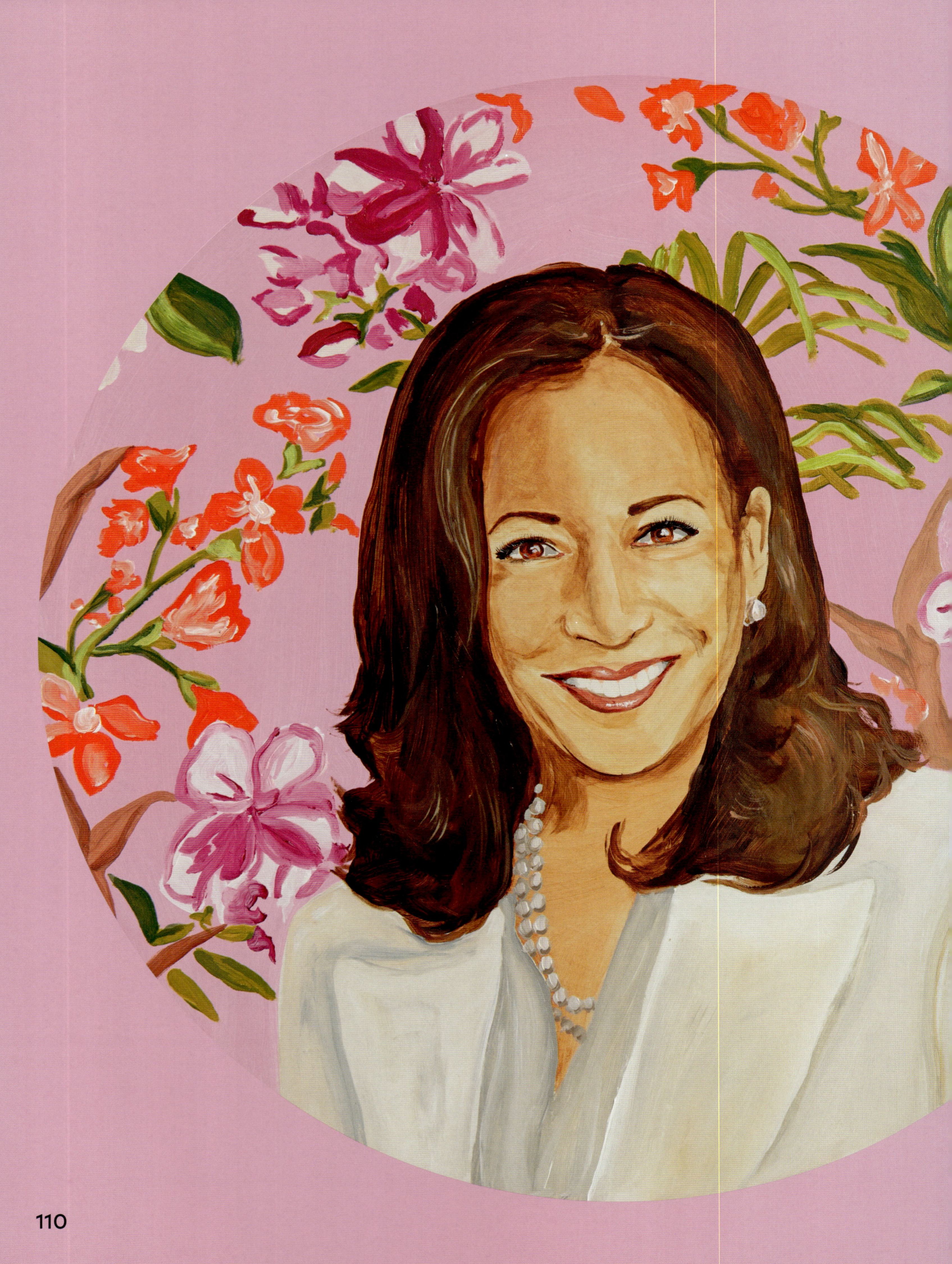

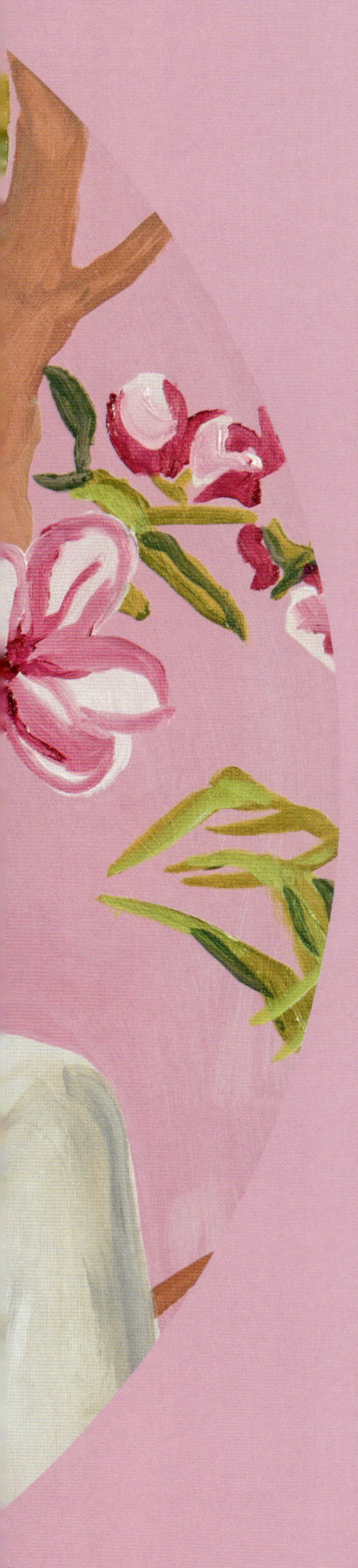

Kamala Harris

Because she is the first woman vice president of the United States. Because she represents the black and Indian communities. She epitomizes possibility, confidence, and determination.

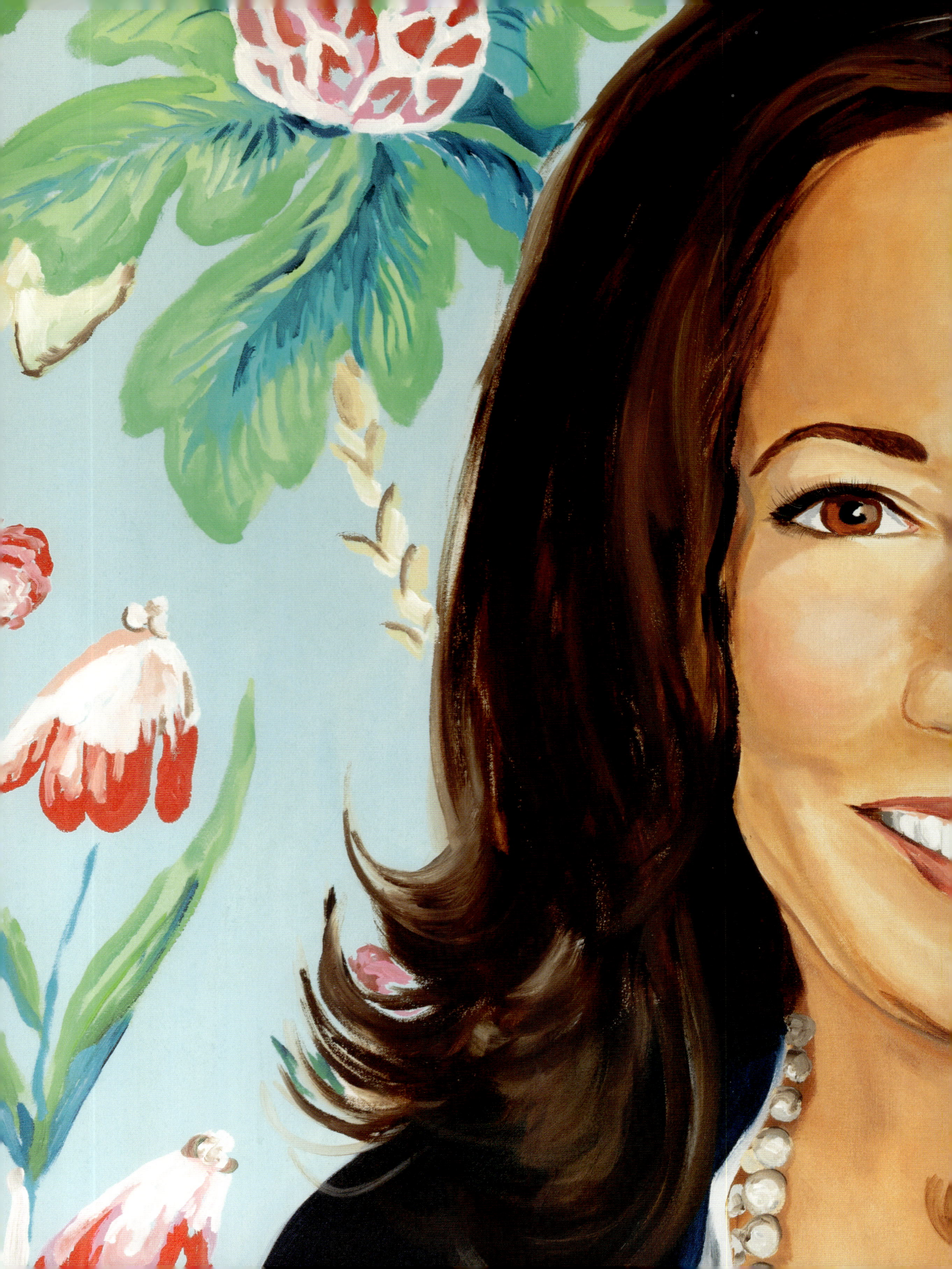

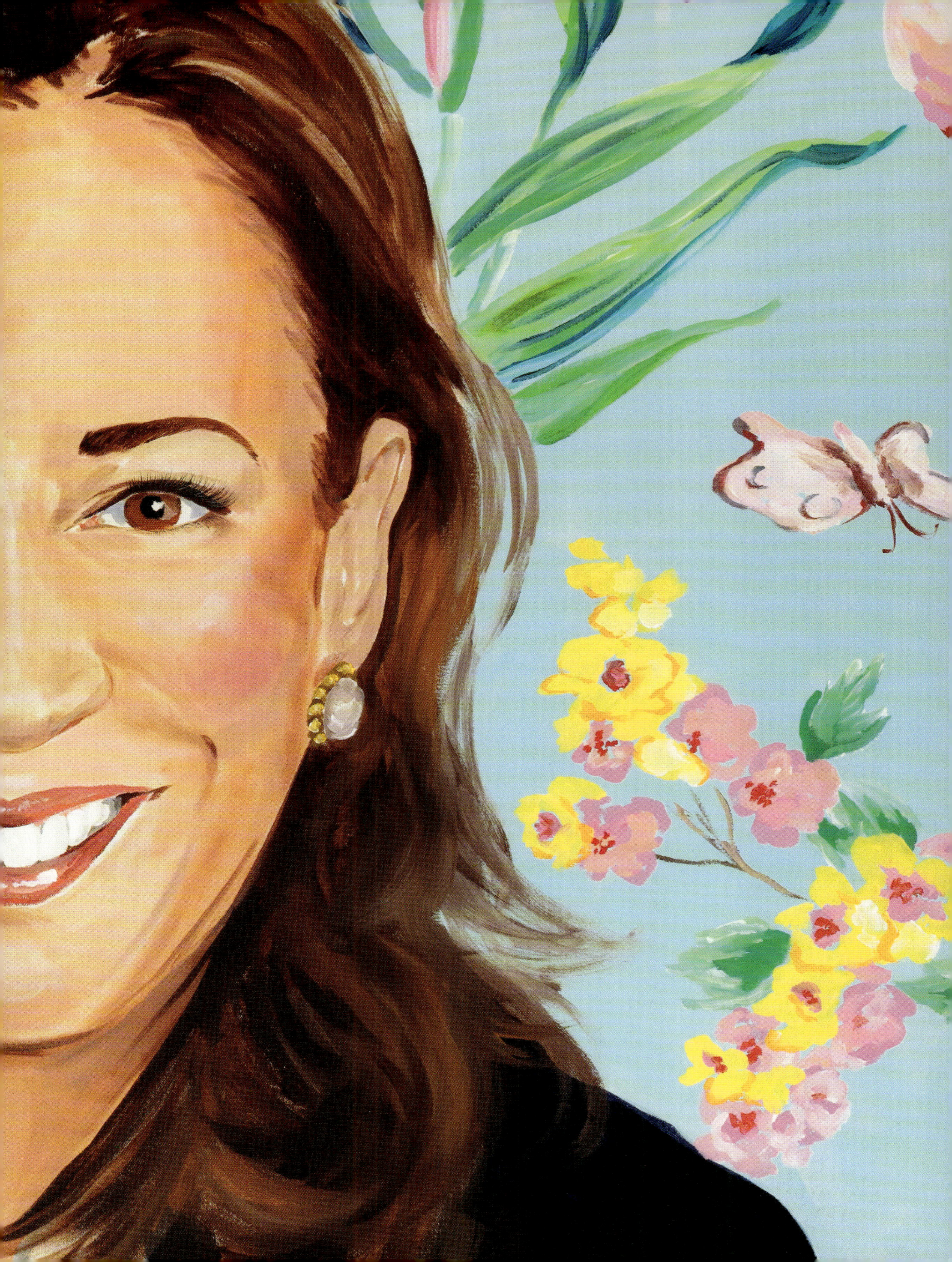

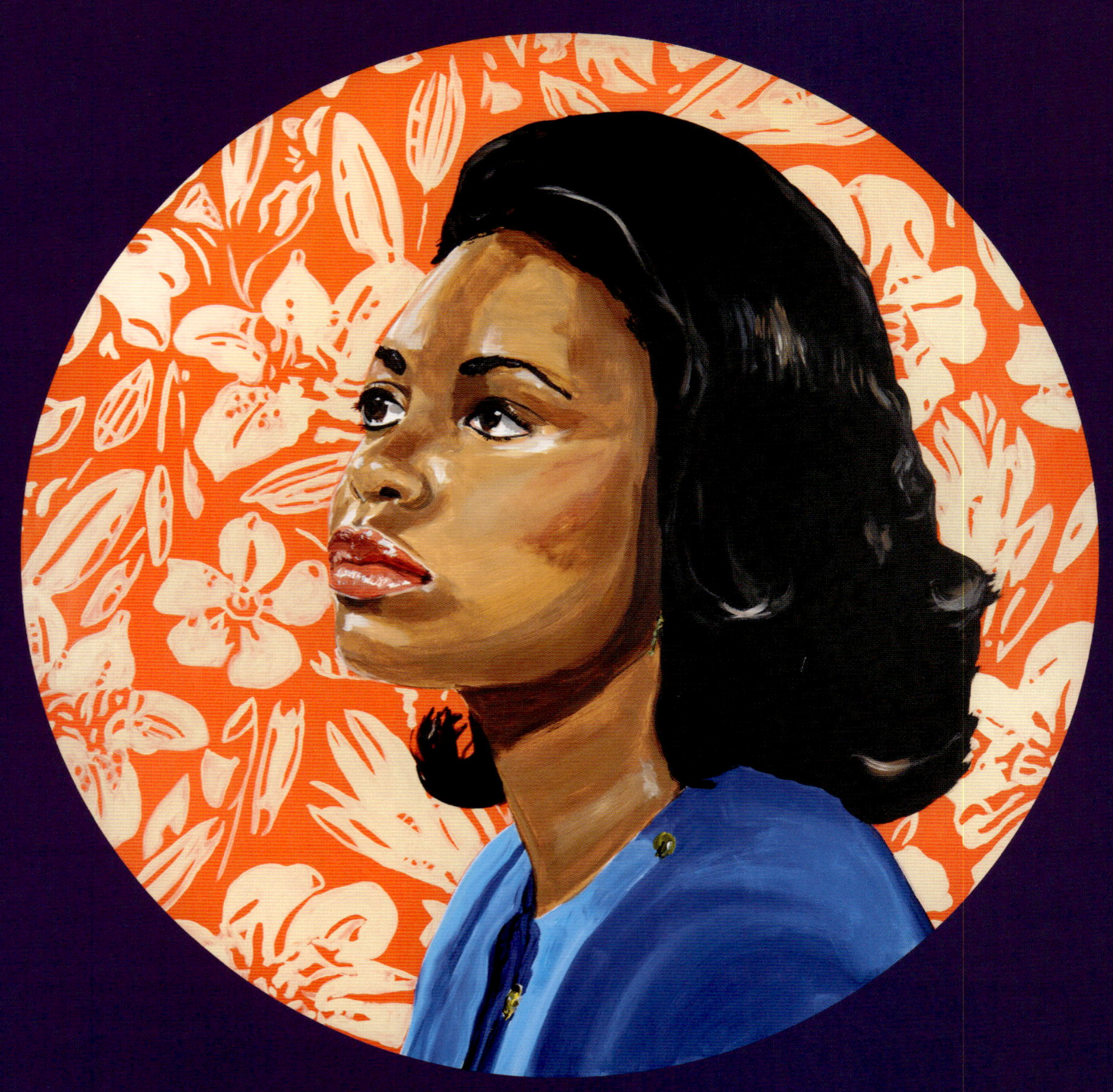

Anita
Hill

Because she is unwavering. She showed us
what courage looked like in the face of injustice
and power imbalances in the workplace.

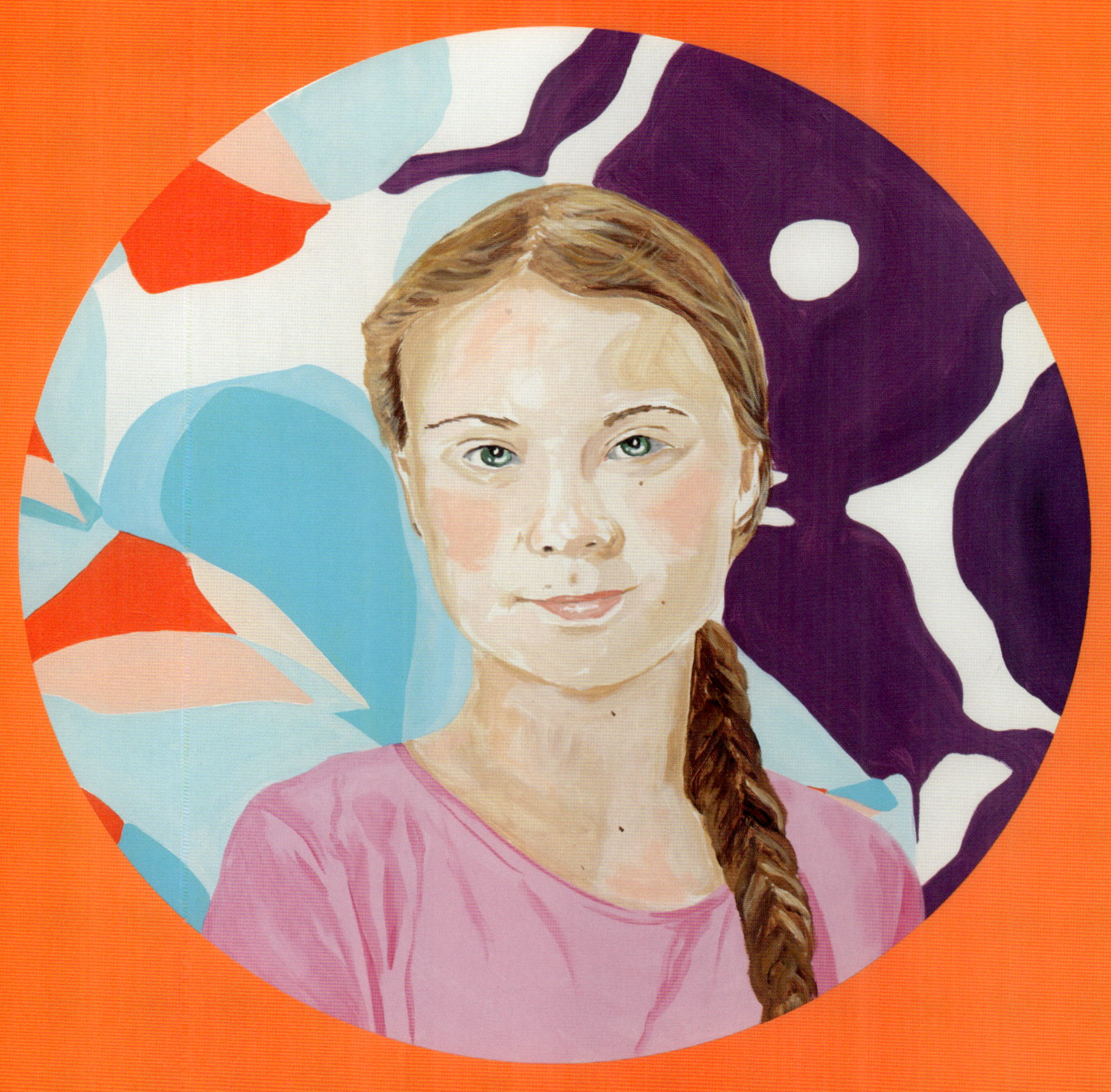

Greta Thunberg

Because she inspires us all to do better and to love our planet. She is a reminder that we must not ignore nature.

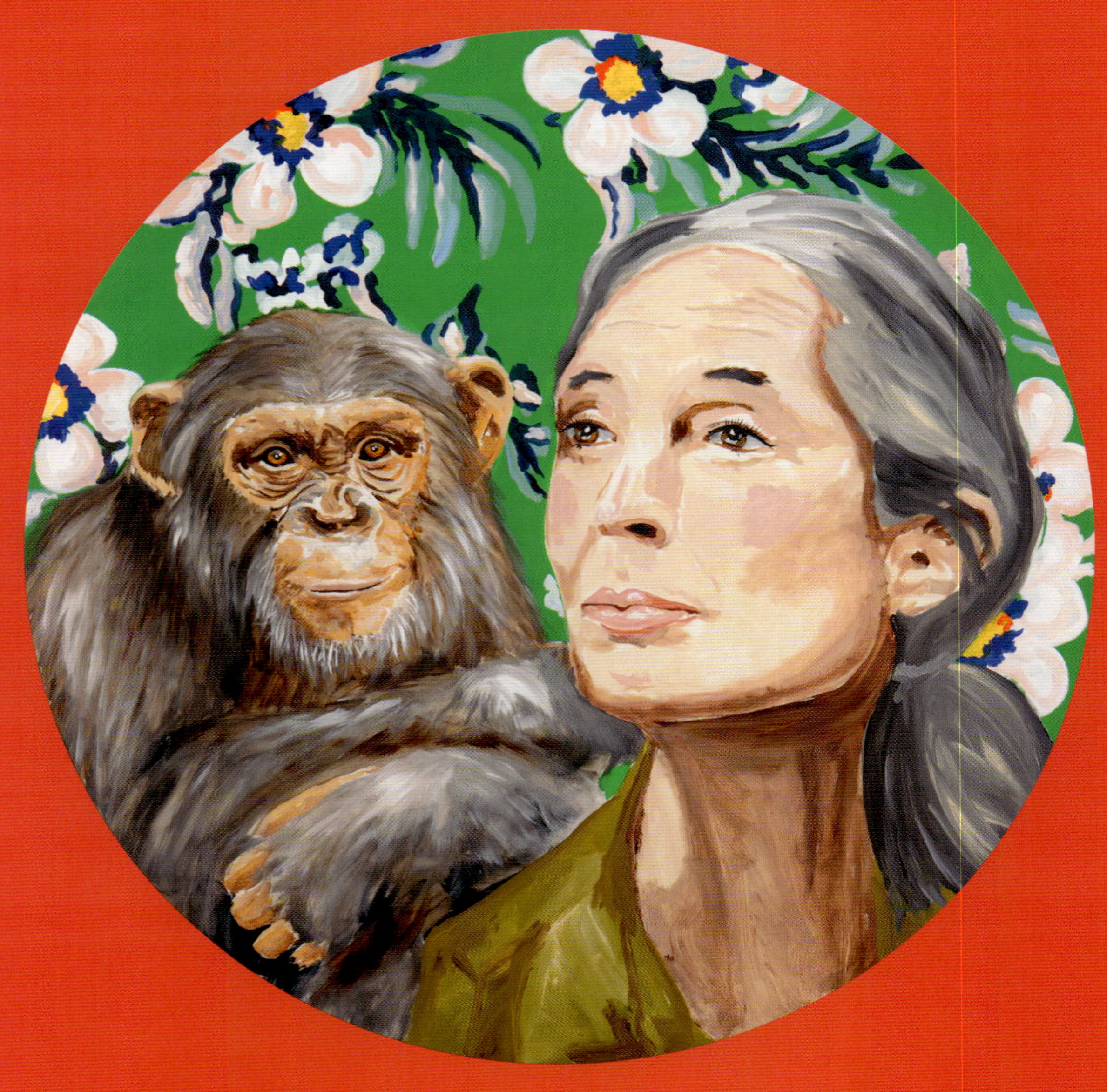

Jane
Goodall

Because she shows us that women can be great
in the field of science—the greatest, actually.

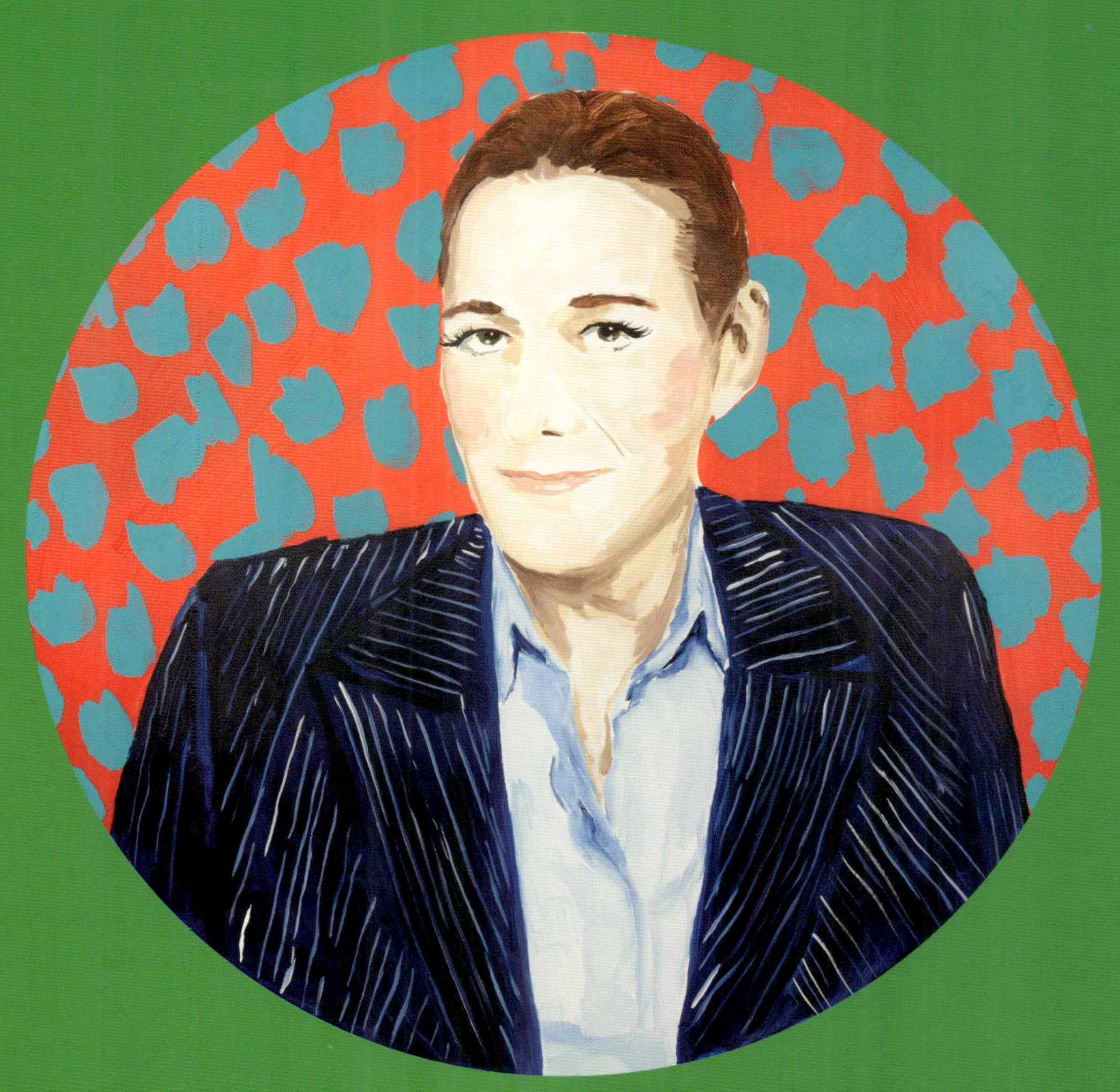

Martine Rothblatt

Because she has set a new standard for how much we can achieve when we are true to ourselves. Her accomplishments run deep, and her awareness is beyond inspiring.

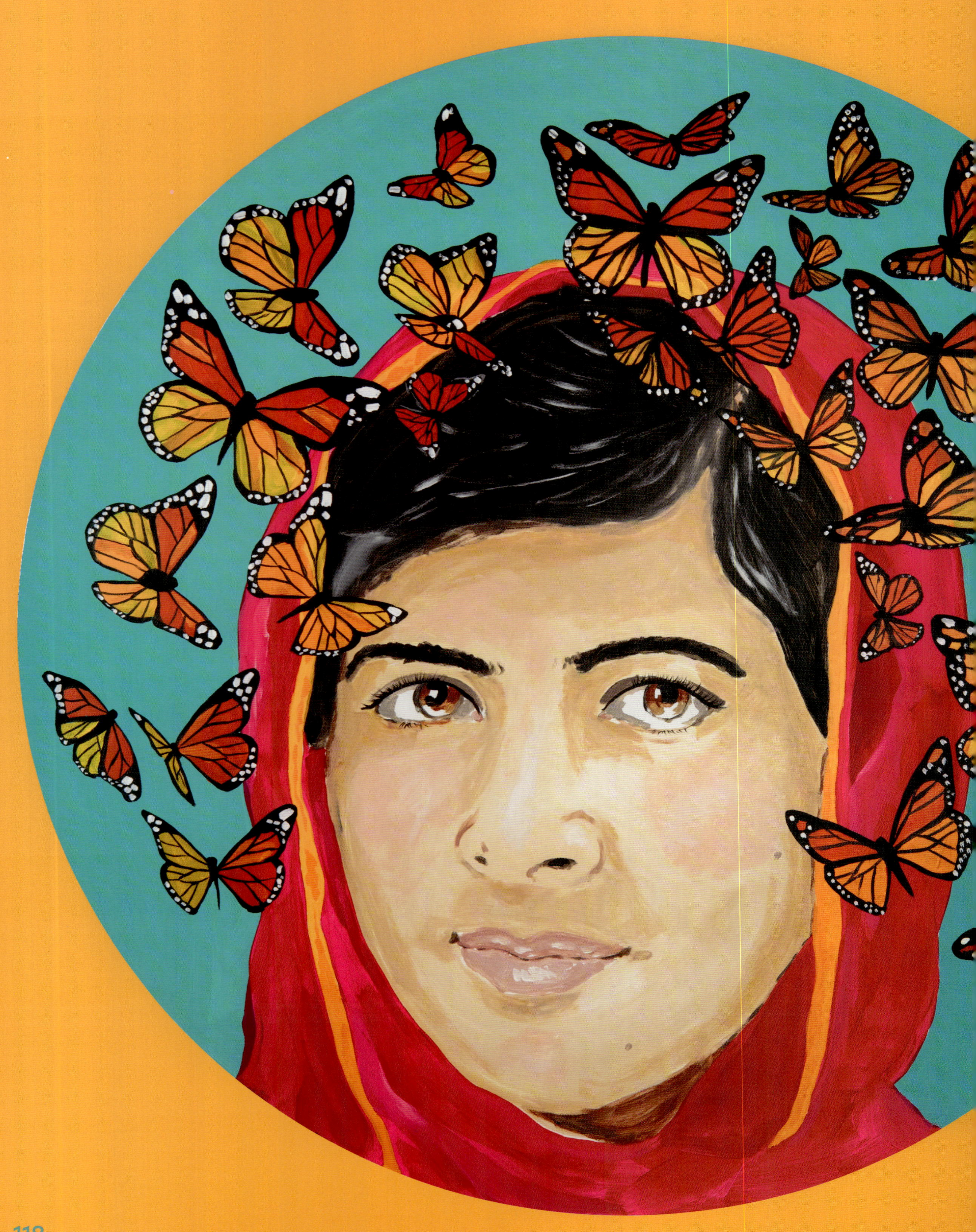

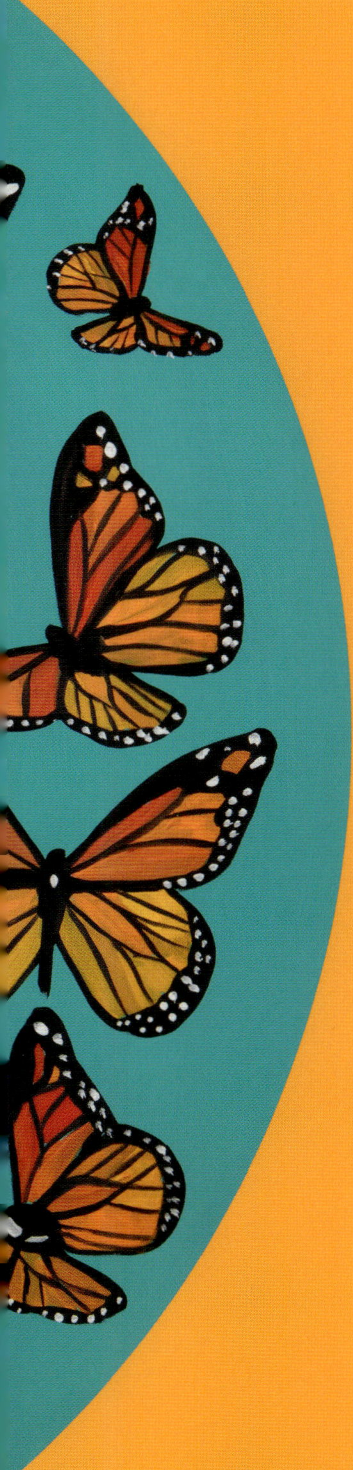

Malala Yousafzai

Because she exemplifies human endurance, decency, and love.

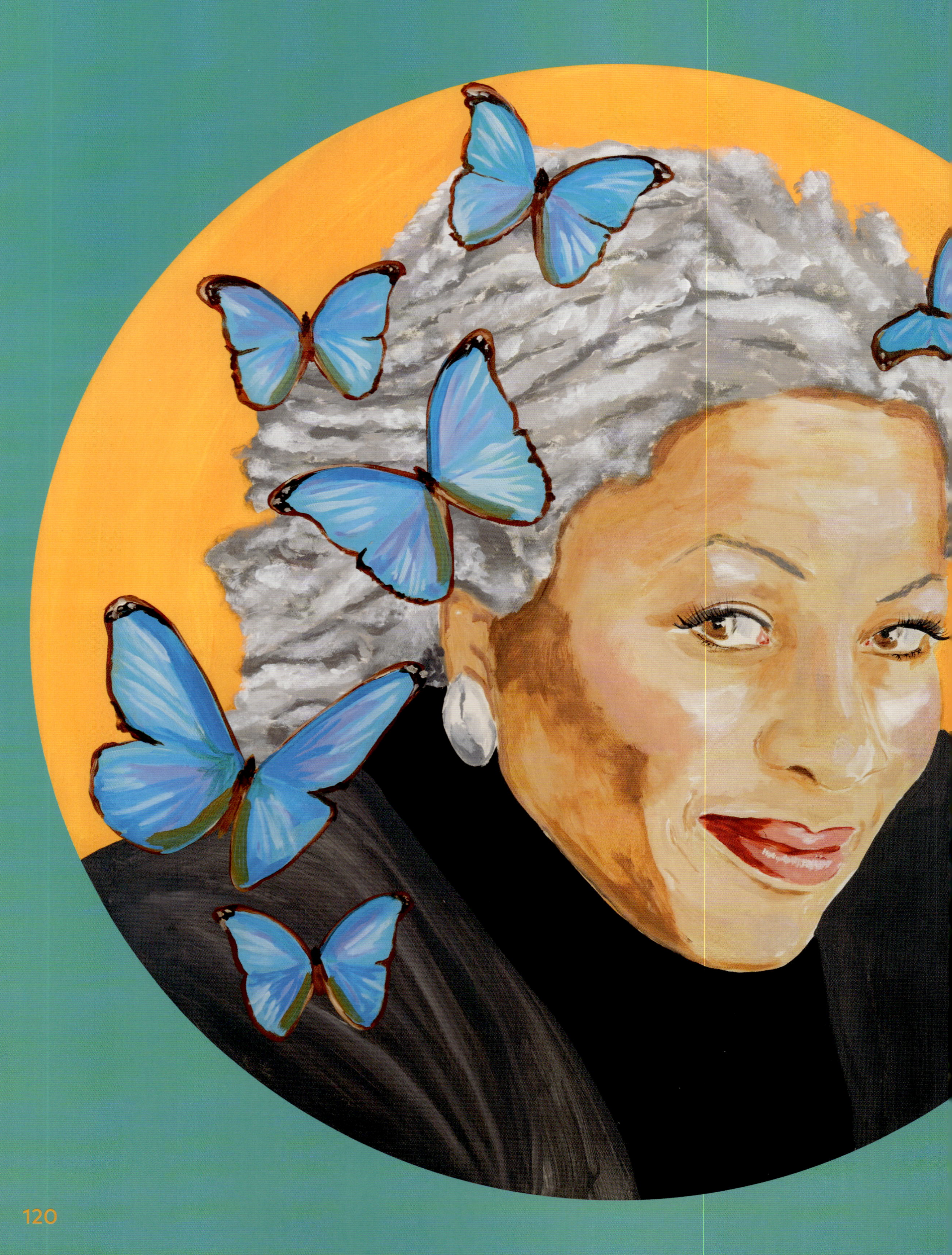

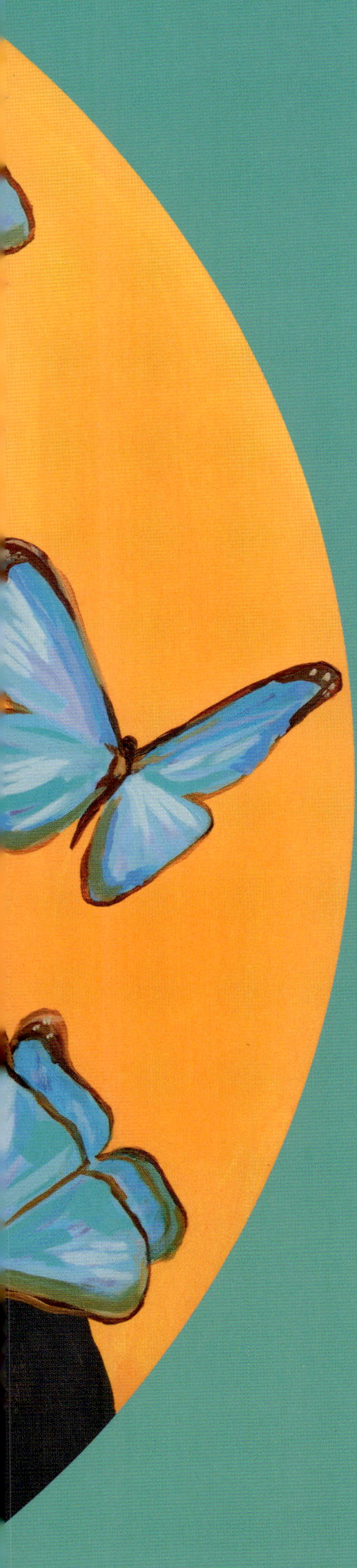

Toni Morrison

Because she opened a window wide and allowed us to participate in the exploration of black identity in America.

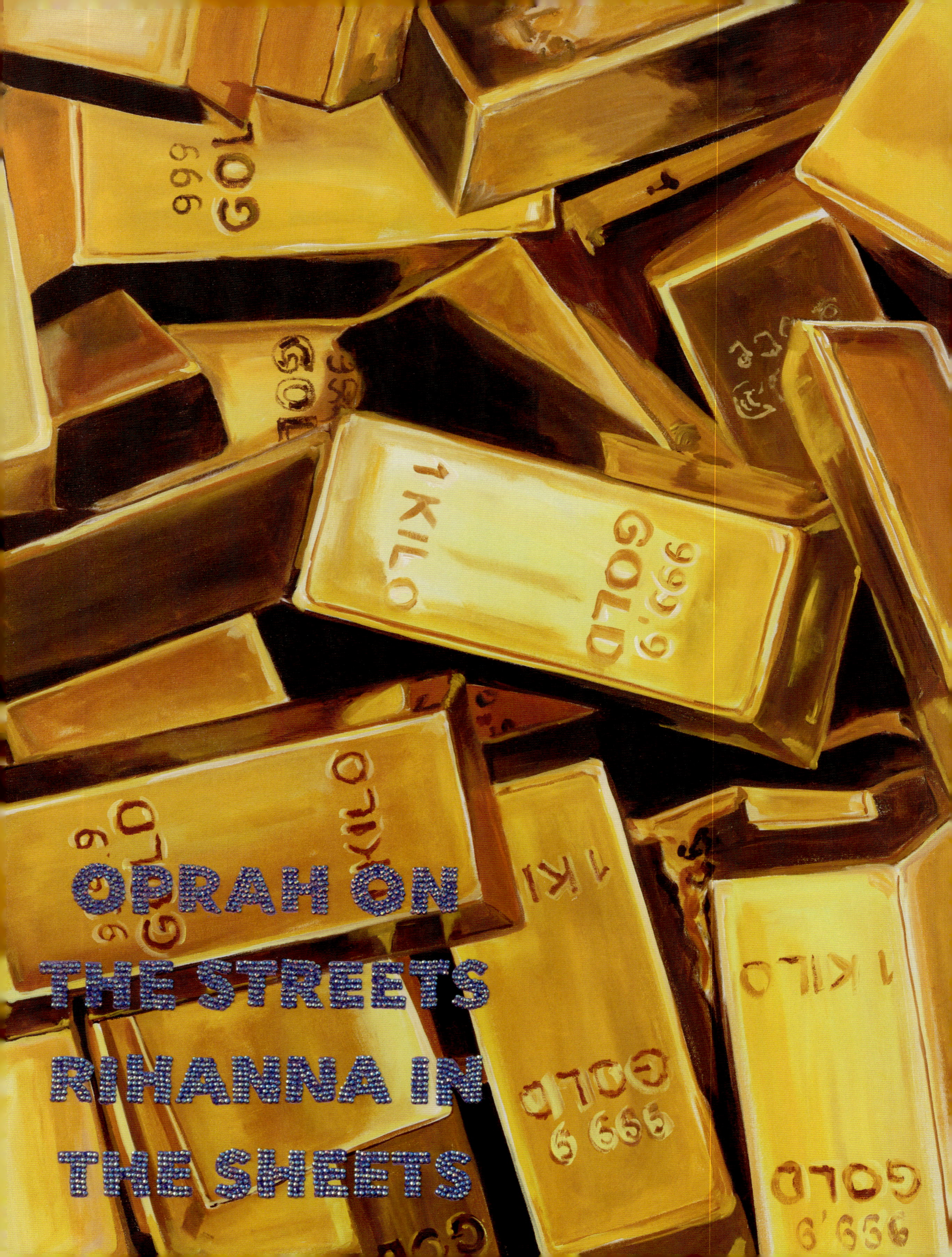

OPRAH ON THE STREETS
RIHANNA IN THE SHEETS

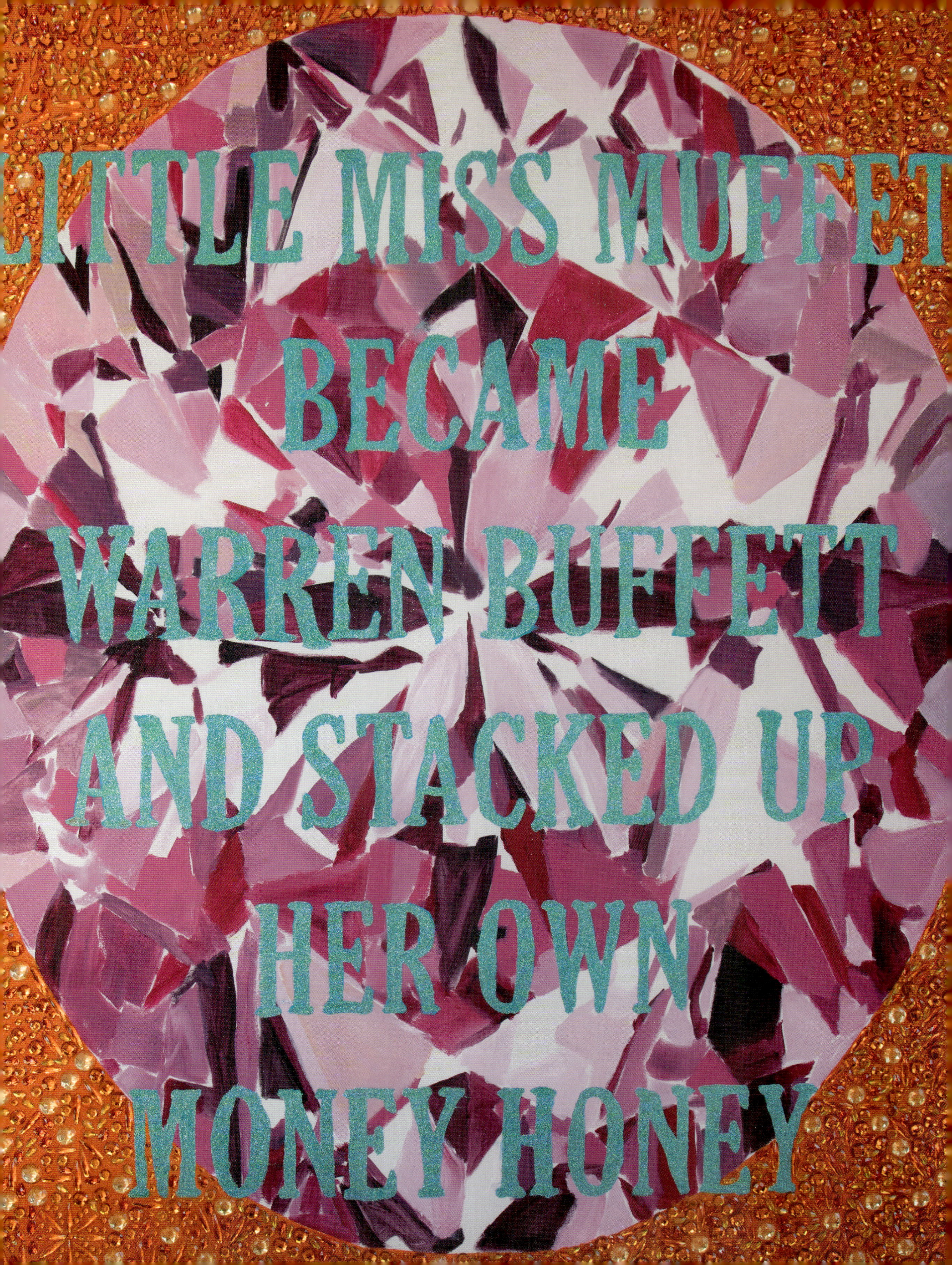

LITTLE MISS MUFFET
BECAME
WARREN BUFFETT
AND STACKED UP
HER OWN
MONEY HONEY

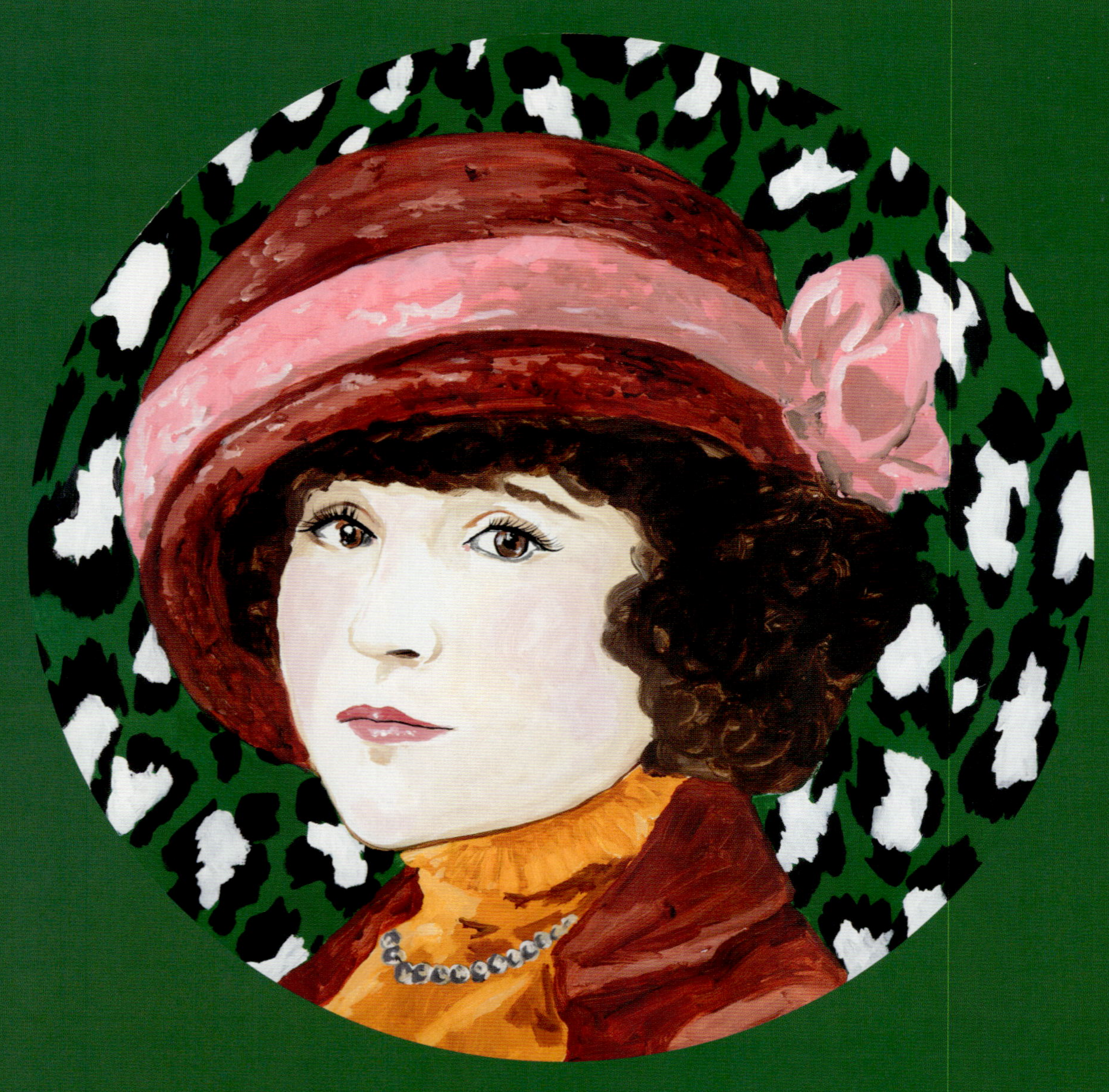

Colette

Because she used her brilliance to magnify her womanhood. She was nominated for the Nobel Prize in literature, no less.

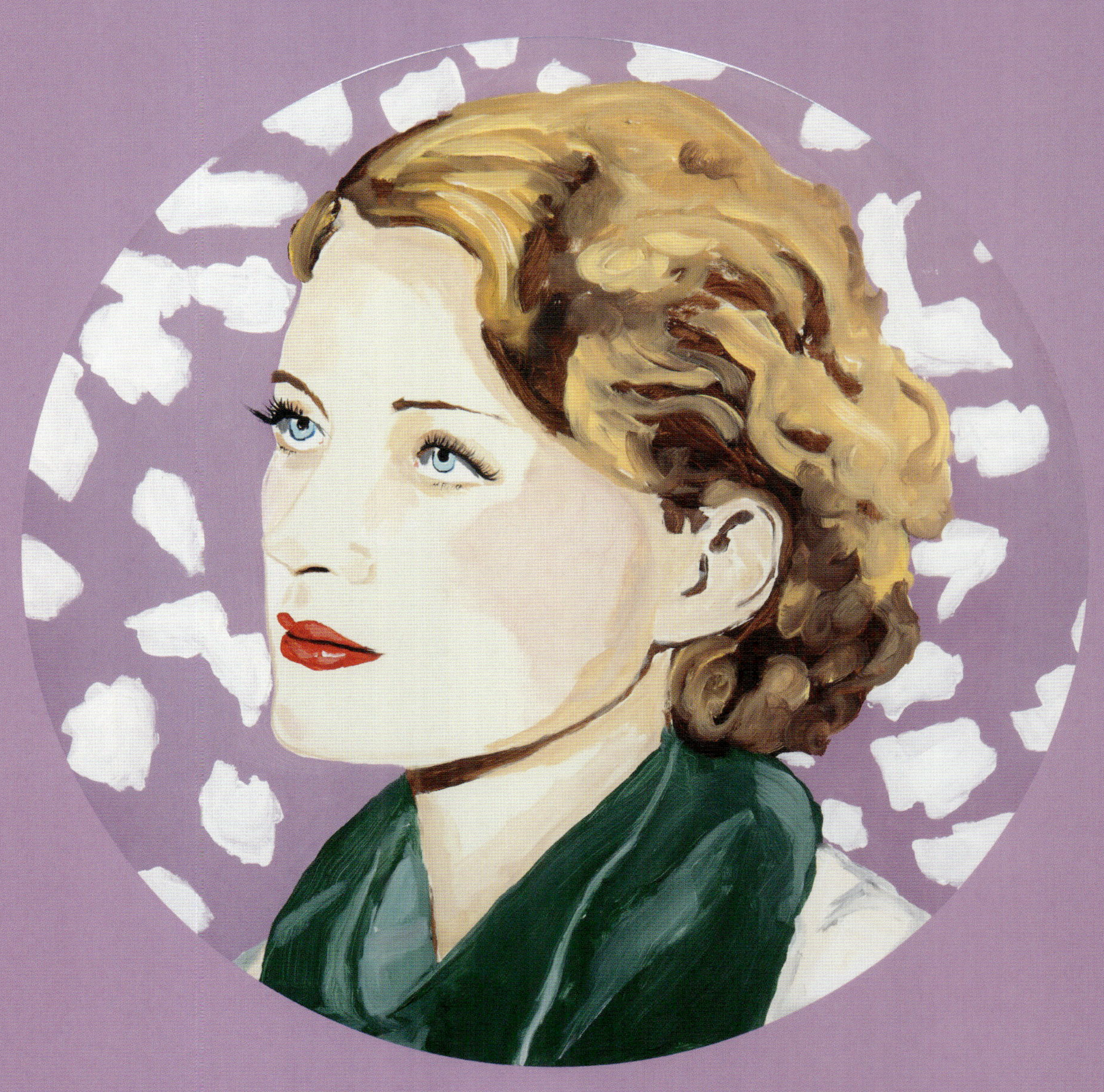

Lee Miller

Because she proved that a woman can cover a war just as well as a man. Before she was a war correspondent for *Vogue*, she appeared on its cover as a fashion model—proving that women can do it all.

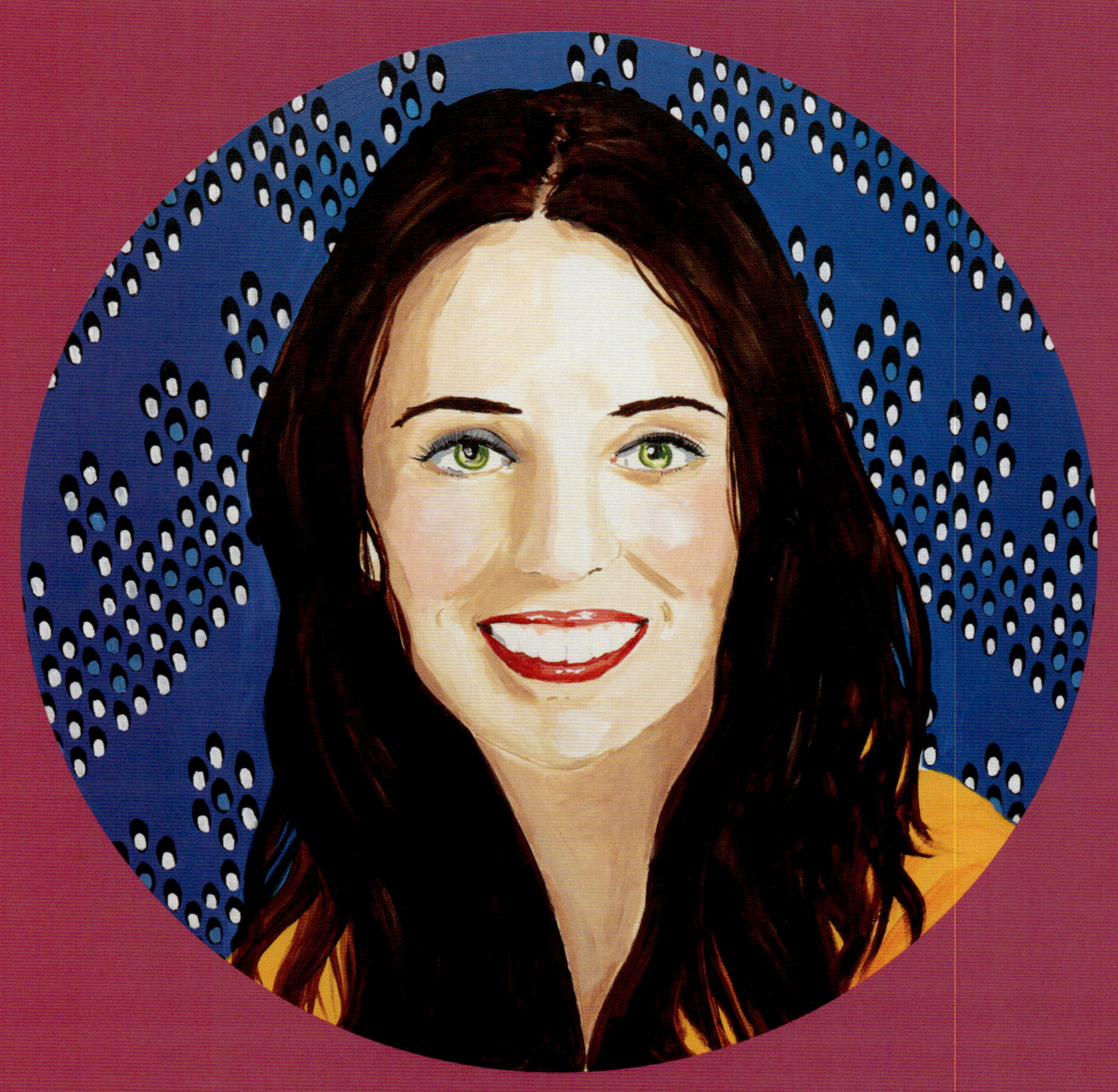

Jacinda Ardern

Because she is breaking boundaries as a female leader, embracing motherhood and family while leading her country by example.

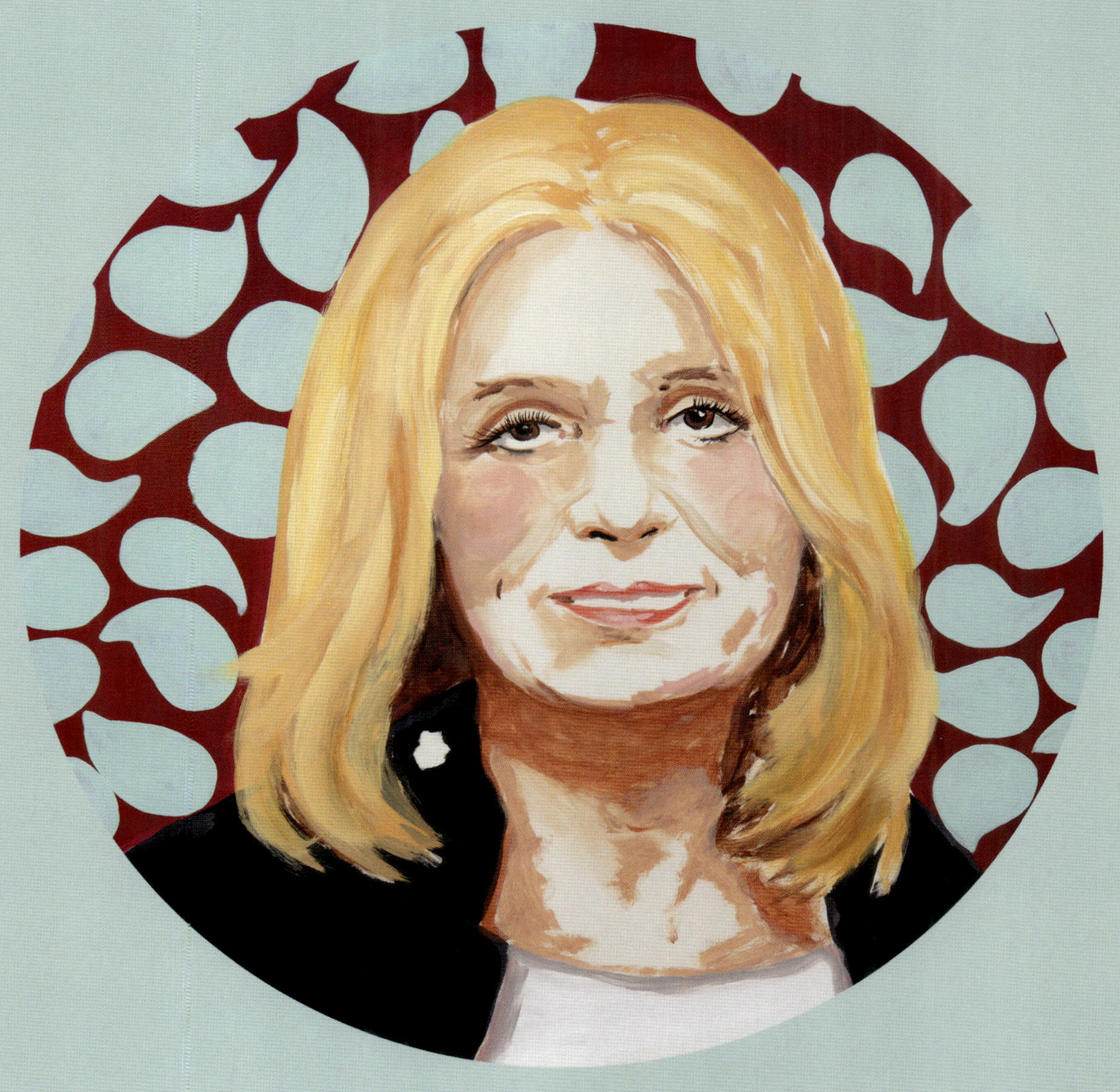

Gloria
Steinem

Because she is the godmother of women's liberation. She is our feminist goddess of gender equality. She is a legend, and I bow at her feet.

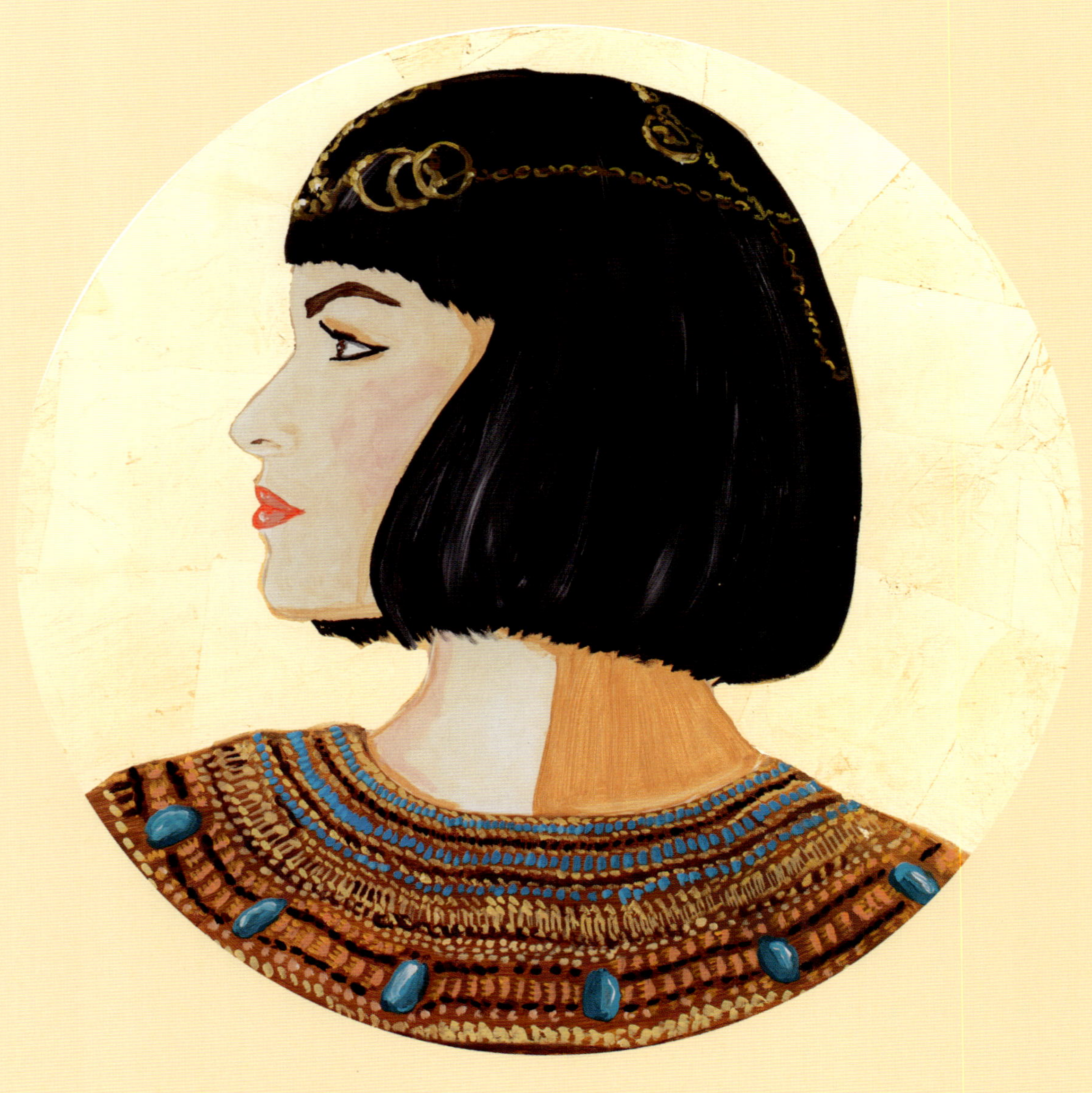

Cleopatra

Because she is an icon of female strength and also, how impressive is it that she spoke five languages? She is one of the most recognizable women in human history.

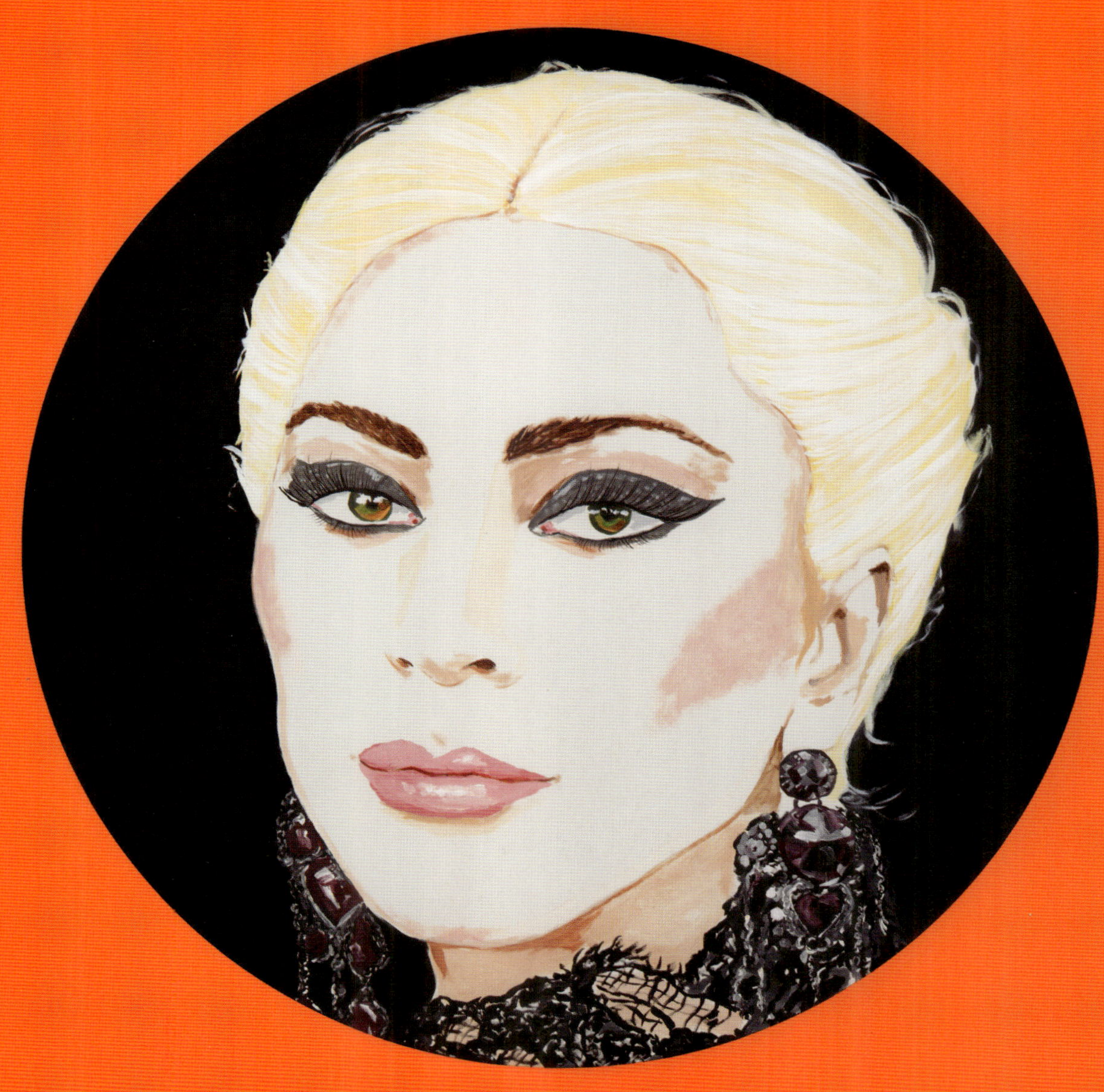

Lady Gaga

Because she shows us her heart. Her talent is absolutely remarkable, and she fights for what she believes in.

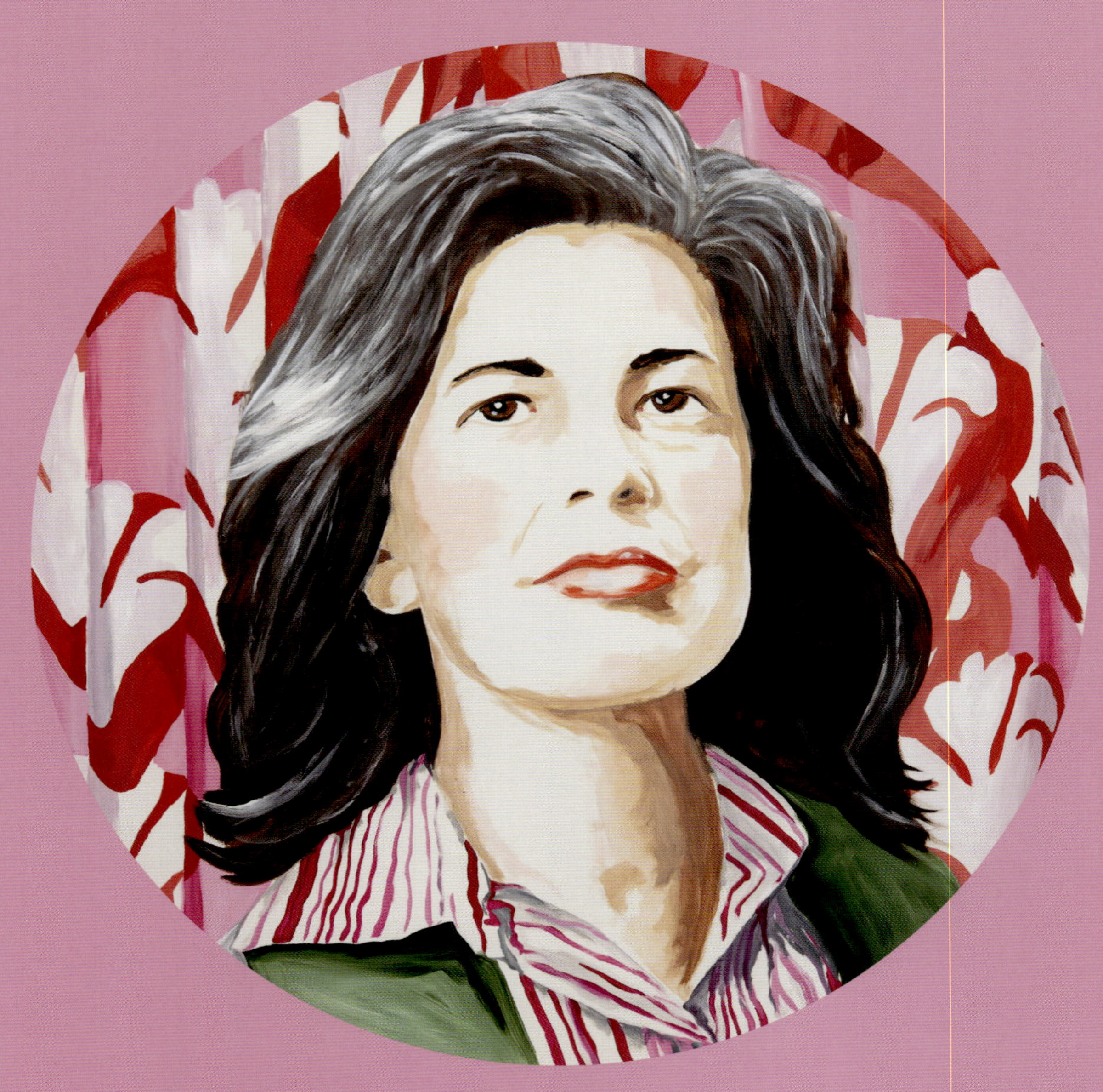

Susan Sontag

Because she was fearless in her craft as a writer. She was a fighter for human rights and one of the greatest critics of our time. She was true to herself.

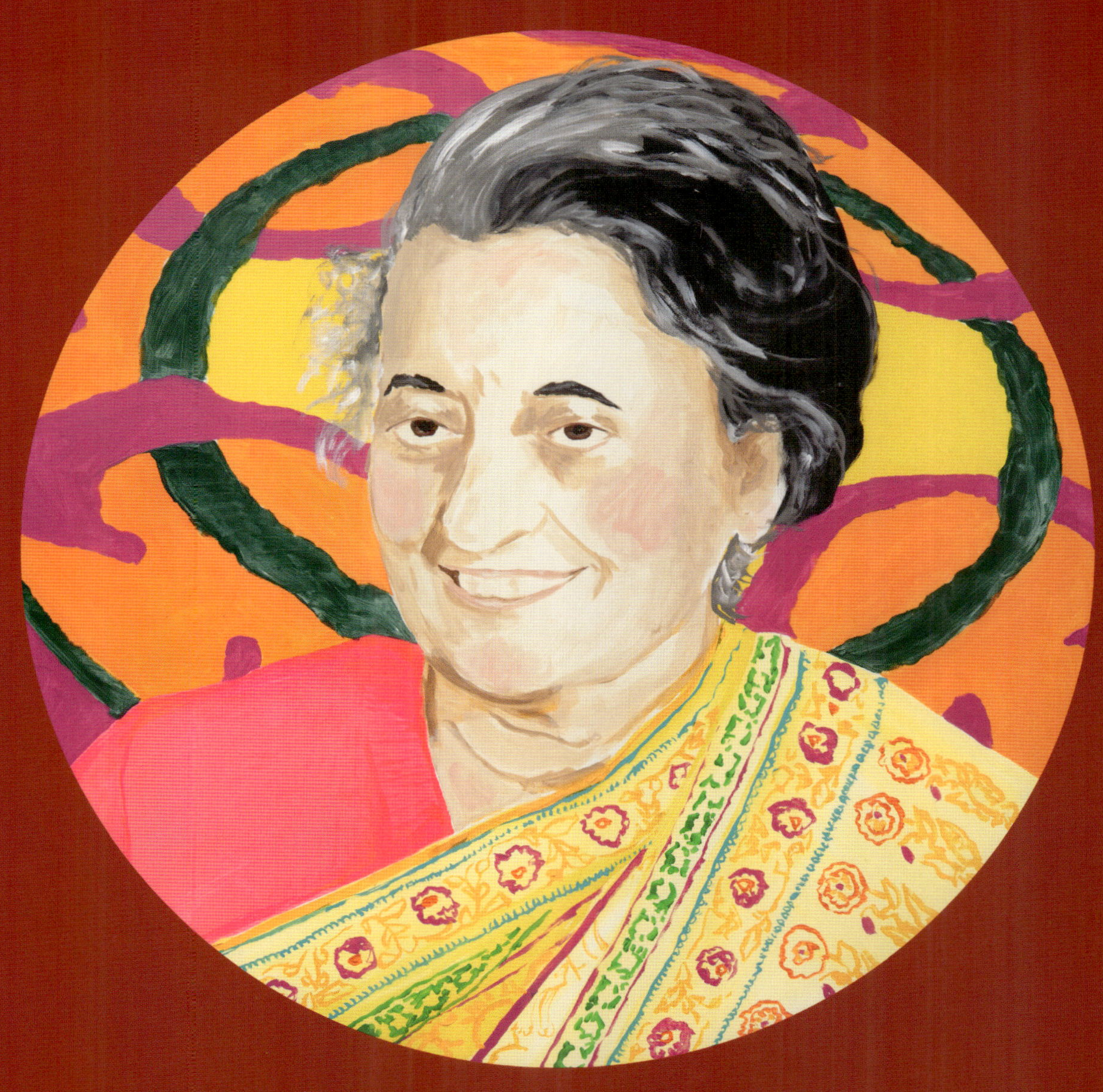

Indira Gandhi

Because she paved a way for women in India as the country's first female prime minister. Her life was taken too soon, but she will never be forgotten.

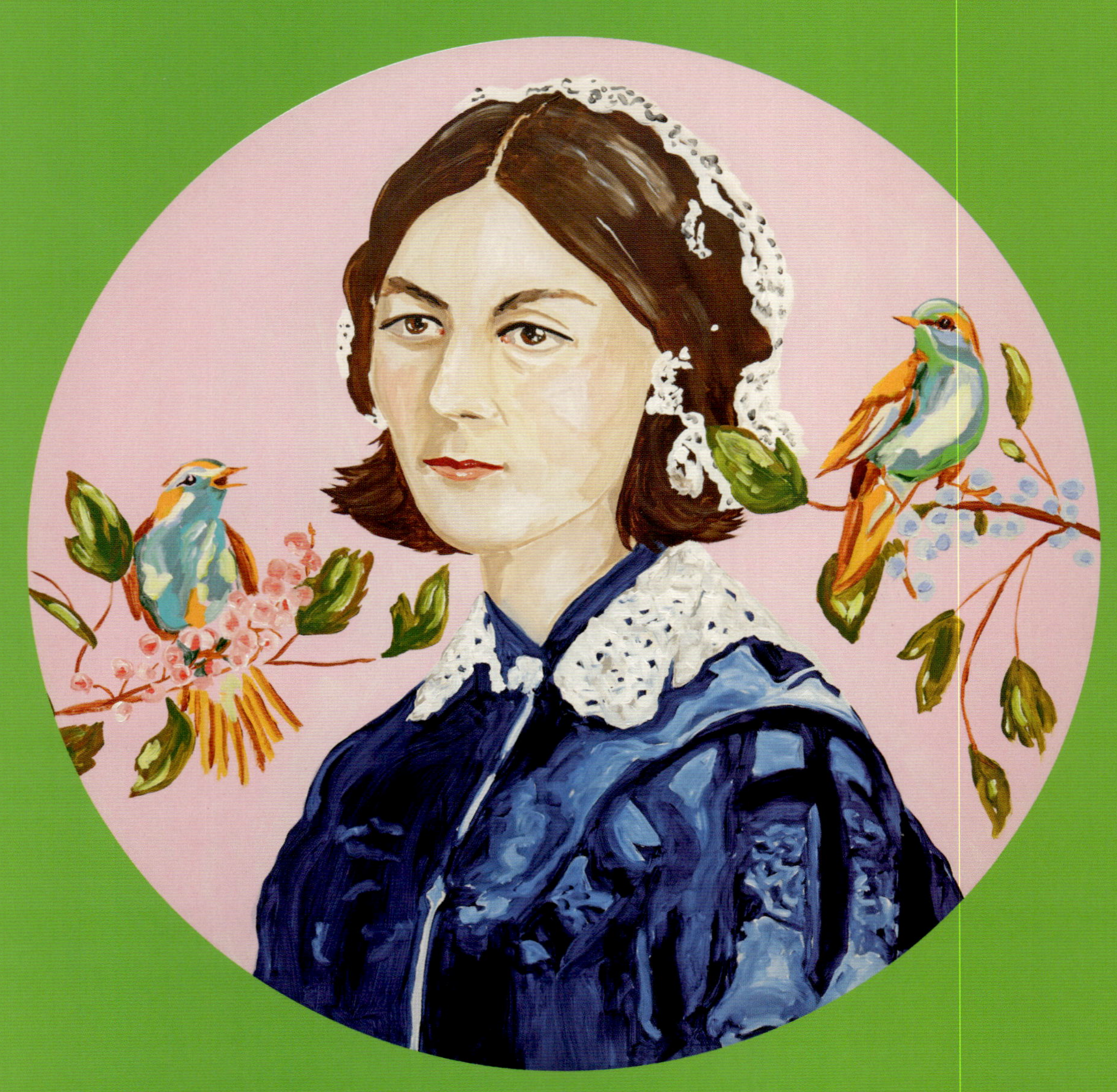

Florence Nightingale

Because she showed us the importance of taking care of others and the critical need for nursing the ill.

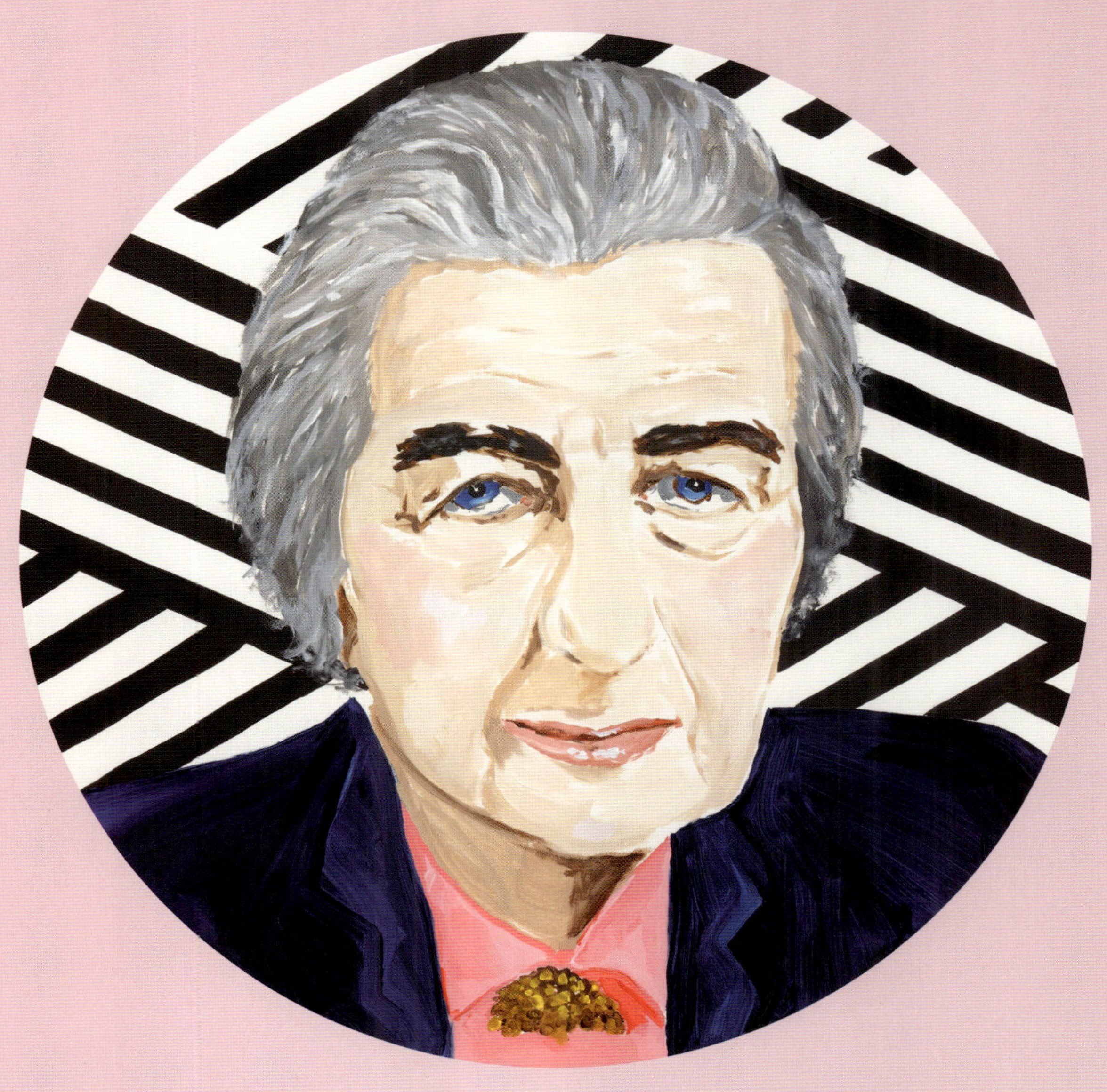

Golda Meir

Because she was the strong-willed, straight-talking, "gray-bunned grandmother of the Jewish people." Because she was called "the best man in government," which she considered a compliment.

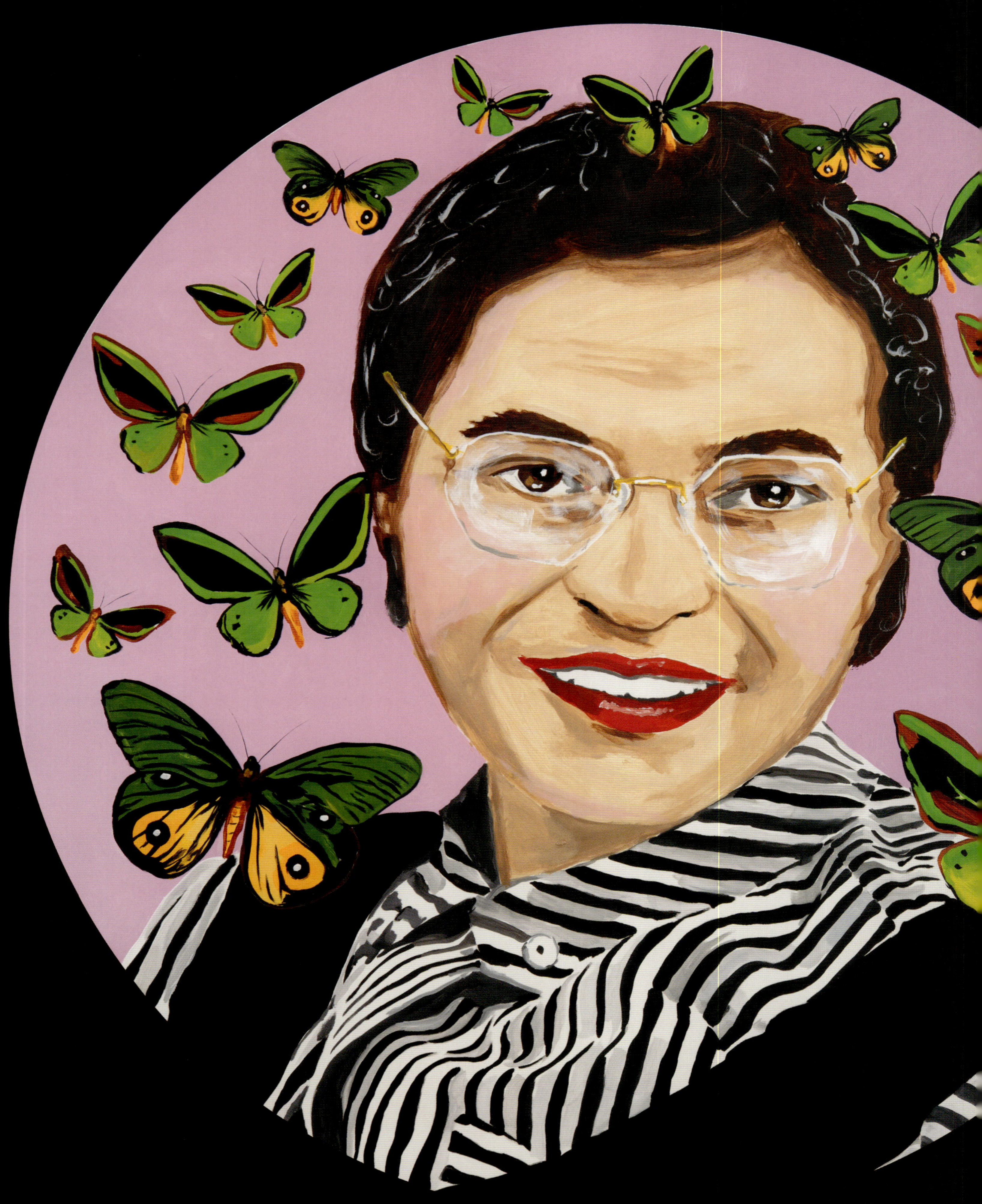

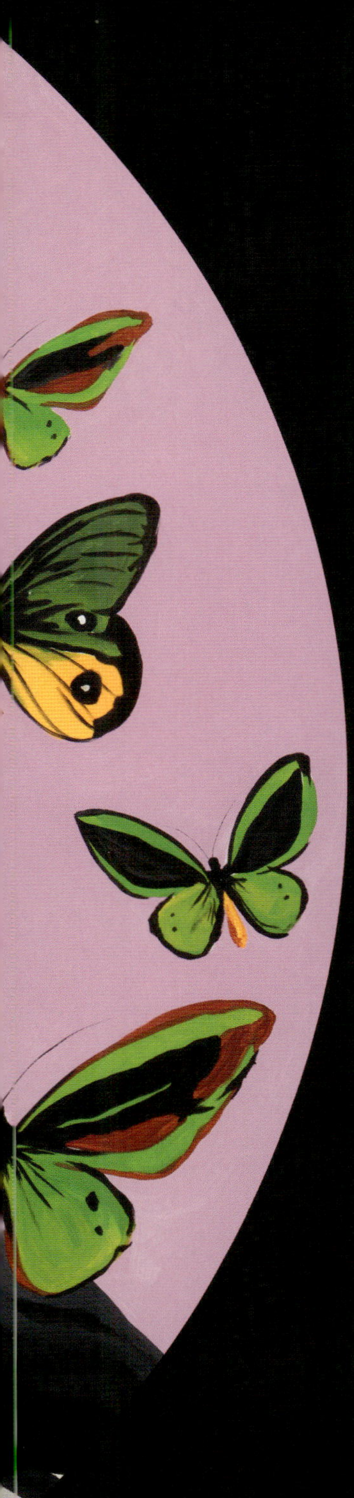

Rosa
Parks

Because she started a movement that is still being fought. Because she was defiant and believed in herself and in equal rights for the black community. She was fearless.

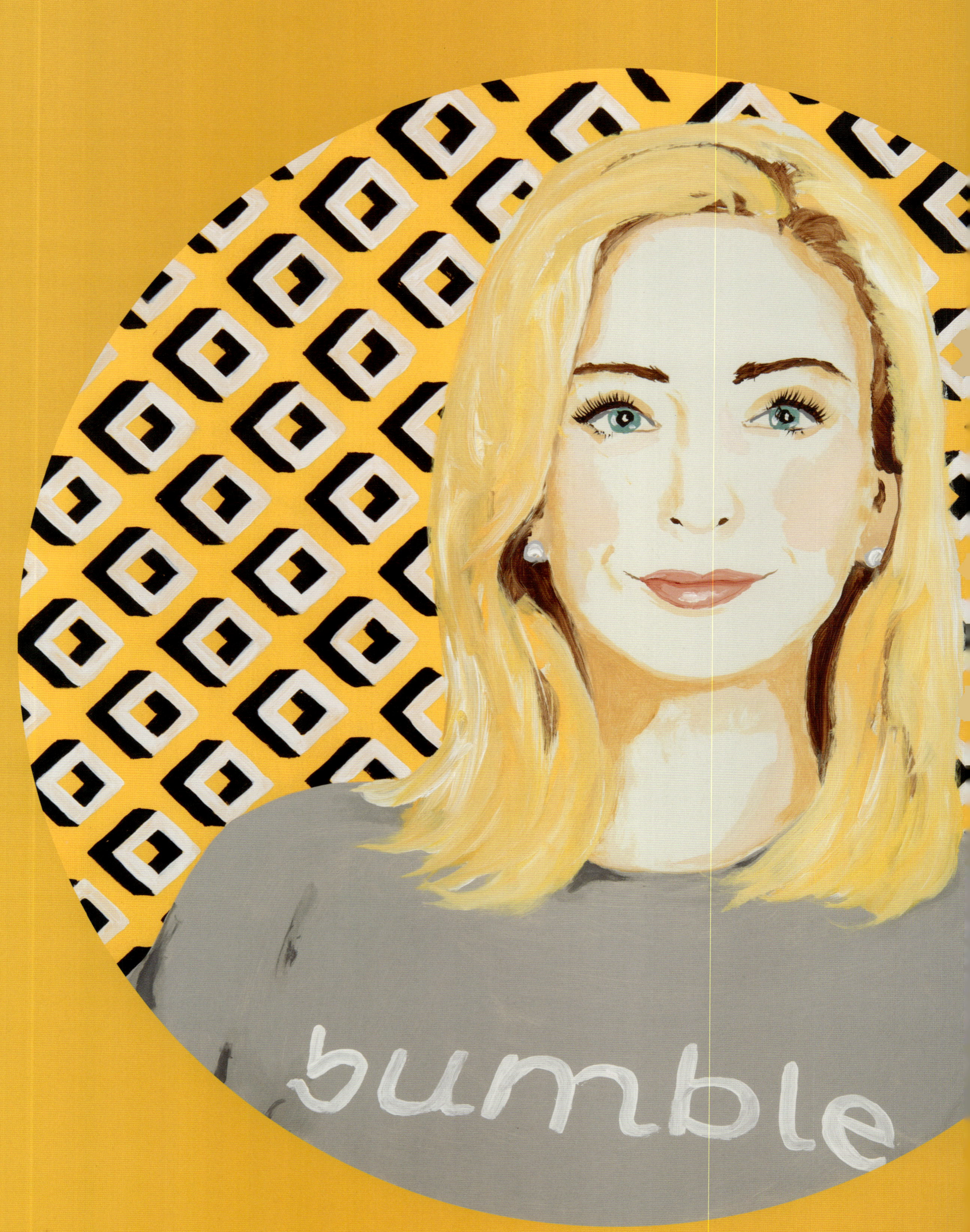
bumble

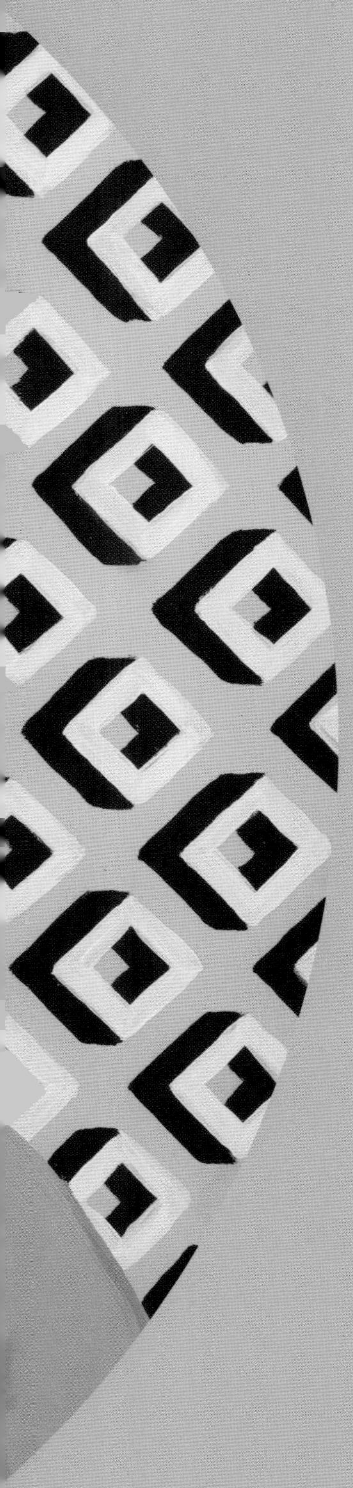

Whitney Wolfe Herd

Because she fights for women, for the respect women deserve, and for women to be decision makers. She is brilliant, kind, and has changed the world for women. I absolutely adore her.

Amelia Earhart

Because she was the first woman to fly solo across the Atlantic Ocean. Because she was an author and an advocate for women. She was a pioneer for women in a man's (aviation) world.

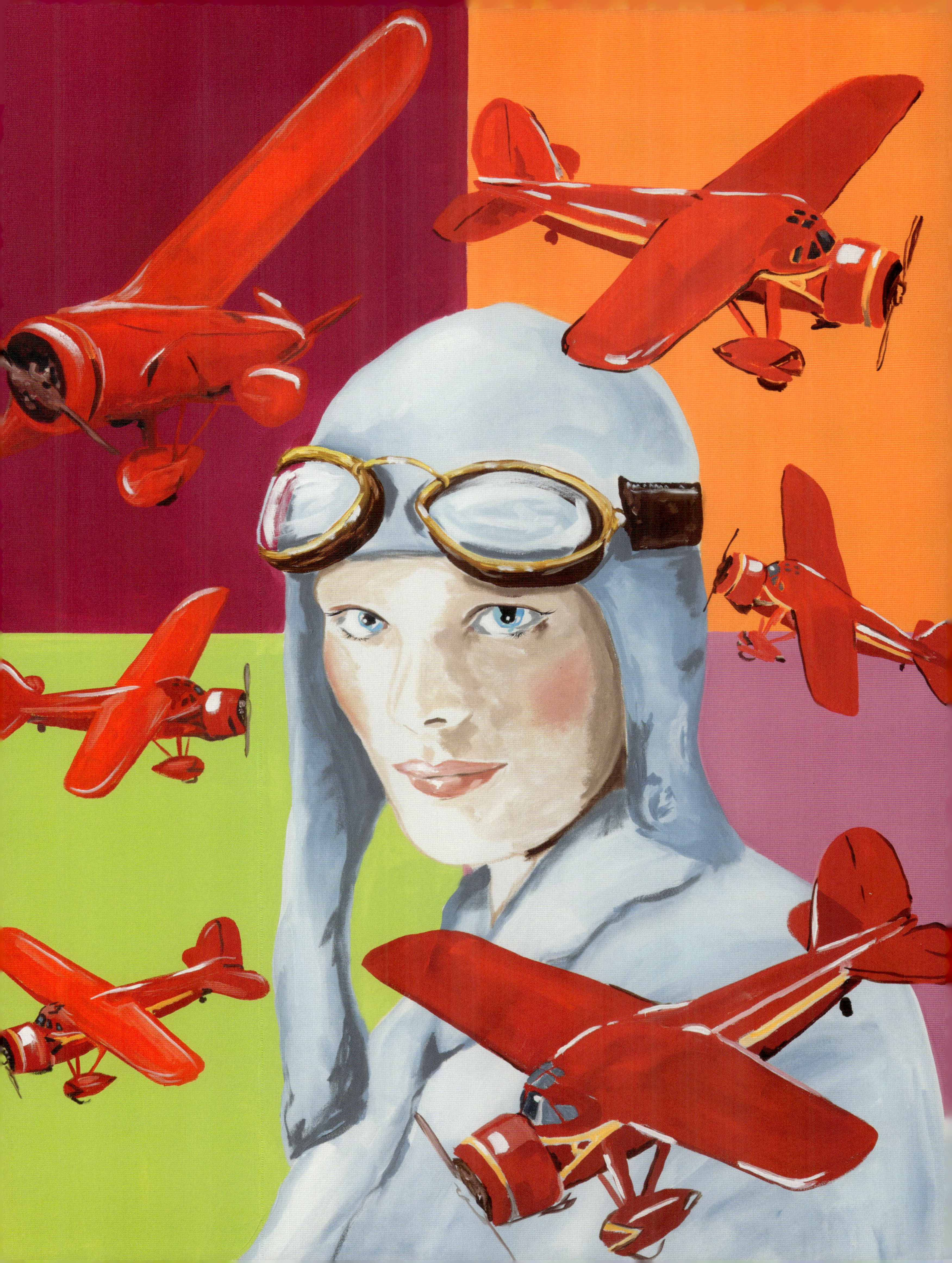

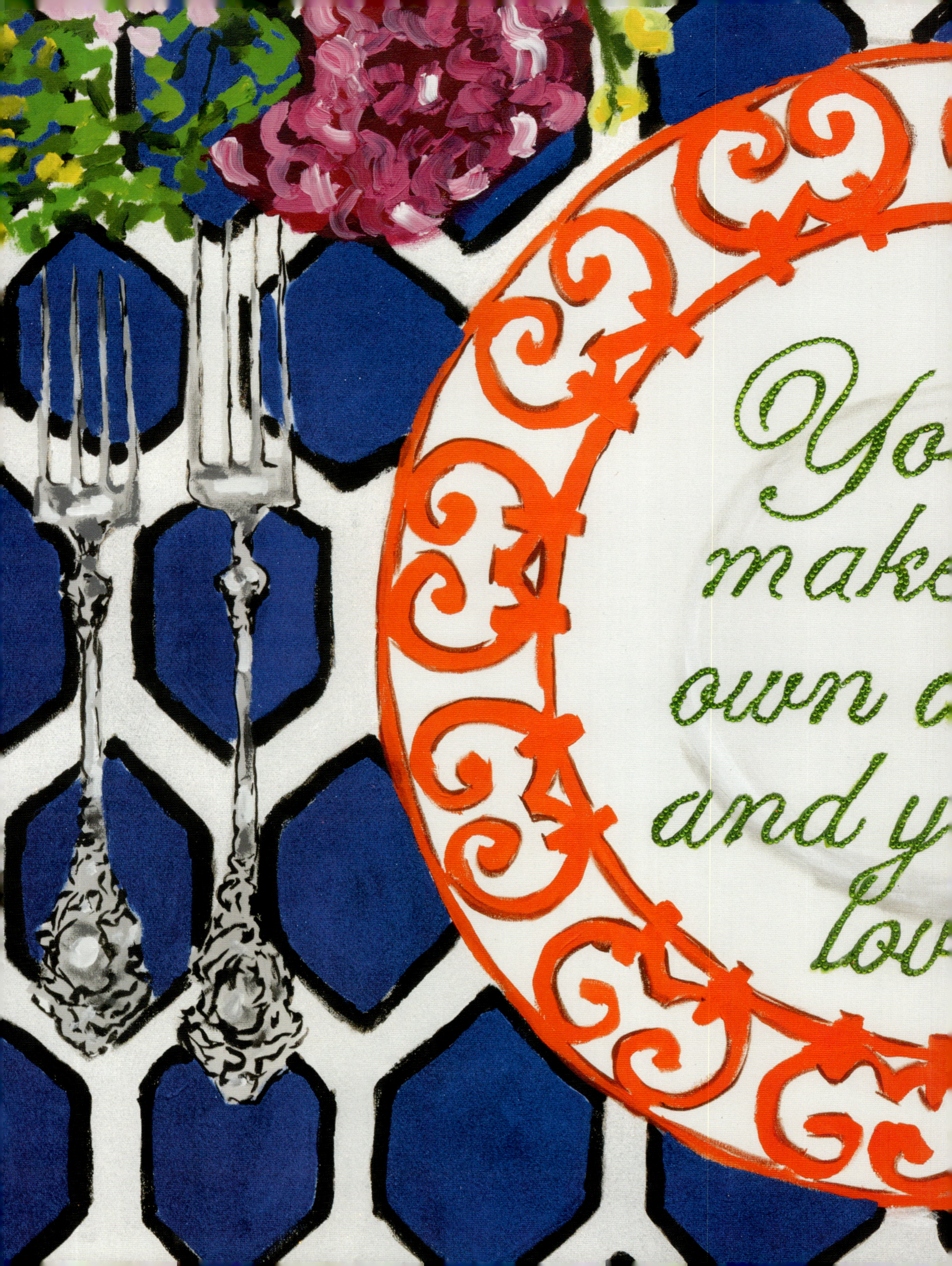
Yo
make
own
and y
lov

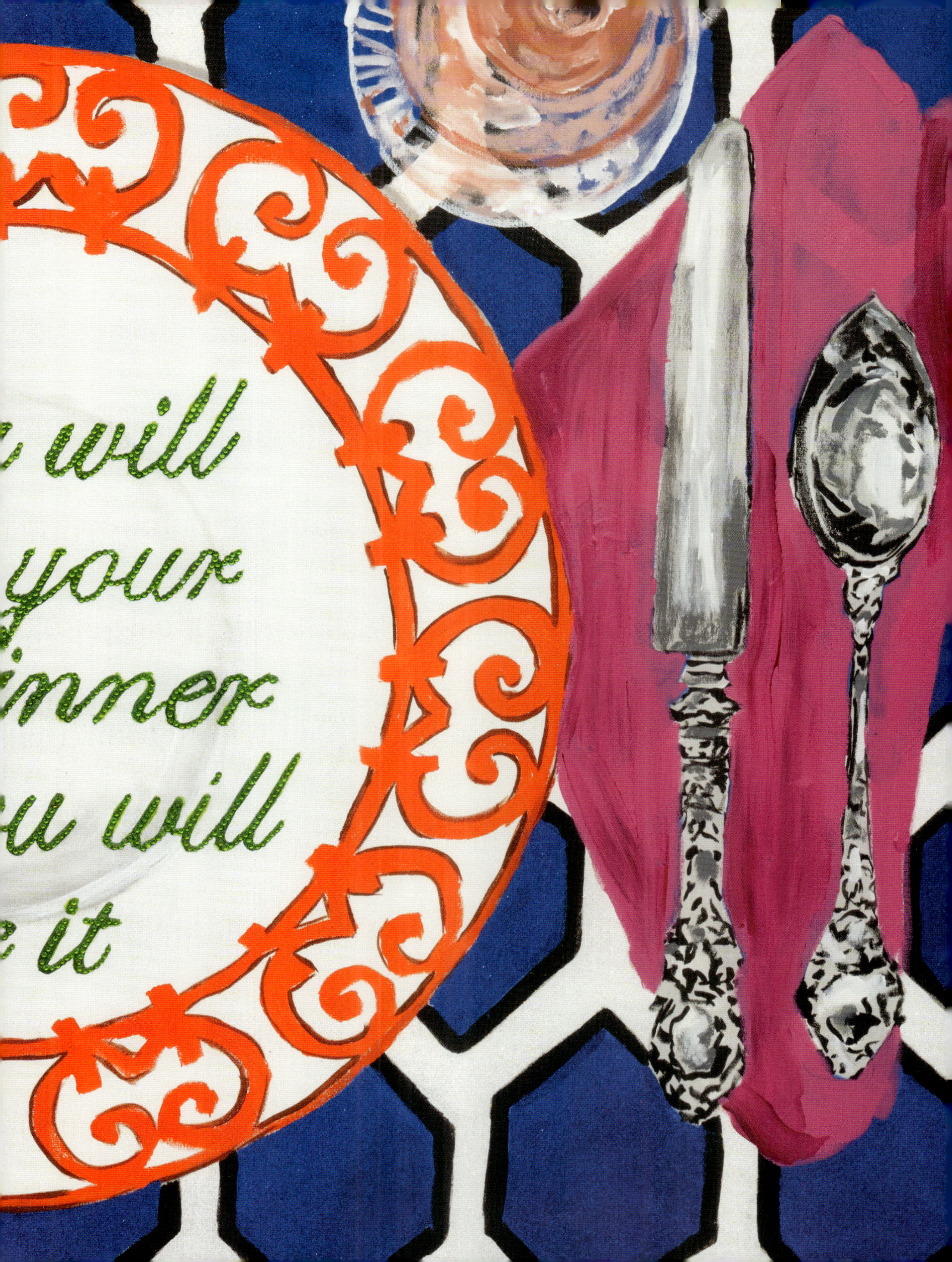
will
your
inner
will
it

Gloria Steinem

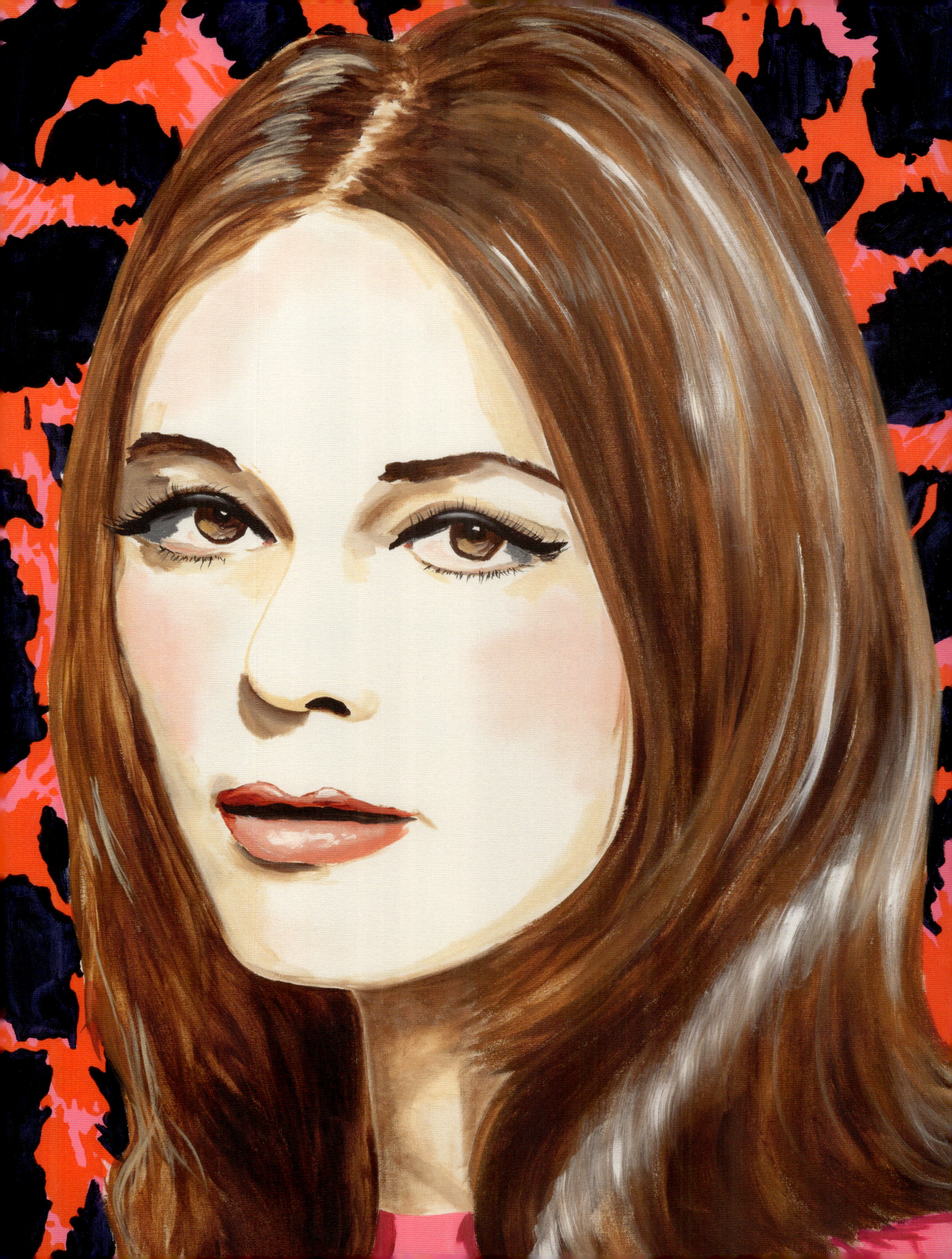

Jane Fonda

Because she jump-started physical health and the well-being movement for women. She is unapologetically vocal about her activism, and her career spans generations.

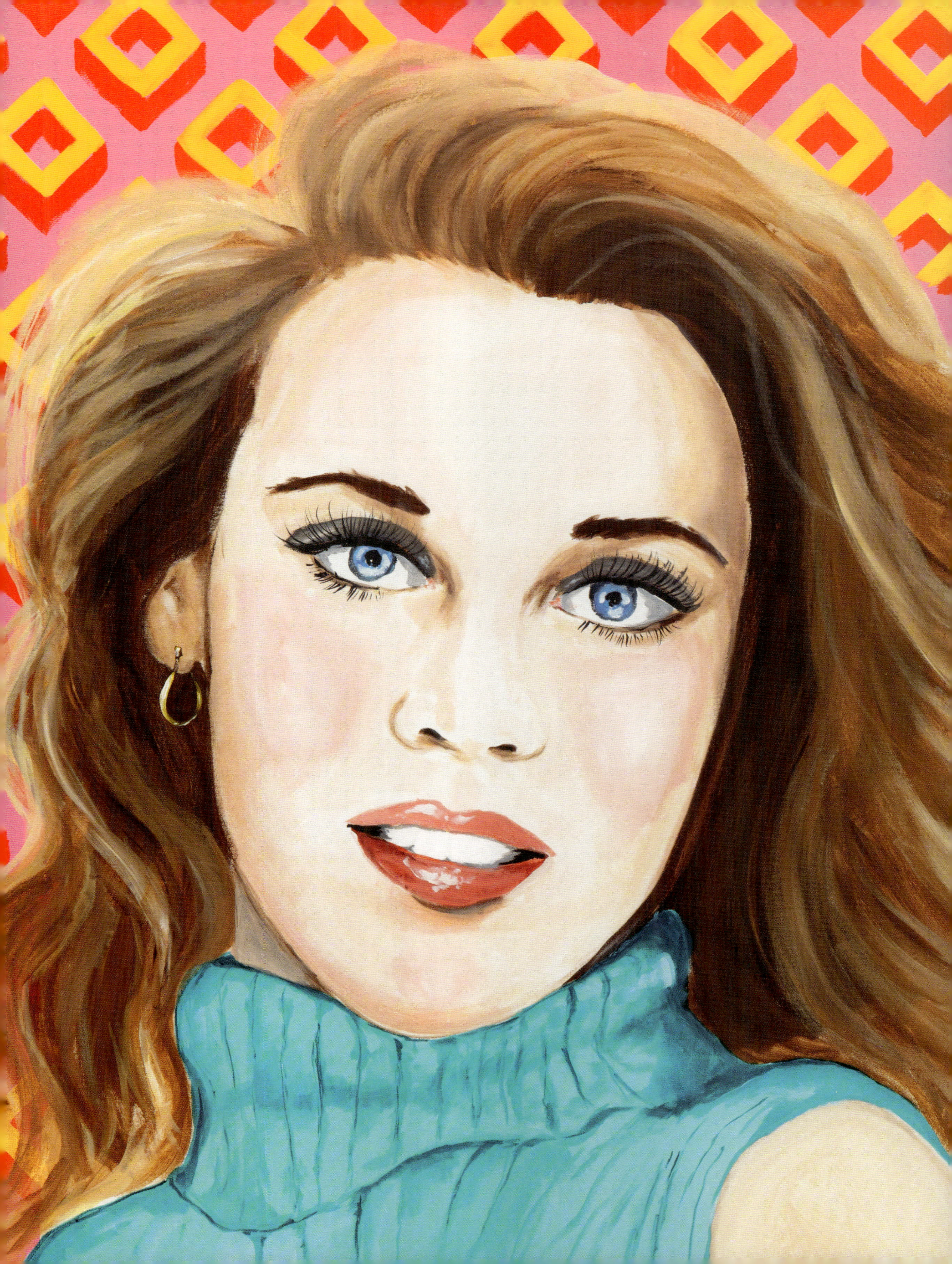

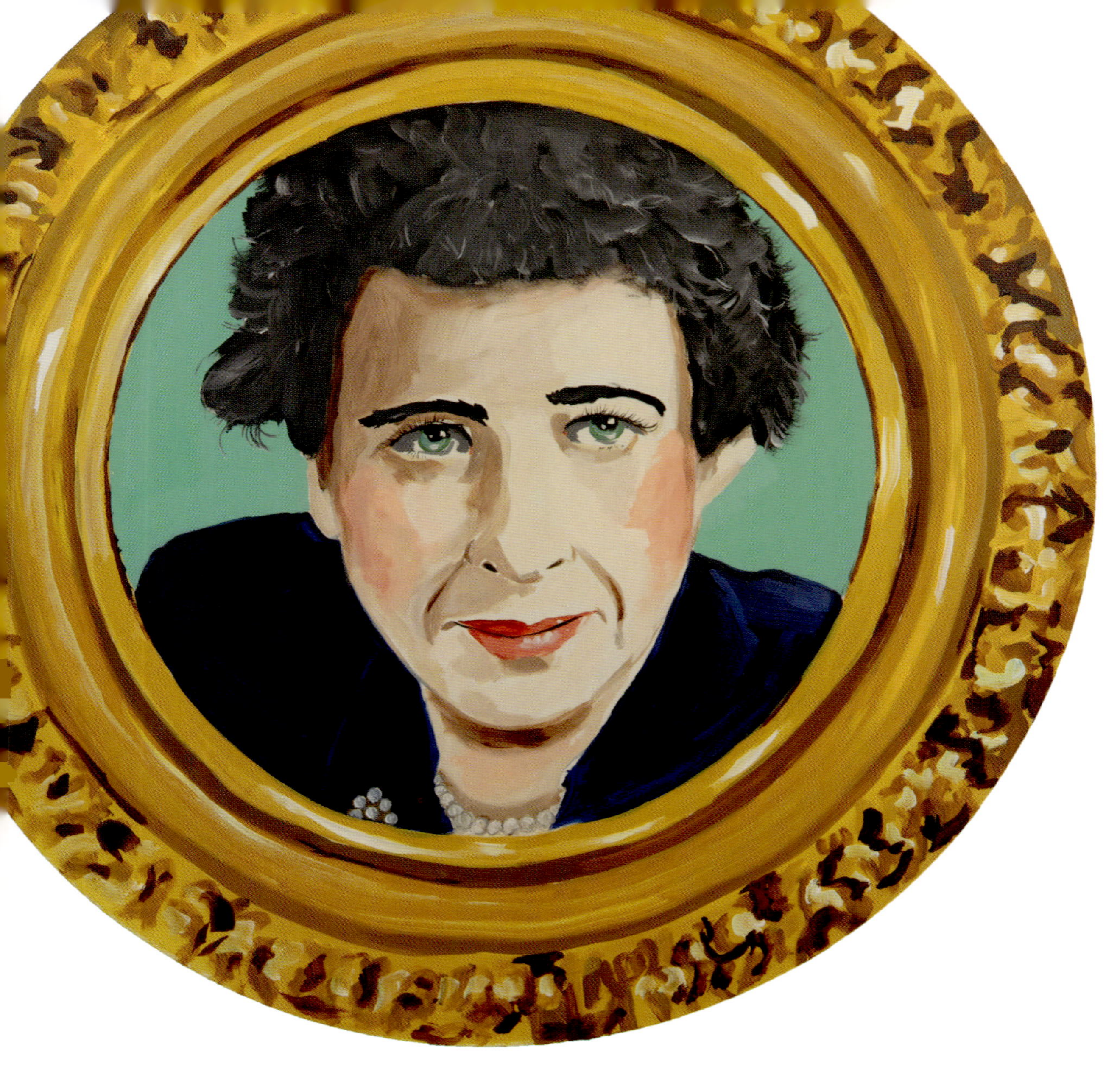

Hannah Arendt

Because she was one of the most important political thinkers of the twentieth century. Her point of view on political theory and philosophy changed the world forever.

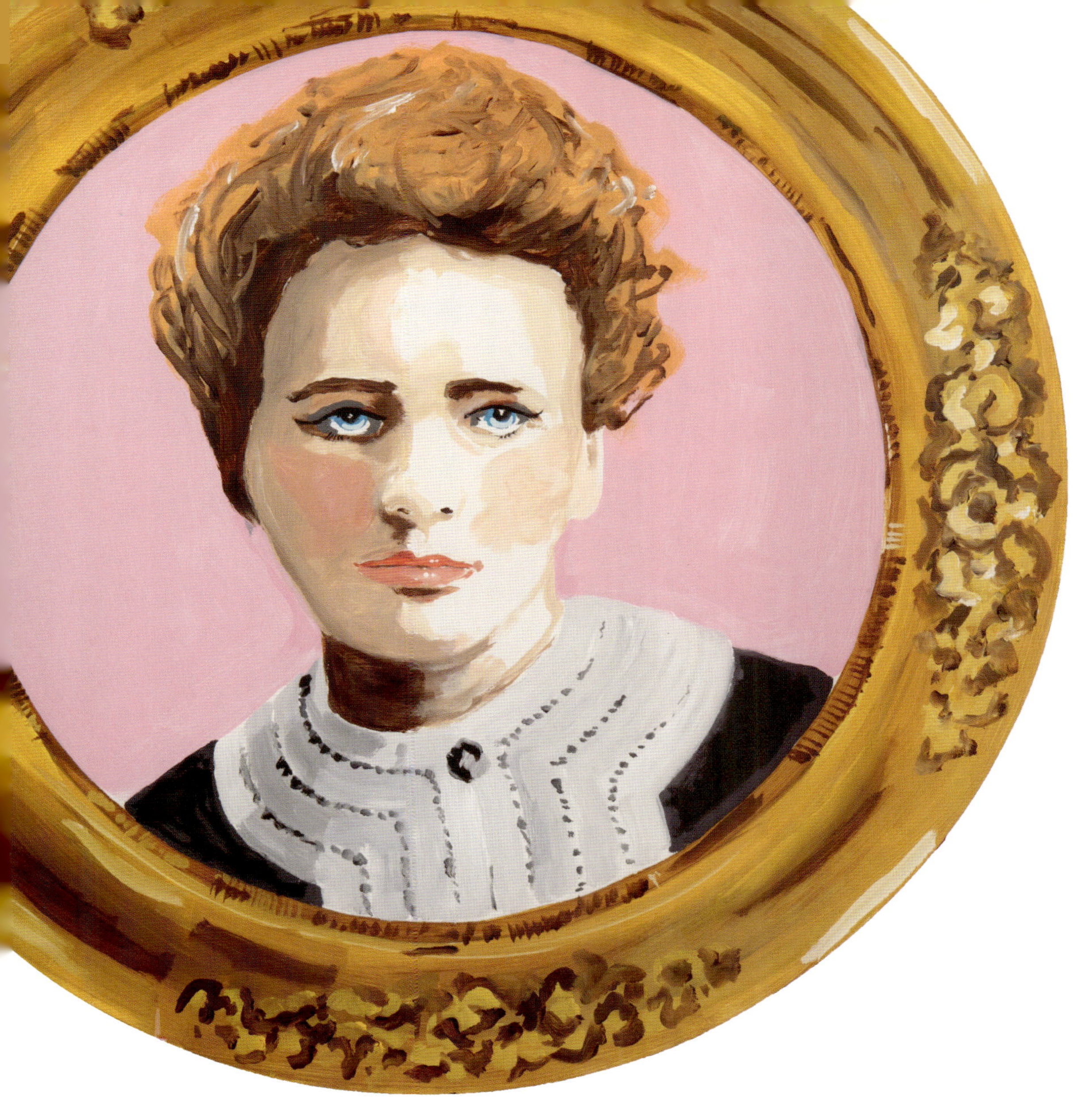

Marie Curie

Because she was the first and, so far, only woman to win a Nobel Prize in two different scientific fields. She blazed a trail for women in science.

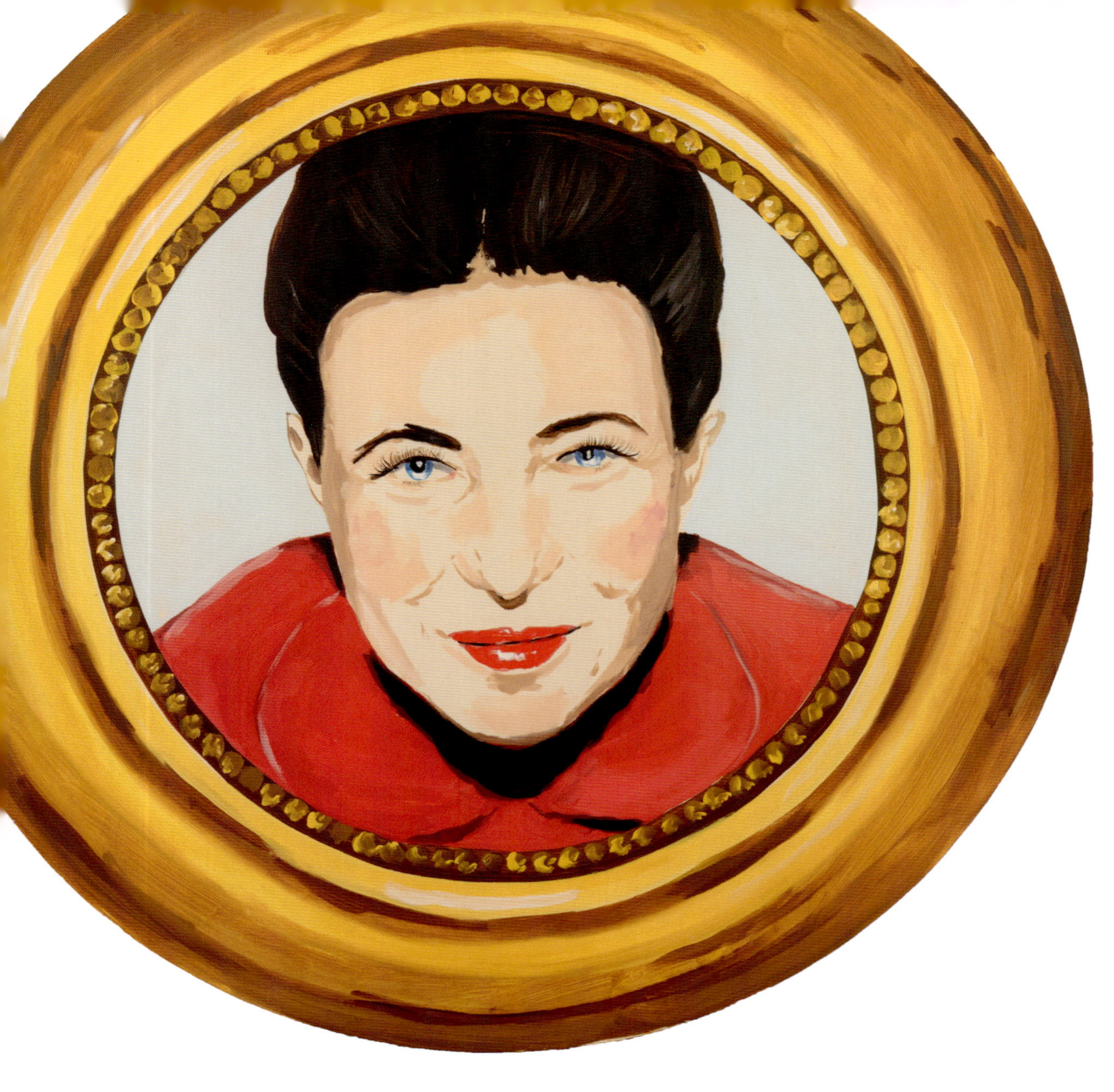

Simone de Beauvoir

Because she was the ultimate feminist. She was a brilliant theorist, and her writing remains a significant influence for its warmth and descriptive power.

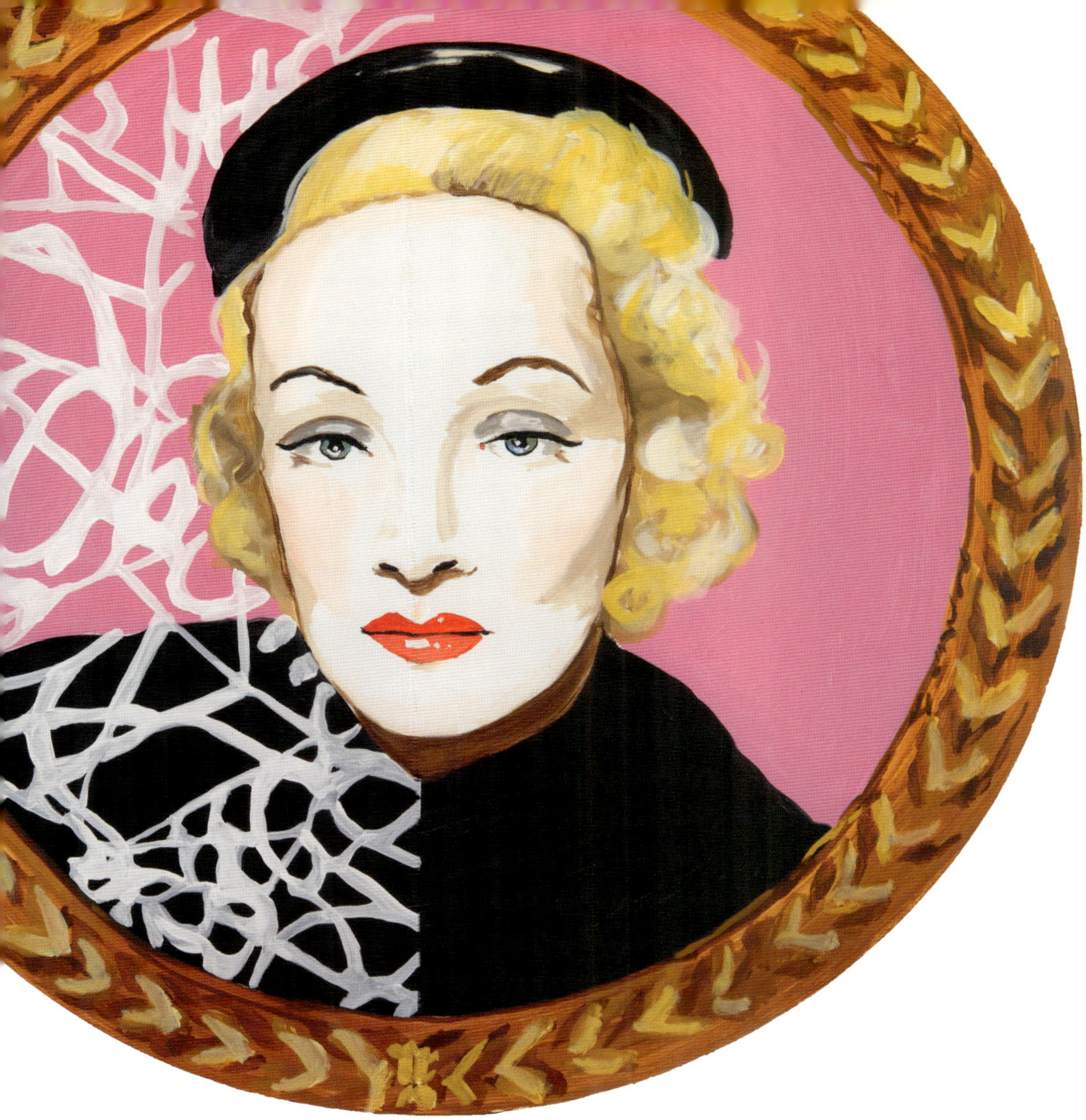

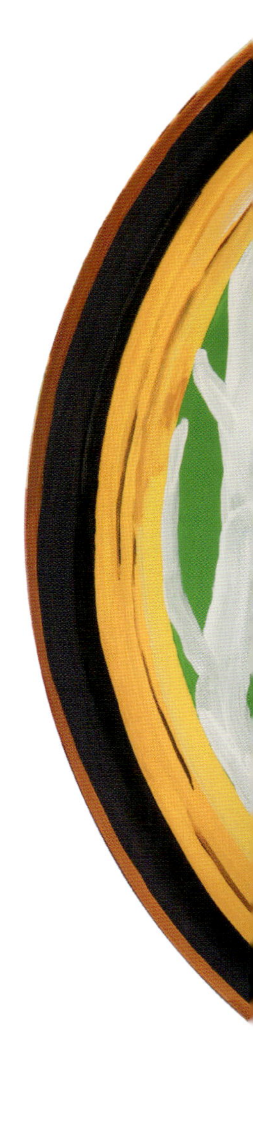

Marlene Dietrich

Because she was a radiant actress and beauty, although her heart and humanitarian efforts are the most notable in regards to her character.

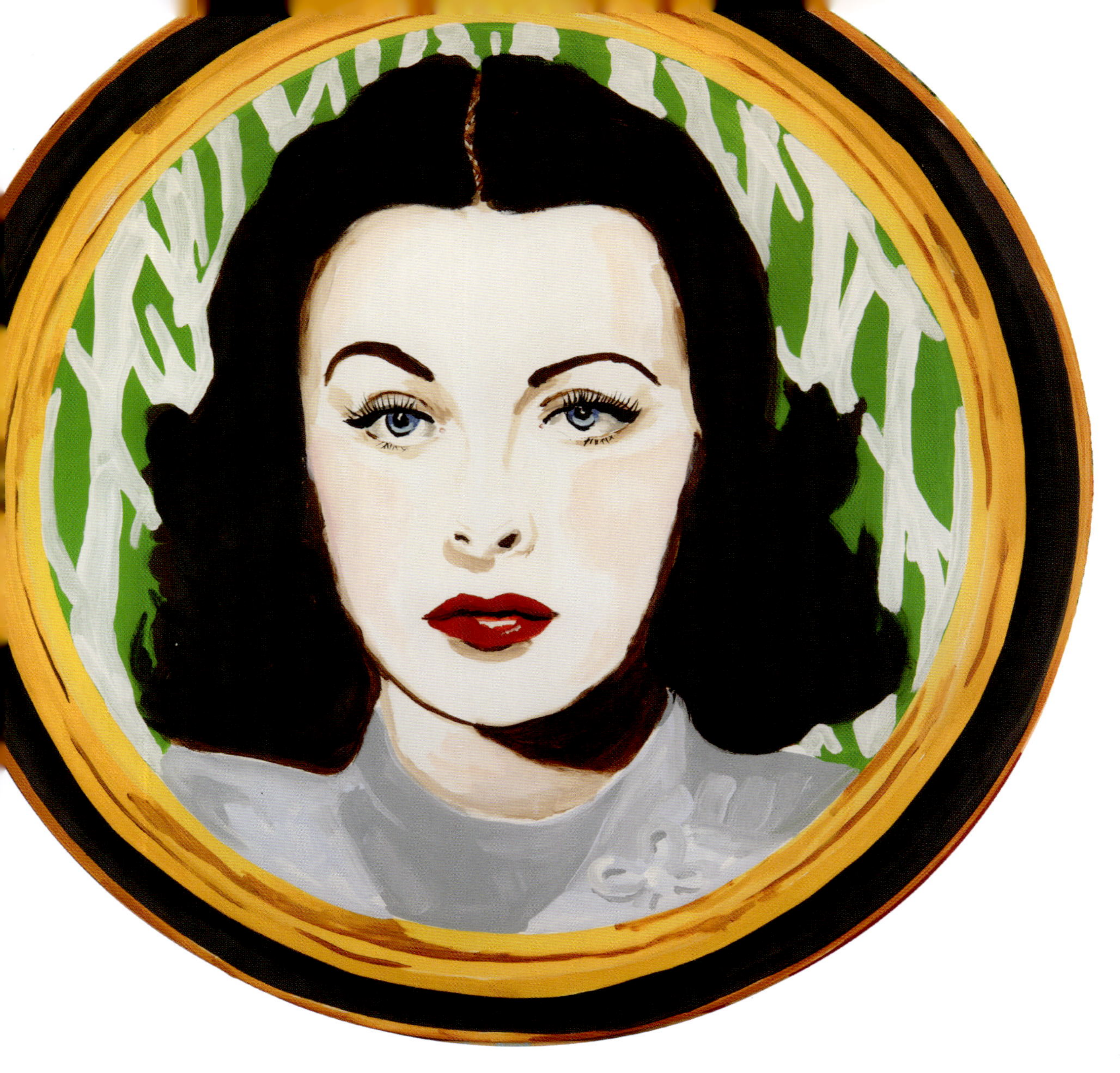

Hedy Lamarr

Because she was a scientific genius and developed the early technology that we now know as Wi-Fi. Because she was also a striking beauty and smoldering actress.

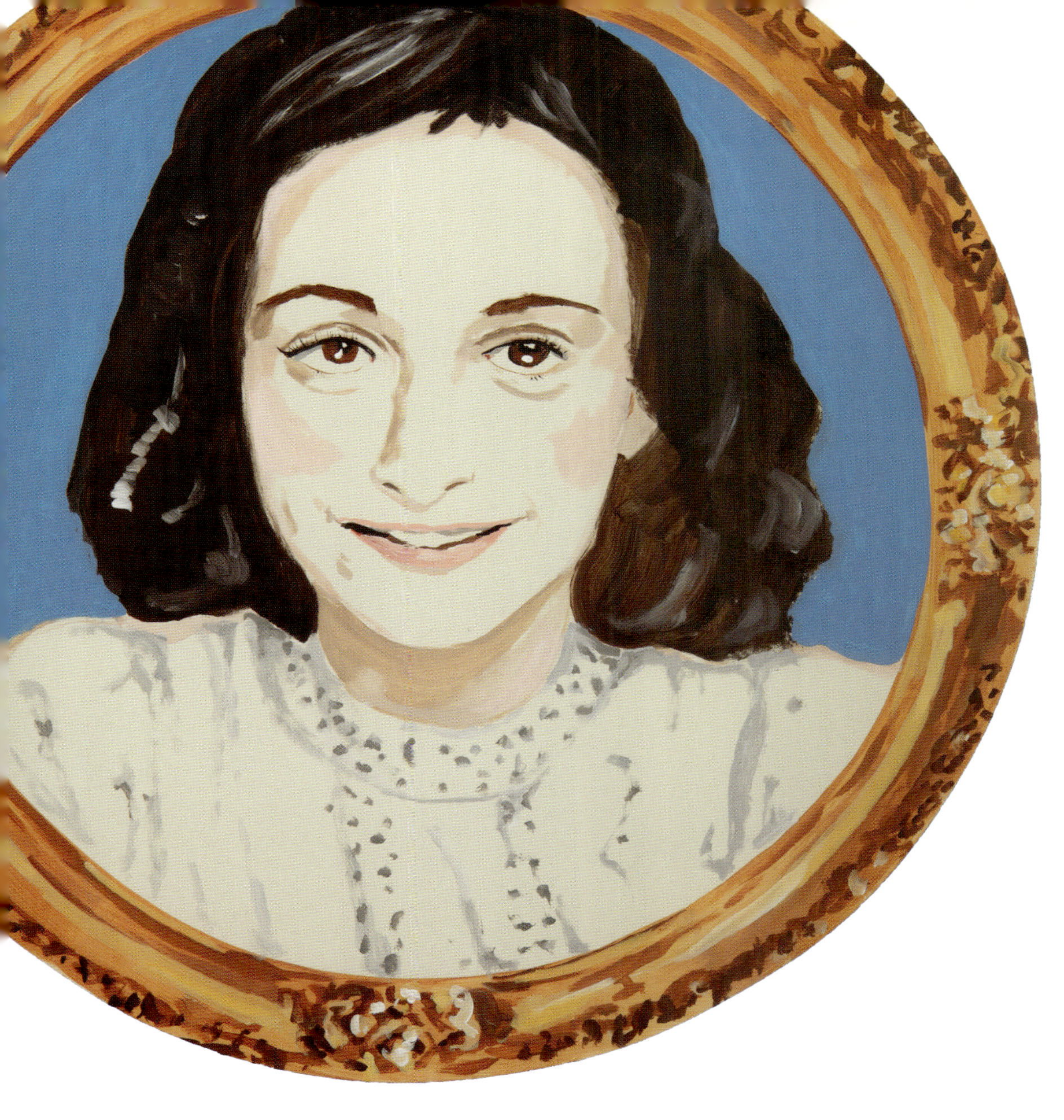

Anne Frank

Because she was courageous enough to document unintentionally and in real time her experience of the most horrific occurrence in European history. Her vulnerability and sincerity continue to inspire others globally all these years later.

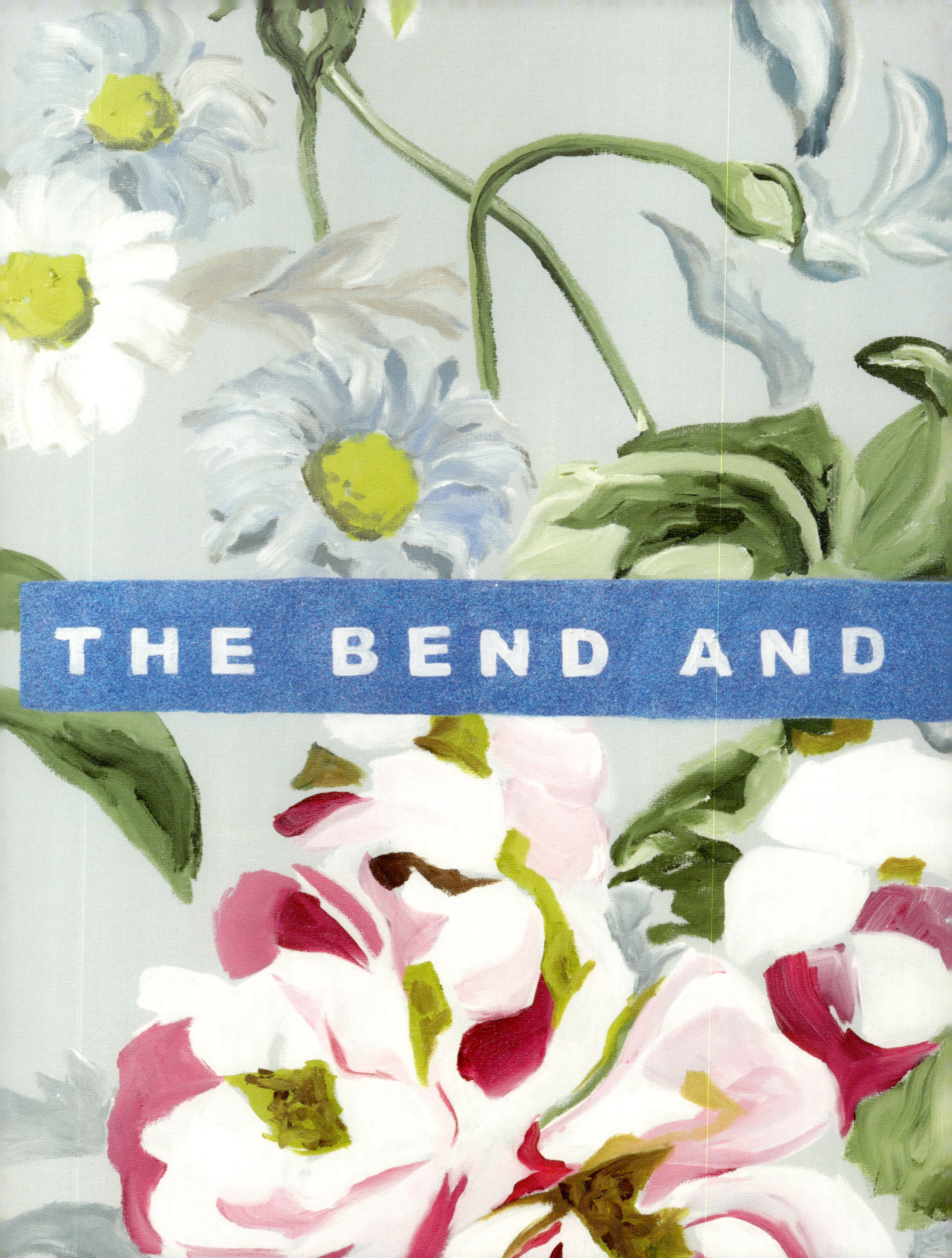
THE BEND AND

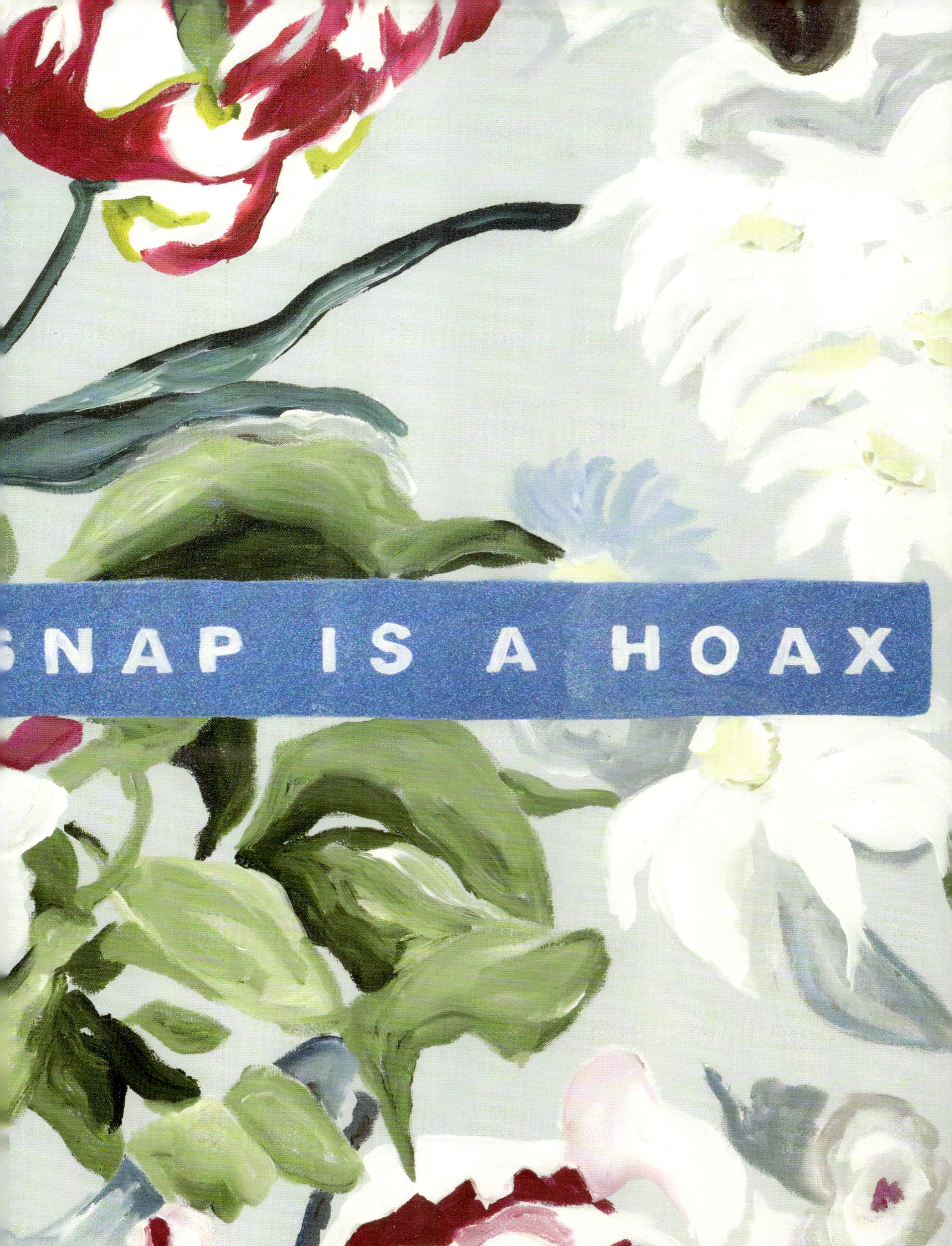
SNAP IS A HOAX

Index

Acknowledgments

I would like to thank all of the women who have been true to themselves, fought through adversity, and graced our lives with beauty and resilience. It isn't the fame or credit that have made all of you so great, but rather how you handle hard times, being misunderstood, fear, and rejection. That is the magic; the legacy you leave is one of hope and joy.

I am grateful to my many mentors but most especially to Diane Von Furstenberg, who gave me the opportunity to create these portraits of remarkable women. Diane, this project is one I am most proud of. You taught me so much and pushed me to grow and learn as an artist. Thank you for your support and for believing in my art. Thank you for all you do to support and promote women. You are a superwoman. I love you. And to the spectacular Sandra Campos, thank you for the introduction. None of this would have happened without you.

And to all of the women in my life, who are there when things are good and when things are bad, to cheer and celebrate and to hug and wipe away tears: I am especially grateful for you. Kelly Brown and Cindy Longshore, I love you both so much. To my brilliant, incredible, magnificent team: I am so grateful for every single one of you. You all work so hard, and I so appreciate your dedication to my art.

And to my father, Spencer Longshore, who is the best dad and mom all in one. You loved me, nurtured me, and gave me the strength to be the woman I am. I love you so much.

Awomen. Amen. Hallelujah!

Copyright

First published in the United States of America in 2021 by
Rizzoli International Publications, Inc.
49 West 27th Street
New York, NY 10001
www.rizzoliusa.com

Publisher: Charles Miers
Editor: Jessica Fuller
Managing Editor: Lynn Scrabis
Editorial Intern: Sophia Francis
Production Manager: Colin Hough-Trapp

Art Direction: GCA

Printed in China
2025 2026 2027 2028 / 10 9 8 7 6 5
ISBN: 978-0-8478-7078-3
Library of Congress Control Number: 2021939998
The authorized representative in the EU for product safety and compliance is
Mondadori Libri S.p.A., via Gian Battista Vico 42, Milan, Italy, 20123,
www.mondadori.it

Visit us online:
Instagram.com/RizzoliBooks
Facebook.com/RizzoliNewYork
X: @Rizzoli_Books
Youtube.com/user/RizzoliNY

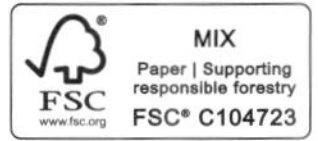

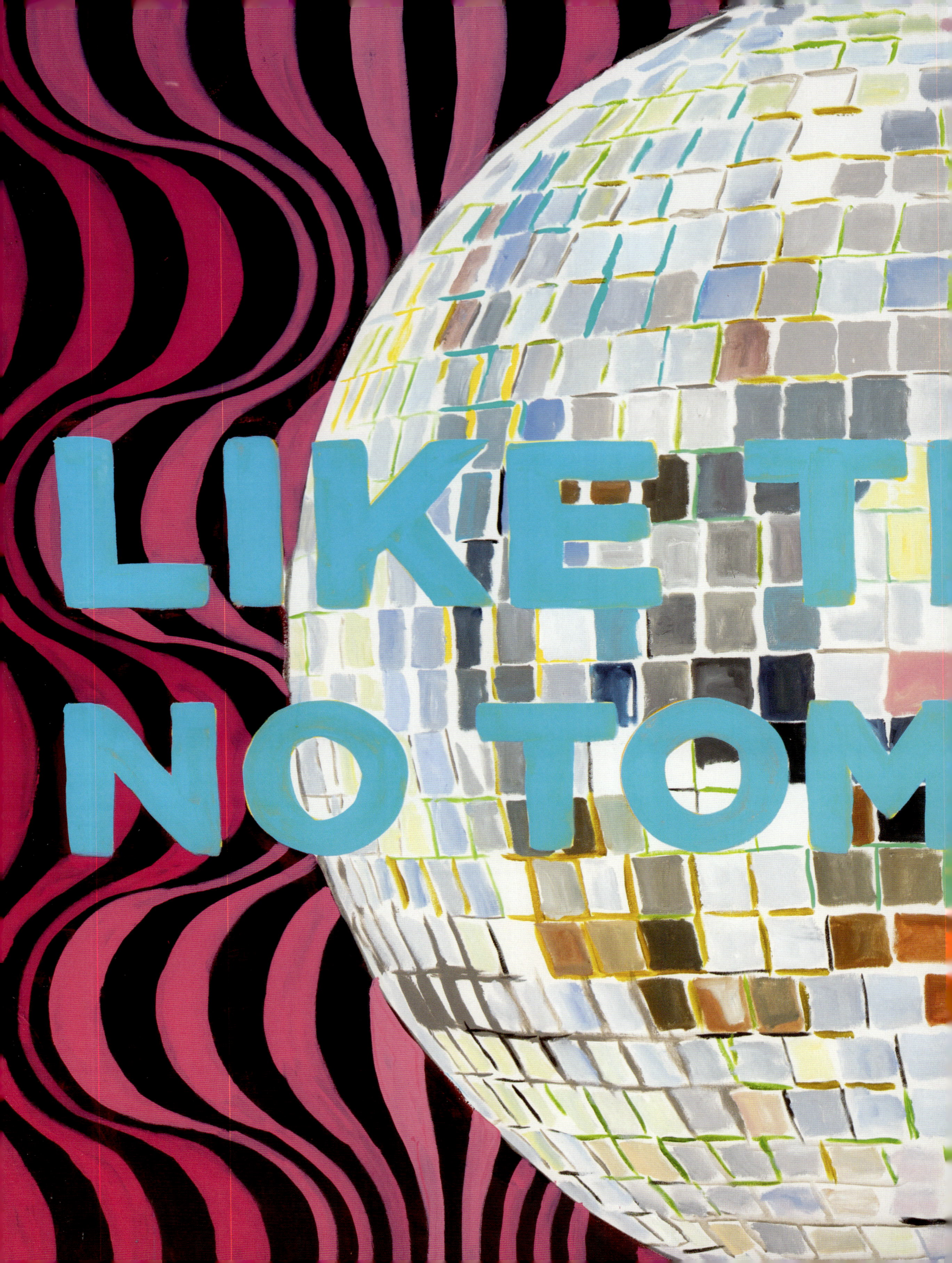

LIKE TH
NO TOM

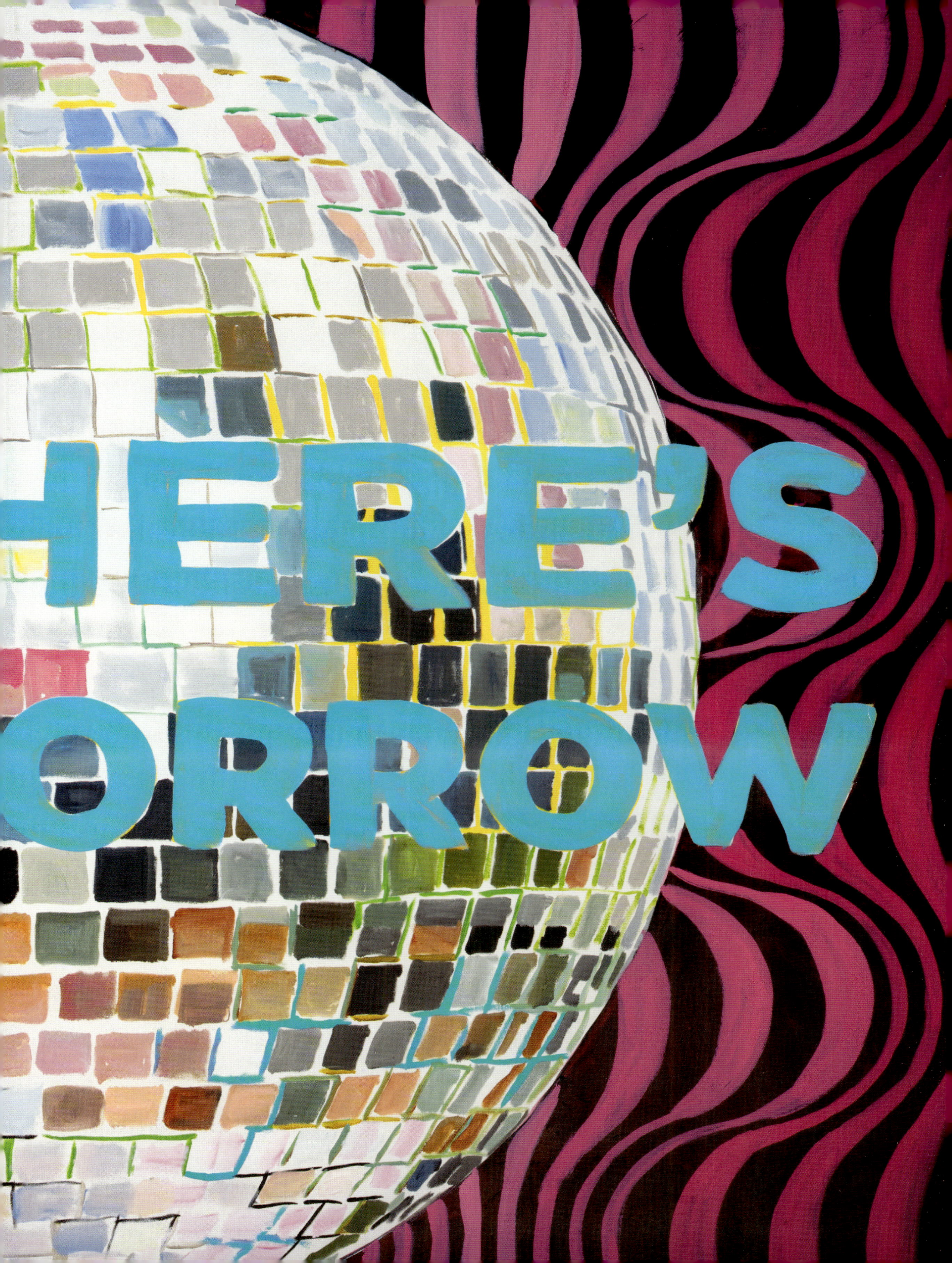

HERE'S
ORROW

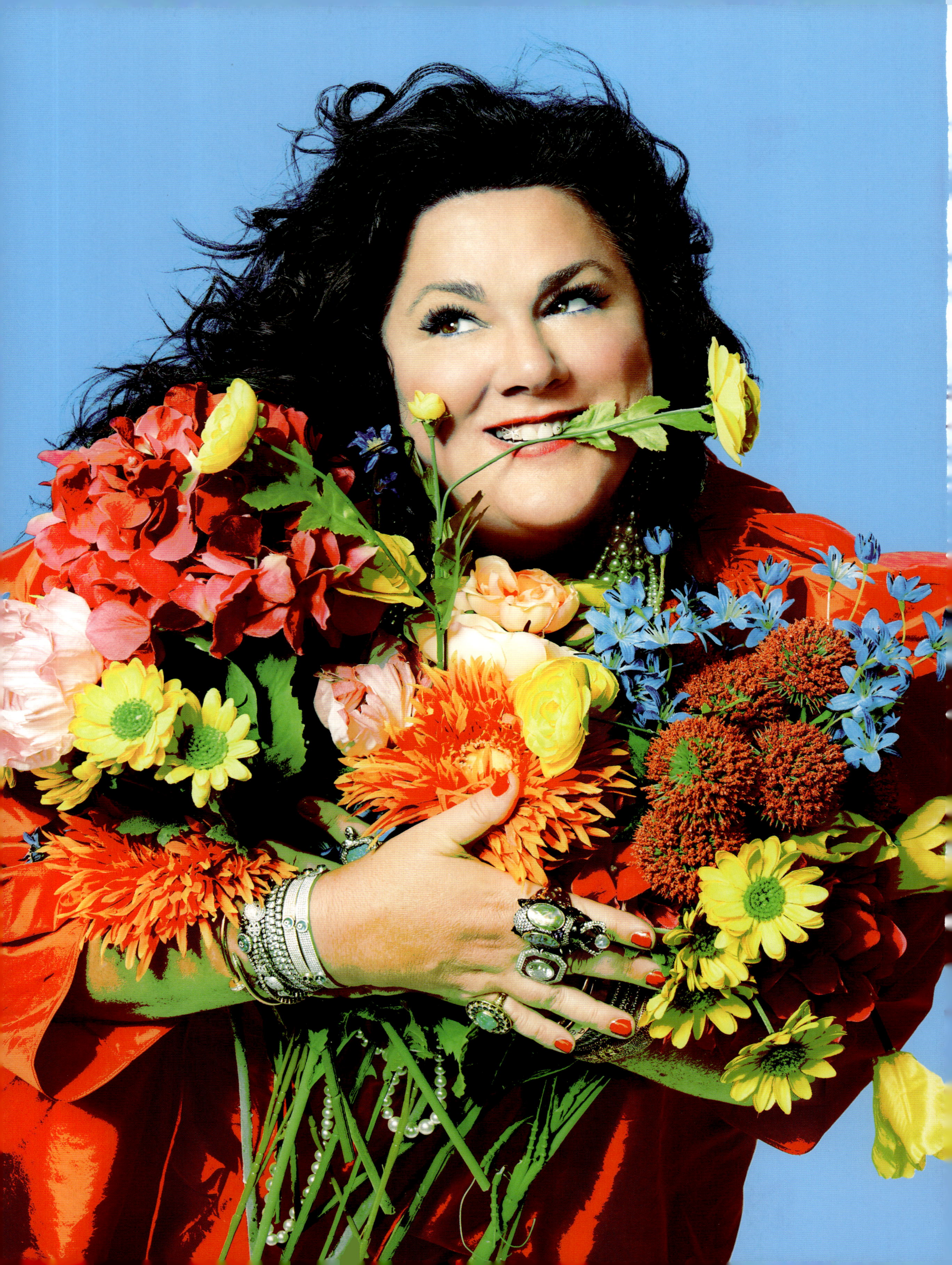

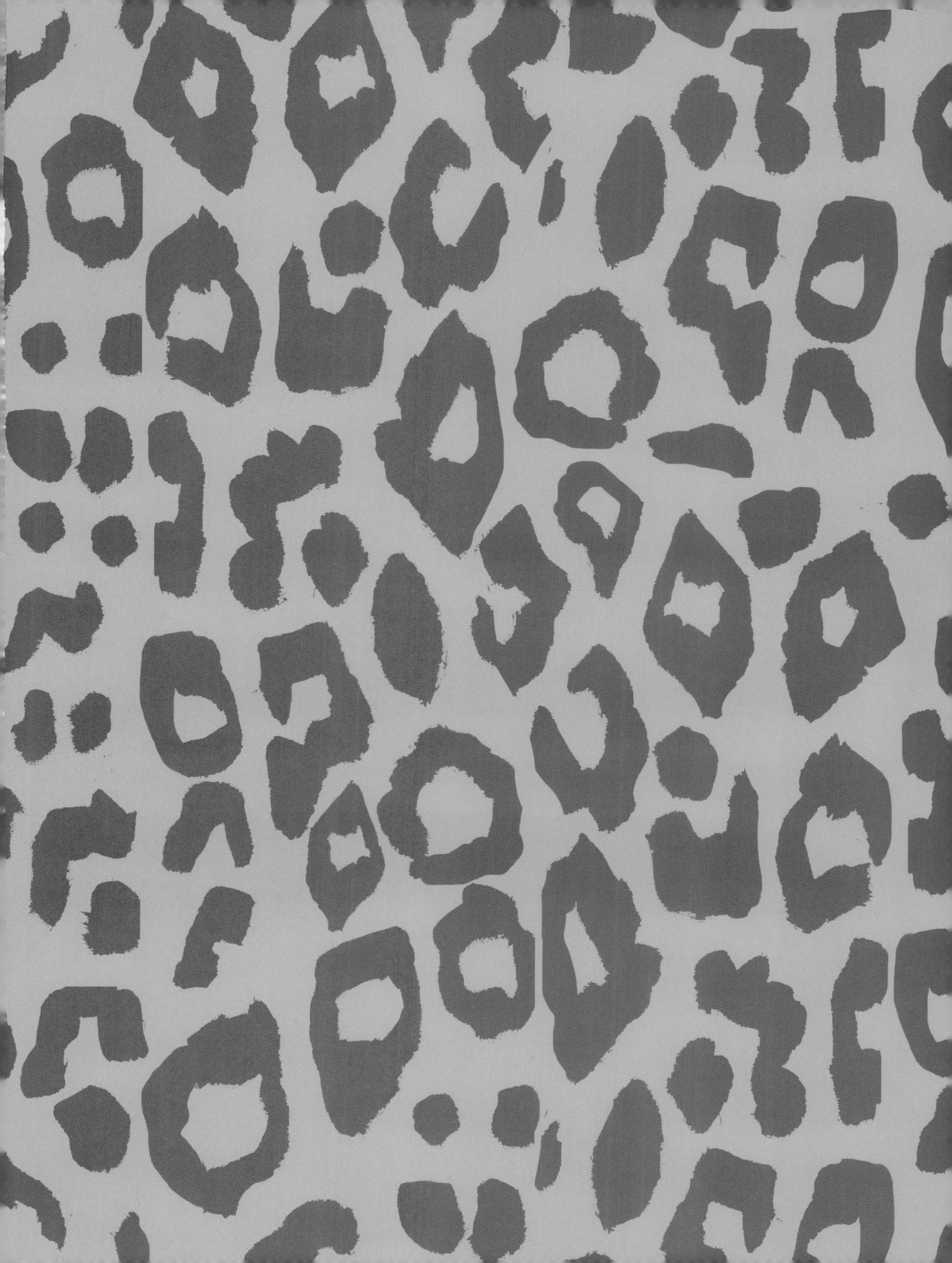

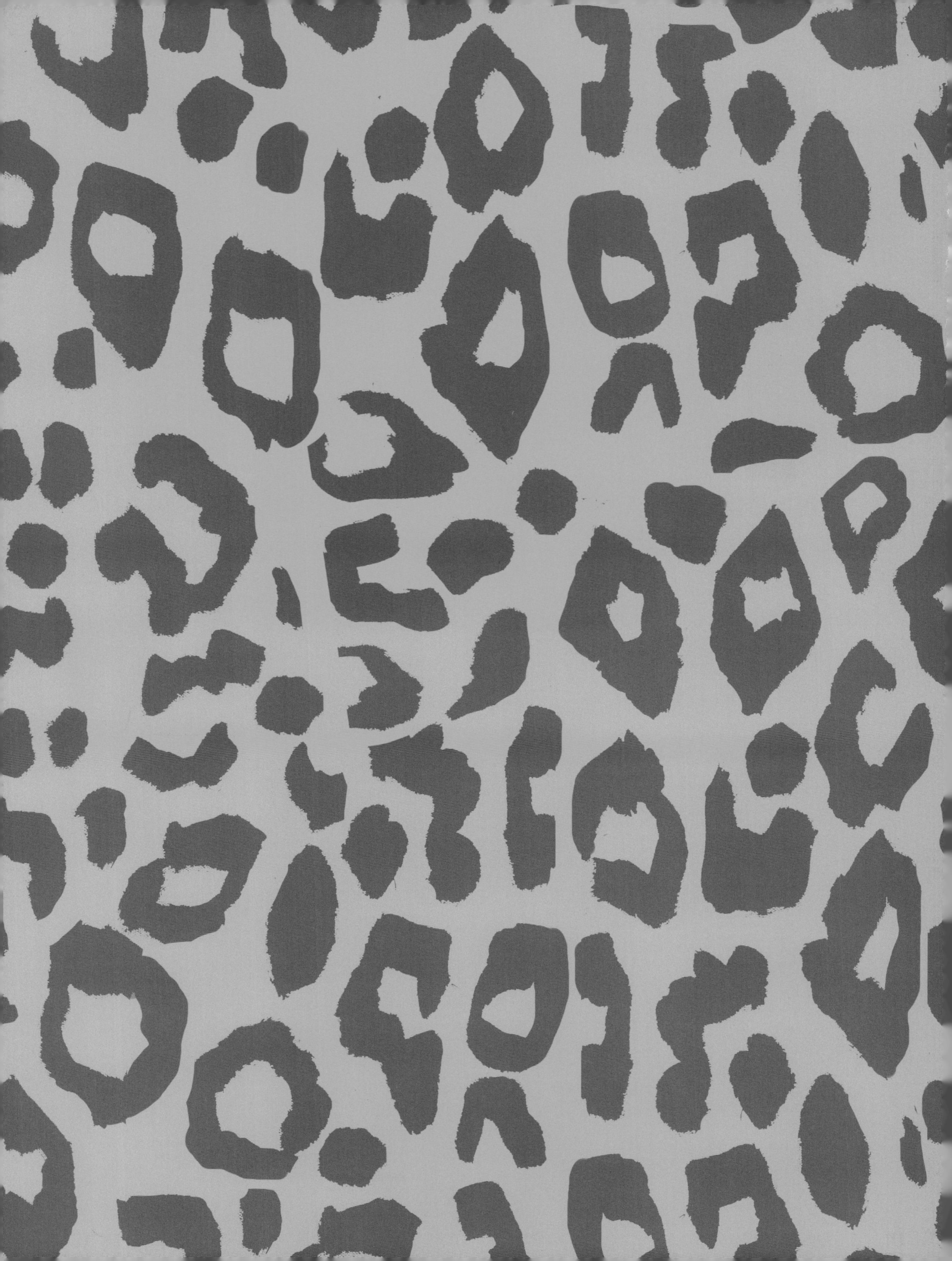